# FAMOUS SHRINES OF
## OUR LADY

# FAMOUS SHRINES

# OF

# OUR LADY

*Volume One*

By H. M. GILLETT

THE NEWMAN PRESS

Westminster, Maryland

1952

*First published, 1950*
*Reprinted, 1952*

𝕹ibil 𝕺bstat:
> Eduardus J. Mahoney, S.T.D.,
> > *Censor deputatus.*

𝕴mprimatur:
> E. Morrogh Bernard,
> > *Vic. Gen.*

*Westmonasterii, die 23a Martii, 1949.*

# CONTENTS

# ILLUSTRATIONS

## DECLARATION

IN conformity with the decree of Pope Urban VIII, dated March 17th, 1625, I declare that if in the course of this work I should give the name of Saint to those not officially recognised as such; and if I make mention of such facts and revelations as might bear the character of the miraculous or prophetic, I do not in any way presume to take upon myself to express, on either persons or facts, a judgment which is reserved to the Church, nor in any way whatsoever to forecast decisions which belong to her alone.

*On May 2nd, 1949, our Holy Father, Pope Pius XII, received the author in special audience, when His Holiness very graciously accepted the first copy of this series of studies of the Famous Shrines of Our Lady and gave His most benign consent that they should be dedicated to Him in the following terms:*

# DEDICATION

TO our Most Holy Father, Pope Pius XII, so outstanding in His devotion to the Holy Mother of God, Blessed Mary ever Virgin; Who fifty years ago offered His first Holy Mass at the feet of Our Lady, Protectress of Rome, in the Borghese Chapel in the Basilica of Saint Mary Major; Who authorised the coronation of the image of Our Blessed Lady, Queen of the Most Holy Rosary, at Fatima; Who brought to a happy conclusion the erection of the Basilica in Her honour at Pompeii; Who has so greatly assisted the faith and devotion of all Catholic peoples by extending to the Universal Church the celebration of the Feast of the Immaculate Heart of Mary; and Who has consecrated the entire world to Her Immaculate Heart:

The author, with His Holiness's most gracious consent, very humbly offers and dedicates this first volume of a series of studies of the living Shrines of Our Blessed Lady; with the earnest desire that they who read them may be inspired to implore the protection of the Mother of God for the Church which, amidst the many adversities by which it is oppressed, places the utmost confidence in Her; and for our very beloved Sovereign Pontiff, Whose great Jubilee this year has afforded all His children so apt an occasion for the expression of their profound gratitude and heartfelt joy.

# DEDICATIO

*Beatissimo Patri Pio XII, qui devotionem erga Mariam, Dei Matrem semperque virginem, maxime promovit ac propagavit; qui abhinc quinquaginta annos sub pedibus ejusdem Virginis, Urbis custodis, in capella Burghesiorum Basilicæ Majoris Sanctæ Mariæ sacrificium eucharisticum primo obtulit; qui Deiparæ simulacrum sub titulo Sacratissimi Rosarii Reginæ Fatimæ coronari libentissime annuit; qui Basilicam in honorem ejusdem Dei Genetricis Pompeii surgentem felicissime confecit; qui tandem universum mundum Immaculato Mariæ Cordi devovendo et ejusdem Festum ut ab Ecclesia toto orbe diffusa celebraretur imperando fidem omnium fidelium ac pietatem tantopere fovit . . .*

*Auctor, ipso Summo Pontifice benigne approbante, hoc sui operis primum volumen de Sanctuariis Beatæ Mariæ Virginis adhuc existentibus et a fidelibus veneratis humillime offert ac dedicat, ut lectores moveantur ad Dei Matris auxilium bono animo impetrandum contra tot tantasque calamitates quæ Dei Ecclesiæ instant, utque Supremus ejus Pastor, cujus Jubilæum sacerdotale hoc in anno celebratur, pro se et universo suo grege gratiarum plenitudinem et perfectam illam felicitatem ac pacem obtinere valeat, quam omnes ejus filii ubique terrarum a Deo enixis precibus postulant.*

# FOREWORD

BY HIS GRACE ARCHBISHOP WILLIAM GODFREY,
APOSTOLIC DELEGATE TO GREAT BRITAIN.

THE author of this volume has done a most useful work, and it will, we feel sure, be welcomed by all devoted children of Mary.

What he has given us in so interesting and readable a form was not possible to obtain without long journeyings from shrine to shrine and painstaking research in the neighbourhood of each sanctuary.

The result is now in our hands, and we read with pleasure and profit of the various phases of devotion to the Blessed Virgin Mary and the large variety of titles under which she is invoked.

Devotion to the Mother of Christ is more and more in evidence in a troubled world.

In the beginning darkness was over the face of the abyss and the Holy Spirit brooded over the waters. Then came order and light. Over the darkness of original sin there arose a bright star, Mary, who, overshadowed by the same Spirit, became the herald of that dawn that was to become full noontide with the coming of the Word made Flesh.

At the present time, dark shadows spread over the face of the globe. The Sun of Justice is well nigh eclipsed in vast regions of the earth's surface. Evil prospers in many parts.

Yet signs are not wanting that the figure of Mary is being seen ever more clearly in the surrounding gloom. There is undying enmity between Satan and the Woman, and her Seed. He lies in wait for her heel.

Writing these lines on the eve of the feast of the Immaculate Conception, one reflects that, if the 19th century was the century of Mary Immaculate, the 20th may be known as the century of her Immaculate Heart, a vessel brimming over with purity, patience, prudence, motherliness and the whole lovely retinue of virtues. As our devotion increases, the more will her bounty be given and the nearer will be brought the victory over the powers of darkness. For she is "terrible as an army set in battle array".

In these days new comets are seen in the skies. Now the light that is Mary must be ever more discovered by the children of God:

> "What said'st thou, Astronomer,
>   When thou did'st discover *her*?
>   When thy hand its tube let fall
>   Thou found'st the fairest star of all!"
>
> *(Francis Thompson.)*

✠ WILLIAM GODFREY,
> *Archbishop of Cius,*
> *Apostolic Delegate.*

*London, December 7th, 1948.*

# INTRODUCTION

SEVERAL years before the 1914-18 War, my father, a well known Hampshire doctor, took me to visit Norfolk where, at Halvergate, our name has been known for generations and where there are family tombs which were put up before the Reformation.

This visit stimulated a profound interest in the numerous medieval churches with which our county abounds. I remember vividly my first impressions of Acle and Ludham, Potter Heigham and Barton, but it was St. Helen's, Ranworth, that excited me so greatly that, at the age of nine, I began to write a "book". This consisted chiefly of notes based on extracts from local guides, illustrated by picture post-cards and snapshots of my own making. Before I was ten, I had a precocious insight into the fascinating subject of "old churches" and could recognise at sight their main architectural and archaeological features. I even knew something about the problems of low-side-windows and squints or "hagioscopes" which, at the age of ten, I preferred to call them.

This hobby was restricted to the holidays because school allowed neither time nor opportunity for such "mouldy" interests, as my preparatory school head-master called them. I owned a bicycle and, as soon as I got home, was off exploring the dozens of churches which abound within a twenty-mile radius of my home at Andover. When I was sixteen, I sold a number of articles on these local churches to the *Andover*

*Advertizer* for what seemed to me to be a princely sum. I am sorry now that my elders—for my father had died by then—did not give me more encouragement.

It was already manifest to me that these old churches had been built for quite a different kind of worship to that I was familiar with in Andover parish church or Blundell's School chapel. Rood-screens without their essential figures, niches without their Saints, empty aumbries and vacant sedilia would, I thought, all look happier if given more reason for their existence. Few of the churches I visited were "high"; many, like Abbots' Ann, were the reverse. I remember being distinctly pleased when I found ritualistic tendencies (of a mild character) at Enham and Amport and I always felt that Longparish was more interesting than certain other places. It used to annoy me intensely that the old Norman priory church of Andover had been pulled down and replaced by the present mock-gothic affair, and that similar vandalism had been done at nearby Charlton.

By degrees my interest shifted, or narrowed. I began to concentrate on Lady Chapels and, for some unaccountable reason, to wish that they might be restored with shrines of the Blessed Virgin. I do not know exactly what gave me this idea for although relatives on my mother's side were "high", I am unaware of any very direct influence that they had on me. At Southsea, my Admiral uncle favoured St. Simon's. At Bournemouth, my aunt was Presbyterian and the church next door was quite as low. But sometimes I would peep in at the Jesuit Church of the Sacred Heart. One day I found Benediction going on, which delighted me, and there I have my first clear memory of a shrine of Our Lady bright with flowers and votive lights. It made an indelible impression.

One holiday, I was taken to visit Walsingham. I

have only hazy recollections of much of that trip but I do remember an old gardener with a beard telling me about the "monks" who lived there, the Lady they "worshipped" and the "wishing wells" they dabbled in. "And they do say as how the day will come when the monks will come back and bring their Lady with them," he told me. And I stood, very small, gazing up at the great, lonely arch which is all that is left of the mighty Priory Church, wondering where they would put "the Lady" when they brought her.

In 1921, my friend Archdale King, so eminent an authority on the Eastern Rites, and who has since become a Catholic, but who was then curate in a Poplar parish, gave me the opportunity of a visit abroad. How eternally grateful I have been to him. We visited Bruges, where I had my first insight into the glories of Catholic Europe, and the joys of true devotion to Mary. For the first time I heard the Litany of Loreto sung in a Catholic church—Notre Dame, Bruges—with several hundred people joining in the responses. It was the Sunday within the Octave of the Assumption, and the Lady Shrine was ablaze with lights. A few weeks later, I took part in the inauguration of a shrine of Our Lady in the (Anglican) parish church of Willesden, seat of a famous medieval shrine. There, I think, began my more active interest in Our Lady's historic sanctuaries as such.

It was a curious turn of circumstances which took me soon after to teach in Cuba. Without particularly seeking for it, I was led to discover the ancient shrine of Our Lady of Cobre, supported by a rather florid devotion. I am not sure that I altogether approved then of the benediction with Our Lady's statue, but I was charmed with her three hundred years old shrine. Other opportunities took me to Guadaloupe, in Mexico, Guatemala City, Panama, and Columbia; and in all these republics I found numerous old shrines and much evidence of the strong faith of Mary's children.

In the United States my Catholic contacts were almost nil, although I spent five years there. I visited St. Vincent Ferrer's in New York and greatly admired the lovely Lady Altar. The Dominican atmosphere took me back to the days a few years previously when I used to stand and watch the growing walls of Blackfriars, Oxford—the builder, Mr. Bell, was one of my father's patients—and plague the very kind architect with questions. I remember, too, what I know now to have been a tremendous privilege, that Father Bede Jarrett gave me my first lesson in Mariology amidst the unfinished walls. It was a great privilege that, before I came back to England, I was enabled to make a trip down the St. Lawrence, to visit the shrine of Our Lady of the Cape, at Three Rivers.

Before I left England in 1922, friends of mine were planning to re-establish a shrine of Our Lady at Walsingham. Sir Frederick Milner (only he was not then Baronet) showed me some plans of his devising at All Saints', North Street, York, where the Anglicans have a very real love for Our Lady. Of course, I did not know anything about King's Lynn, or the efforts of some Catholics to have a shrine erected in the Slipper Chapel, though Miss Boyd had been an actual friend of my grandfather's and was well known by my mother. On my return to England, I hastened to Walsingham to learn of advanced plans for the building of a permanent Anglican shrine (before the "Romans" did) near the priory. Later on, with Theodore Gobat, Rector of Gedney, I witnessed the opening.

But the sand was low. A very serious illness obliged me to leave England for the Mediterranean where I got a job which enabled me to travel and re-travel through Italy, Sicily, Malta and along the Riviera to Spain. Before long, I had gained what I thought was quite a comprehensive insight into the subject of Marial

shrines. Then one day, the thought occurred to me:
"All these are real shrines of Our Lady. They have
a continuous history. They are Catholic. Our Lady's
revelations made at Lourdes, at La Salette, at Pontmain
(yes, even at Fatima, for I had by then read something
about it), were made to "her people" with singularly
little reference to Anglicans. I came rapidly to the
conclusion that devotion to Mary was a Catholic
essential and that it had no legal or proper place—
except in a very truncated form—in the Church of
England. Our Lady demanded the Rosary. How,
within the framework of the Anglican body, could,
openly and above board, those demands be fulfilled.
I made a Novena for guidance to Our Lady of
Perpetual Succour. Within a few days an unexpected
opportunity came and I found myself in a train bound
for Rome. At a late hour, I rang the door-bell of the
Beda College and next morning Mgr. Moss, the Vice-
Rector, started me on my first "official" instructions.
During that stay in Rome, I received tremendous
kindness from many Catholics, was able to make my
thanksgiving at the shrine of Perpetual Succour, and
was given a semi-private audience of Pope Pius XI.
I was received into the Church at the London Oratory,
and made my first Holy Communion at the Christmas
Midnight Mass. Was it just coincidence that I was
given a seat almost at the foot of the magnificent Lady
Altar which came from Brescia?

A few weeks later, I was invited to write my first
book about "Walsingham and its Shrine" (Burns
Oates, 1934). Bishop Youens suggested I ask Father
Francis Devas, S.J., to write the foreword, which he
kindly did; and Cardinal Bourne himself advised me
to proceed. This little book was well received. It
came out just in time for the Cardinal's great
pilgrimage. I still have the charming letter of
appreciation that he wrote me.

Thereupon I was called to lecture for Our Lady of Walsingham, and to organise some of the earliest pilgrimages. For example, in July 1935, with Father Harold Purney, we accomplished the "first" walking pilgrimage all the way from London, following what were believed to be the old routes, in company with W. R. Titterton and his brave wife, in a wheel-chair, Egerton Clarke, and a number of others.

Personally, I wanted to go back to writing and did complete two other books; a short history of the Relics of the Passion (Basil Blackwell) and a life of St. Bede (Burns Oates) to which Abbot Vonier, one of my kindest good friends, contributed a characteristically charming foreword. It was he who urged me to go on with the work for Our Lady. So I did. I cannot say how many lectures I gave, or how many places I visited. Mr. John Boland, K.C.S.G., of the Catholic Truth Society, helped me much by allowing me to edit the C.T.S. set of Walsingham slides which I have used on many occasions. I lectured in over two hundred towns and, when we were organising the National Pilgrimage of Catholic Youth in 1938, I spoke in quite as many schools. Mrs. Hope-Nicholson, of Tite Street, Chelsea, drove me round to many in her car. Thus I was called upon to lecture for the Westminster Catholic Federation, and for the Youth Organisers, with Cardinal Hinsley in the chair.

But Walsingham did not absorb all my devotion. I began to take interest in others of Our Lady's shrines in this country—Willesden, Penrhys, Guisborough, Brewood and others. Some people, I fear, thought I was deserting my first love. Far from it; but I am firmly convinced that England will be converted by Our Lady—is not that the intention of the magnificent prayer so often said at Benediction?—and that, one by one, the more important shrines will be restored. Penrhys is already reclaimed if not yet rebuilt. This will increase, not diminish, the worth of Walsingham, chief centre of this, Our Lady's Dowry. I began to amass notes for an up-to-date version of Waterton's *Pietas Mariana Britannica*.

In the meantime, a large number of questions assailed me. What was a shrine? What was the distinction between a shrine and any other Lady Chapel or Lady Altar in hundreds of churches? What process went towards the selection of any one particular sanctuary? Was it arbitrary, or what made for the decision? Apart from the universal honour given by Catholics to the Mother of God, who decided upon their particular shape and form? What factors went to the making of a shrine? How did the images of Our Lady come into being? Apart from this honour was there any other common factor between the old English shrines, now destroyed, and those still functioning across the Channel and the Atlantic? These thoughts weighed heavily upon me. Was I competent to write further on so vast a subject. I had visited many shrines, perhaps as many as any other Englishman, but what did I really know of the history, or even the legends, of their origins?

Before I went further, then, in my researches for the English shrines, I decided that it would be as well to learn rather more about those of our Continental neighbours. From the story of their unbroken continuity I would surely learn much of value. I must learn about what exists before I started to unearth what has been buried for centuries.

Then I found to my chagrin how little had been written in English about these Shrines abroad. The *Catholic Encyclopædia* gave some useful, critical, information about Loreto. There were about a dozen other useful books to which I could safely refer. From Father Martindale I learned that some of the most popular works on Lourdes, for example, were far from accurate. The great majority of shrines was hardly touched upon.

I determined, then, insofar as I was able, to visit as many of the more historic sanctuaries as time and means allowed; to collect and make note of all I could of their history, legends, and descriptions of their present-day status.

These notes form the basis of the ensuing thirty-one chapters. With the exception of Lujan, in the Argentine, and Fatima, I have visited every one of the shrines here described since 1946. There has been no process of selection. No one is more aware than I, of many that are omitted that are of greater importance than some that I include. Boulogne, Mount Carmel, Barcelona, Maastricht, Kevelaar, Guadaloupe are but a few that merit attention. I have visited those, except Mount Carmel, at one time or another. But it has not been possible to include them in this volume. In some cases, I am not yet satisfied with notes and translations I have made. In 1948, I spent a week in Maastricht and have an accurate account of all that Fra Henry Sedulius wrote in 1609; but there is so much material covering its subsequent history that it has proved impossible to digest it in time for this volume. I can never be sufficiently grateful to the good Pastor of Maastricht, who went out of his way to put me on the right path.

There is a surprising number of popular shrines in Central and South America, the names of which are rarely heard in Europe. Lujan is one. Father Moore, the Passionist Provincial, whom I met in Rome on a certain great occasion, kindly sent me all the history which I include. Cobre is another that I have visited, and there is Quito several days' journey beyond the Panama Canal. Before I write about them, I must try and go back to South America and distances are considerable.

On my last visit to Italy, I was assured at Ancona that I could easily get to Tersatto, on the other side of the Adriatic. That is where the Holy House of Loreto was first set after its translation from Nazareth. The site is marked by a wonderful shrine. It should be studied. Easy enough to get there in a fishing boat perhaps, but would it be as easy to come back? Post-war circumstances have rendered it difficult to go to some parts of Europe, impossible beyond the "Iron Curtain". Further East, in the Balkans, Syria and India, there are many shrines, others in Abyssinia.

How gigantic a task this is to make an adequate survey of Our Blessed Lady's shrines, it must suffice to point out that in France alone there are more than three thousand, fully sixty of which have been honoured with Papal encoronation. In Belgium there are more than thirty such, which attract thousands of pilgrims each year.

Of the thirty sanctuaries included in this volume, several date back to primitive times. More than half belong to what we would call the pre-Reformation period. Some sprang to fame during the counter-Reformation and proved to be towers of strength against attacks on the Faith. Eleven have come into being since 1800, and three during this century. Paris, La Salette, Lourdes, Pontmain, Fatima, Beauraing and Banneux all offer sanctuaries, the scenes of Apparitions of Our Blessed Lady accredited by canonical enquiry and approved by ecclesiastical authority. Likewise the cultus at Pellevoisin is approved even if authority has remained silent about Estelle Faguette's experiences. The stories of these comparatively modern centres of Marial devotion form an important group towards the end of the book. Devotion to Our Lady is living and not static. Some shrines have passed away altogether. Others linger on like the still glowing embers of a once great fire. Yet others have sprung into existence as if to replace those that are lost and to remind us that however transitory time may be, Our Lady's prayers go on for ever. And some there are which seem to possess the gift of perpetual vitality.

It is sometimes said that no shrine that has·"died" may be restored again. Certainly there are many, like Chartres and Le Puy, which were murdered yet lived on. Surely the decision rests with us mortals only in our determination in the matter, to restore what was once given and then snatched away? It is, apparently, Our Lady, by the grace of God, who decides where her chosen shrines will be. Almost every shrine here mentioned has suffered severe tests, crushing disasters, but every one is today a focus of fervent, quickening devotion.

Even this small survey was achieved only with a great deal of help, and to all who have made it possible I express my heartfelt gratitude.

Foremost, I thank most sincerely His Grace, Archbishop Godfrey, Delegate of His Holiness to Great Britain. Not only has he contributed the thought-provoking foreword to this volume, but he has paved the way for almost every visit to Our Lady's shrines that I have made during the past three years, with letters of introduction. Than he, Our Lady can have no more devoted a servant. One has only to mention that some work is connected with her devotion and he is ready to do his utmost to assist. England owes him a great debt of gratitude for his unstinted services for the welfare of the Faith.

In Rome I was greatly helped by Bishop Addeo, of the Order of Saint Augustine, the best living authority on Our Lady of Good Counsel; and Father Clement Henzë, C.SS.R., concerning Our Lady of Perpetual Succour and St. Mary Major. I have found Professor Carlo Cecchelli's very recent volumes entitled *Mater*

*Christi* of the utmost value. Father Hilario of Malta, personally guided me at Loreto. Dom Anselm Albareda, O.S.B., Prefect of the Vatican Library, sent me a mass of matter and excellent pictures for Montserrat, his own monastery in Spain. Father Lawrence, the ubiquitous and many-tongued guest-master at Einsiedeln did much to make my stay profitable.

Concerning the shrines in France, so many people have advised me that I am embarrassed where to begin with my thanks. At the Rue du Bac all my help was gained from no less than Père Edmund Crapez, S.M., the chief postulator in the cause of Saint Catherine Labouré. It was a great honour when he gave me, autographed, a first edition of his own great work on the Miraculous Medal Apparitions, corrected for future editions in his own hand. From there I went on to La Salette. I alone know the tremendous kindness I received and the ever ready help accorded me. Père L. Sorrel, who acted as Superior General of the Missionaries of La Salette throughout the war, did all in his power and in particular read and advised me on the translation I made of the Message of La Salette. Father Ferec, who was guest-master during the Centenary, gave me access to many original documents. Father Jalbert and Father Lawrence, the present Superior on the Holy Mountain, have been kind and helpful beyond words. La Salette deserves a book all to itself, and I am glad to assure my friends there that all the valuable documentation they put at my disposal is nearly ready for publication.

From La Salette, I paid my first visit to Le Laus so soon after the war that the military took me for an escaped German and detained me. I cannot be sufficiently grateful as the very rapid transport they provided to Gap police station enabled me to catch what was in those days the only transport back to Lyons for some time.

At Le Puy, Monseigneur Faurie, the Vicar General, went out of his way to see that I met those who could give me the most accurate information, showed me much personally, and presented me to the Bishop, who blessed this part of my work.

At Rocamadour, it was Mgr. Cros, Superior of the Chaplains of the sanctuary, who entertained me at the château for some time and explained much. Elsewhere in France, I owe debts of gratitude to both Mgr. Boucher, the Administrator, and the Sacristan of Chartres, and the Father Sacristan of Fourvière, all of whom showed me round and directed my enquiries for the histories of those shrines.

It was Mgr. Michel Evan who advised me about Pontmain. I was deeply sorry to find him no longer there. Likewise Chanoîne David, Professor of Lille, in his day the greatest authority on Mount Sinaï, died on the day I reached Lille to discuss matters with him. His works and his letters have proved most valuable. May they both rest in peace.

It was my very kind friend, Abbot Wilfrid Upson, of Prinknash, who introduced me to the Belgian Abbots of St. André and Mont César, both of whom gave me hospitality and great help. Likewise their guest-masters, Dom Emmanuel Meester and Dom David Maffei, went to great trouble to advise me as to shrines in the Netherlands and Belgium. In particular Dom David spent many hours in seeing that I got correct advice. Father Boniface Luyckx, of Postel Abbey, and Canon Van de Walle, of Bruges, eminent authorities in history and art, did much to advise me. It was a great thrill to discover at the English Convent, Bruges, such ardent devotion towards Walsingham and the actual records of Miss Charlotte Boyd's reception into the Church. The Rectors of Hal and Montaigu themselves showed me the famous treasures of their respective sanctuaries.

At Beauraing it was Chanoîne Massart, chief Chaplain and pioneer of the present great developments, who proved such an assiduous and generous guide. Never shall I forget his hospitality over the 1948 Feast of the Immaculate Heart, Beauraing's chief festival, and the opportunity of meeting and conversing with the Papal Nuncio and so many members of the Ecclesiastical Commissions. Monseigneur Charue, the Bishop of Namur, very graciously received me and accepted the text of the chapter on Beauraing which now appears.

At Banneaux, the Abbé Arendt, founder of the world's largest Marial Library, welcomed me drenched to the skin and made me feel that it was good to be a Christian. I shall not forget his attentions or his help in giving me the best documentation on these, the latest of Our Lady's Apparitions to receive Ecclesiastical approval.

In conclusion it should be mentioned that in the majority of cases the chapters on each European shrine have been submitted to the relative local authorities.

Father Gordon Wheeler, Editor of the *Westminster Cathedral Chronicle* has kindly allowed me to include parts of articles of mine that have appeared in past numbers of the distinguished monthly which he edits.

Lastly, but by means least, Mr. L. J. Sullivan, Editor of the *Catholic Fireside*, has read the proofs of every one of thirty articles which appeared in his popular weekly, which form the basis on which this volume has been composed. Never once has he complained! In these days of restricted papers, not many Catholic periodicals, however willing, would have undertaken to find space, over years, for so many articles. It is encouraging that as a result there have been so many requests for them to appear in more permanent form.

The illustrations have been drawn from every conceivable source. They have not been easy to obtain and, in some cases, it has been impossible to trace original ownership. I am very grateful to all from whom they have been derived and hope that their publication, all in one collection, may do much to promote honour and devotion to Our Blessed Lady, whose cause we all desire to serve.

# I: OUR LADY OF THE CATACOMBS

IT is curious that so many people, even among Catholics, have an idea that devotion to Our Blessed Lady is something rather new; something which must be justified and apologised for, especially among Protestants. Non-Catholics in particular are prone to consider the Church's teaching with regard to the Mother of Our Lord as an "innovation", unknown to the early Christians. For example, one quite recent and important book, widely sold and read (*The Cathedrals of England,* published in 1935 by Batsford: a beautiful book in its way) talks of the "rising cult of Our Lady" as being of the thirteenth century.

It will be a surprise, then, to such folk, and of great importance to all Catholics, to know how old is the oldest surviving picture of Our Blessed Lady; and also what advanced symbolism this very ancient portrayal has to present. The painting is to be found in the depths of one of the most interesting of the Roman Catacombs; the "Cemetery" of St. Priscilla underneath the Basilica of St. Silvester, the Pope whose feast day occurs on December 31st.

Here, among the decorations of one of these fascinating underground chambers, is a portrait of the Madonna and Holy Child which experts are agreed must have been painted by a skilled artist during, and certainly not later than, the second half of the second century; that is somewhere about A.D. 175.

This was at a period when Roman art was still at

27

a high level, before the decline of the Imperial City had brought a serious decline in artistic standards.

Although the lower part of the picture has been damaged—not to be wondered at, considering its antiquity—enough remains for it to be clearly distinguishable and to astonish one with its advanced symbolism which demonstrates how well developed was devotion to Our Lady at that early date.

The Blessed Mother is shown seated, wearing a *stola,* the long woollen garment usually worn by Roman matrons, and with her head covered with a short veil. The full significance of this can be appreciated only by comparison with another picture of Our Lady, almost as ancient, close by: it is the veil used to cover the heads of dedicated virgins.

The Holy Child is seated upon His Mother's knee, turned towards her breast yet glancing back to look at someone who is, apparently, approaching. The whole posture and attitude of this Mother and Child is natural and charming. The delightful Bambino is the sort of little baby attractive to every mother.

But this does not complete the study. Standing beside Our Lady is the figure of a man dressed in the cloak which was reserved for philosophers of distinction, who is pointing upwards to a star—only faintly discernible—above the Madonna's head. This figure is now recognised as representing the prophet Isaias. He it was who proclaimed: "The Lord Himself shall give you a sign. Behold a Virgin shall conceive, and bear a Son, and His Name shall be called Emmanuel." The star symbolises the divinity of Christ and is reminiscent also of the Star of Bethlehem.

This group is depicted beneath a large and flourishing tree which has burst into blossoms of a formalised nature.

In Paschal-time, in the Proper of the Mass of March 25th, the Annunciation of Our Blessed Lady,

*The second century picture of Our Blessed Lady in the Catacomb of St. Priscilla*

(Page 27)

*Our Lady of Rome in St. Mary Major's,*
*attributed to St. Luke*

(Page 31)

certain verses are sung instead of the Gradual. These repeat the Messianic prophecy and combine with it the first part of the Angelic Salutation and the text of that other great prophecy: "The rod of Jesse hath blossomed: a Virgin hath brought forth God and man . . ."

The presence of this very early, and highly symbolic, picture of Our Lady, is all the more significant when one recalls that quite possibly it was seen and admired by no less a person than St. Irenaeus, who was a disciple of St. Polycarp, himself a disciple of St. John, to whose care Our Divine Lord bequeathed His Mother from the Cross.

St. Polycarp visited Rome to settle the date of Easter. Later, St. Irenaeus came to Rome bringing letters to the Pope from the Martyr Christians of Lyons, where he became Bishop: at very much the same date when this picture was painted.

St. Irenaeus was outspoken about this matter of reverence to Our Lady. His teaching may be said to be reflected in this very portrait; it shows the parallel between Eve and Our Lady; between what he terms "the mortal fruit of the one and the Blessed Fruit of the other". "As Eve," he wrote, "by her disobedience was for herself and the whole human race the cause of death, so Mary, by her obedience, has become the means of salvation . . . The Virgin Mary has become the Advocate of Eve."

There, in the second century, was proclaimed, by one who was taught by a direct disciple of the Beloved Disciple, a title of Our Blessed Lady which was to resound through all subsequent ages of Marial devotion. Advocate of Eve! How aptly may this title be applied to this particular picture in the Catacombs of St. Priscilla; for this earliest known painting of Our Lady is surely a worthy attempt to portray the root Mystery of the Incarnation.

The effect of this picture upon those early, heroic Christians can be gauged by the other, painted close by in the same Catacombs a few decades later. This shows the tall figure of a robed and veiled Virgin standing with her arms widely outstretched in the primitive posture of prayer. On one side a bishop, the Pope, for all the world reminiscent of traditional portraits of St. Peter, is shown engaged, with two assistants, in placing the ceremonial veil upon the head of an avowed Virgin—in other words, the most primitive form of veiling a nun is being performed by one who represents the Pope himself.

On the opposite side is enthroned a figure of Our Lady, vested in a long dalmatic, with the Holy Child, looking towards the scene of the veiling. The Virgin Mother, Advocate of that other virgin, Eve, is included in this group as being the true and eternal model of Virginity.

It is an inspiration to remember that these two pictures were painted respectively more than sixteen and seventeen hundred years ago, and revered by Christians at a time when fierce persecutions raged and threatened the Church in Rome. At such a time Our Lady was not forgotten. In their secret hiding places Christians thought fit to portray, thus wonderfully, symbolic pictures of the Mediatrix of all Graces from which undoubtedly they derived great comfort.

It was pictures such as these that were the prototypes and forerunners of all future eikons and figures of Our Lady. It is good to know that such splendid examples have been spared through all these centuries to enlighten us today.

## II: OUR LADY, PROTECTRESS OF ROME

A S soon as Saint Augustine and his fellow-missionaries had made any substantial progress in the conversion of pagan Kent, there came the need of restoring the old churches which local Christians had used in late Roman times, and of building new ones. Already, under Queen Bertha and her bishop-chaplain, Luidhard, St. Martin's Canterbury, had been repaired and the Holy Sacrifice had been offered there for more than a decade.

Now it is obvious that these brave missionaries, inspired in Rome and sent by the great Pope St. Gregory from his own monastic house of St. Andrew's on the Coelian Hill, would have drawn on their own monastery and the same Pope's generosity for all the things they needed for furnishing these new churches. It was not until a good deal later when, under St. Benet Biscop of Northumbria, special training had been given, that local craftsmen were able successfully to undertake such jobs.

Devotion to Our Blessed Lady was as intense among Catholics in the sixth century as it is today. In fact, not to regard Our Lady as Mother of God was one of the worst heresies at that date. A large number of new churches built then were dedicated to Our Lady. Into all of them was introduced a beautiful picture of her, likely to inspire devotion in the hearts of the faithful.

One wonders what these early pictures and shrines of Our Lady were like and what influence these early "Our Lady's" had upon later English pictures and

figures of the Blessed Mother. It is rather thrilling to
discover that one does not have to search far to find
that the picture of Our Lady most beloved of St.
Gregory still exists, and, because of its important
influence at that time, there is little reason to doubt
that it was universally popular.

This painting is still the centre and magnet of the
most celebrated Shrine of Our Lady in Rome and is to
be found in the most important church of Our Lady
in the eternal city, that of the Major Basilica of Saint
Mary Major, which has its own special feast day on
the 5th of August under the title of *Sta. Maria ad Nives,*
Our Lady of the Snows.

This Basilica, as most Catholics know, was built on
the Esquiline Hill by a wealthy Roman and his wife
during the pontificate of Liberius. They were guided
in their choice of a site at the command of Our Lady,
who appeared to them in a dream, and the subsequent
miraculous fall of snow in mid-summer confined to this
particular hill-top. The snow is said to have covered
a piece of ground of the form and size necessary for a
large church and no more.

Later, on the occasion of the General Council of
Ephesus, at which the Blessed Virgin was declared to
be truly the Mother of God, Pope Sixtus III rebuilt
this Basilica and greatly enriched it in honour of the
event. It was marvellously adorned with silver
furnishings and the walls were covered with large and
elaborate mosaic pictures, commemorative of Our
Lady as Mother of God. Thus the Basilica of Saint
Mary Major became one of the four chief basilicas of
the eternal city.

A few years later this same church was enriched
with a famous relic, the manger from the stable at
Bethlehem in which the Infant Jesus had been laid at
birth. So yet another title was conferred on the church,
that of *Sta. Maria ad Praesepe,* St. Mary at the Crib.

But not even this wondrous gift outshone the original glory, the picture of Our Lady that had been enshrined in the basilica which Pope Liberius built.

According to an ancient tradition, this picture was brought to Rome by the Empress Saint Helena, at the time when she rescued from oblivion the Holy Places of Palestine and the Relics of the Passion. It is claimed of this picture that it was painted by St. Luke the Evangelist. This is a tradition which no Catholic is bound to accept, although the Lessons of the Divine Office approved for the use of the Canons of the Chapter of St. Mary Major's speak of it as a "pious belief, warranted by an old and constant tradition".

Protestants, very often through ignorance, throw scorn on the tradition that Saint Luke was an artist and are fond of asserting that there are so many of these "Lucan Madonnas" that had the Evangelist painted them all, he would have had no time to write the Gospel, let alone the "Acts of the Apostles". As a matter of fact, the tradition of Saint Luke as a painter is ancient and is founded on authority by no means unworthy. The Evangelist was born and educated in Antioch, a city of great culture and under Greek influence. The author of writing so beautiful as that found in the Gospel and the "Acts of the Apostles" must have had a superior education. Antioch was renowned for its art, and there is nothing impossible or even improbable in a distinguished author also being an artist. Likewise, St. Luke is the writer who tells us most about Our Lady.

The suggestion that these pictures called "Lucan Madonnas" were painted by another "saint" of the same name does not help. They are all older than the earliest date these critics give for this other imaginary Luke. He could have lived only about 1050, but the picture in St. Mary Major was venerated five hundred years before then.

At any rate, as soon as the great Basilica was built, this wonderful eikon of Our Lady was enshrined therein, considered to be by Saint Luke, and the most authentic portrait of the Mother of God.   Not even the later acquisition of the Crib made this shrine any less popular.   It was already pre-eminent in the hearts of the Romans and of all Christians drawn to Rome. No other shrine of Our Lady, in consequence, has been visited by so many Popes, Princes and Prelates in the history of the Church.

From England's point of view, the picture had an important part to play.   No Pope excelled in devotion towards it more than Pope Gregory the Great, who ordained that St. Augustine should lead the famous Mission to Kent in 597.   It was this picture which he chose to bear in solemn procession from St. Mary Major's to St. Peter's, deprecating God's wrath and imploring His mercy to stay the terrors of a plague which was then decimating the population.   It was during that famous procession, according to tradition, that choirs of angels were heard to sing around it:

> *"Regina coeli, laetare*
> *Quia quem meruisti portare*
> *Resurrexit sicut dixit,"*

to which the holy Pontiff immediately added, *"Ora pro nobis Deum"*.   Thus was formed, according to this delightful legend, the whole antiphon which the Church has adopted for especial use at Easter.   It was later in this same remarkable procession that St. Gregory was privileged to see the figure of St. Michael the Archangel over the Mausoleum of Hadrian, now called San Angelo, sheathing his sword, in token that the plague had ceased.

As this was Saint Gregory's "favourite" picture of Our Lady, one can easily imagine the great Pope praying earnestly before it for the success of the English

Mission which he had sent; and that the picture of Our Lady which St. Augustine brought to Kent was likely to have been a fair replica of it.

On numerous other occasions the same picture—the most historic picture of Our Lady in the world—has been carried in public processions, by various Popes. The last time was by the last Pope named Gregory, in 1837, again in intercession for the cessation of cholera; and the prayer was granted. Then the Pope, in public thanksgiving, affixed two crowns of gold to the picture, enriched with numerous precious stones, one for the Mother, the other for the Son, which may still be seen.

It was not until 1613 that this painting was removed from its original shrine behind the high altar. Then Pope Paul V built a magnificent Lady Chapel, on the north side of the church, expressly for its reception. The ceremony of removal was celebrated with extraordinary pomp. In a brief the Pope indicates his reasons for the change, namely that he felt such honour was due to the picture which "ancient records testify to have been always distinguished by the devotion of the faithful, and that many and wonderful miracles have proceeded from it".

This, then, is a fragment of the history of one of the most important of Our Blessed Lady's sanctuaries. It is one that must have had some influence on England, through St. Gregory, who loved England so much, and St. Augustine, who was his friend. Both had great devotion to Our Lady of St. Mary Major.

When St. Cuthbert died, a picture of Our Lady was painted on his coffin and enough of it has been spared for us to know how strong was the influence of this Roman Madonna. There is no need to wonder why. St. Benet Biscop, who played an important part in the Evangelisation of Northumbria, spent many years in Rome and must surely have paid his dues at St. Mary Major's on occasion.

A careful study of this prototype Madonna is worth while: but how seldom have good photographs been taken of it; how few of us get the chance to go to Rome. Our Lady is wrapped in a mantle of blue, which covers her head and shoulders, and which is bordered with a golden edge. Her features are depicted in true Greek style: her countenance, thrown into relief by the addition of a halo, is royal and dignified, intensely and fittingly lovely. The Holy Child is clasped upon her left arm. A large halo surrounds His curly hair and He gazes upward at His Mother. His right hand is extended in blessing: His left clasps a Gospel-book to remind us that He Himself is the *Logos,* or Word of God.

The portrait shows only the head and body of Our Lady. It is impossible to deduce exactly whether she stands or sits, though probably the former. In many respects there is a resemblance between the details of this picture and what we believe to have been the figure of Our Lady of Walsingham, except that she was enthroned. For all that Our Lady of St. Mary Major is at least 1500 years old, possibly older, the colours are still fresh and vigorous; as a portrait it rivals any picture to be seen in the National Gallery.

Today, as much as ever, this sanctuary is thronged with a constant stream of suppliants and pilgrims. One wonders if ever our present Pope makes pilgrimages in secret, as Pope Pius IX did so often, at midnight and barefoot; for it was at the altar of this very shrine that, fifty years ago, on April 3rd, 1899, Eugenio Pacelli, just ordained, said his first Mass. Forty years later, in 1939, he returned as Pope Pius XII, to kneel in prayer at this beloved shrine and then to Pontificate at the Solemn Mass which followed. According to recent announcements, the Holy Father proposes to celebrate the fiftieth anniversary of his priesthood with a similar pilgrimage.

# III:  LORETO

**E**IGHTEEN miles south of Ancona, and about three
miles from the Adriatic coast of Italy, stands the
city of Loreto on the summit of an abrupt hillside,
prominent for the great bastions which ring it round,
even more outstanding for the dome of the vast basilica
which crowns every aspect of the hilltop.  This great
church and some of the adjacent buildings, form the
most treasured of all the Pope's "extra-territorial"
Vatican State properties—like Castel Gandolfo—
enshrining as it does the most sacred and important of
all Our Lady's Shrines in Christendom: the Home of
the Holy Family, Our Lady's own dwelling-place, the
Holy House of Loreto.

On entering the basilica, one finds beneath the central
dome, and just behind the high altar, a singular,
rectangular edifice, of no great height, apparently of
white marble, richly adorned with statues and
sculpture.  The white marble, however, forms only a
protective crust.  Within, the contrast between the
exterior richness and the poverty of the interior is
startling.  As seen from inside, the walls are the plain,
rough walls of a cottage of great antiquity, 30 feet long
by 15 feet wide and about 15 feet high to the cornices.

Written at the door of the basilica is this text:

*Let those who are impure tremble to enter into this
sanctuary.  The whole world has no place more sacred.
This building is more holy even than the Basilica of
Saint Peter, Prince of the Apostles.  For here was the
Word made Flesh, and here was born the Virgin
Mother.  From the West, where the sun goes down,*

37

*to the East, where it rises from the waters, no place
is more holy.*

This, then, is none other than the Shrine of the
Incarnation which is here preserved and which has been
styled by numerous Popes as the premier shrine of
Our Lady. How comes it to be today in Italy and so
far from its original site in Palestine? The ridicule of
one half of the world and the devotion of the other has
made famous the strange story of its translation—how,
towards the end of the thirteenth century, the Holy
House was borne by the hands of angels, first from
Galilee to Dalmatia, and thence to Loreto, where it
has remained ever since.

The House of Our Lady stood undestroyed in
Nazareth for more than twelve hundred years. Early
tradition asserted that the house was set apart from
secular uses by the Apostles. Then, ancient, and
usually reliable, authorities record that when the
Empress, St. Helen, visited the Holy Places, she "went
to Nazareth and found there the House of the Angelic
Salutation, where she built a very beautiful church to
the Mother of God". It was a common practice to
enshrine entire houses associated with saints beneath
churches. Numerous examples of a similar date remain
elsewhere. There is no need to suppose that the Holy
House was destroyed to make way for the basilica.

John Phocas, a Greek priest, visited Nazareth in
1185. The Holy House was still there, built with its
back against, and opening into, a cave or grotto, down
below the basilica. That was the local custom, to build
houses on steep terraces, backing on to caves. St.
Louis, King of France, heard Mass in Nazareth in 1253
"in the exact chamber where the Virgin Mary was
declared the Mother of God" and then heard another
Mass at the High Altar up above. This is clear evidence
that the Holy House was at Nazareth under the basilica
at that date.

In 1291, on May 10th, some Dalmatian shepherds found a strange building in their field, at Tersatto, close to Fiume, where the evening before there had been neither house nor building materials. Their parish priest, Dom Alessandro di Giorgio, came to examine it. He had been warned in a dream of the true origin of the cottage. Within were found an ancient altar, a Greek Cross beautifully painted, and a curious statue of the Holy Mother of God.

Then did Nicolo Frangipane, the Governor of Dalmatia, send envoys to Nazareth, who verified the story and brought back valuable evidence. The Holy House could no longer be found at Nazareth, but the length and breadth of the walls of the cottage at Tersatto agreed exactly with those of some foundations which they could see beneath the Basilica of the Annunciation. The materials used, limestone, mortar, and cedar-wood, were the same as those used at Nazareth and were unobtainable in that part of Dalmatia.

Three-and-a-half years later, on December 10th, 1294, this same Holy House was removed from Dalmatia and set down at Loreto, on the opposite side of the Adriatic, in the midst of a wood called Lauretum. Tradition goes on to say that it was visited there by innumerable persons, but that evil men hid themselves in the woods and robbed the pilgrims so that the house was soon taken to a more open site. But there, two brothers quarrelled so bitterly that again the house was lifted up and set, where it is today, on a spot in the middle of the high road to Recanati.

The loss of the Holy House was a great grief to the people of Tersatto. St. Nicholas of Tolentino, who had a great devotion to it when it was in Dalmatia, was overjoyed by an apparition of Our Lady, telling him that the house was near Recanati.

Pope Boniface VIII deputed a Commission to inquire into and report fully on the whole matter, both at Tersatto and Nazareth as well as Loreto. From then onward, the Dalmatians flocked annually, on December 10th, across to Loreto to visit "their shrine" and to bewail that Our Lady had removed it from them. They refused even to be consoled by the building of a replica as a substitute at Tersatto.

From 1294 onwards pilgrims began to throng the roads to Loreto. The great Jubilee year of 1300 seemed to bring all Christian Europe to the "City of Mary", as it was called, for few strangers visited Rome without calling at the Holy House on their return journey.

The list of famous persons who have paid homage at Loreto would, if published, be interminable. Some forty-seven Popes have knelt there as Popes, calling the history and traditions "most worthy of belief". Many others, including our own Holy Father, have gone there before they were raised to the Papacy. Pope Paul II was cured of the plague there. Pope after Pope has added to the testimony in favour of belief. An Archconfraternity has long been established, conferring extraordinary benefits on its members. The Sacred Congregation of Rites has paid tribute by appointing December 10th as the Feast, "Of the Translation of the Holy House," with special Office, Mass and lessons.

To such testimony must be added the witness of the Saints. It was here that St. Francis Xavier was inspired to devote himself to the East. In the list of other saints who have visited and acclaimed Our Lady's Dwelling, there are the names of St. Francis Borgia, St. Peter of Alcantara, St. Joseph of Cupertino, St. Camillus of Lellis, St. Charles Borromeo, St. Stanislaus Kostka, St. Aloysius, St. Francis of Sales, and so through the centuries to St. Benedict Joseph Labre.

So much for the history of the Holy House, and the reasons for the immense veneration shown to it by the faithful of the Church. Having entered the great outer Basilica and reached the door of the marble-encrusted shrine, what does the present-day pilgrim find on entering?

The original House had only one door, a small window to the right of that, a hearth for a charcoal fire at the (left) end opposite the window, the Apostle's Altar opposite the door, with Our Lady set on a pedestal beside the altar, and a wooden roof, painted blue and spangled with golden stars.

Pope Clement VII made certain drastic alterations to meet the requirements of the press of pilgrims. Four doors were opened at the corners of the side walls and the stones were used for blocking up the original entrance and for raising the height of the ceiling at the cornices. The altar was moved to the "east" end; Our Lady of Loreto was enthroned in a bejewelled niche behind it, and above the "Holy Hearth".

The figure of Our Lady of Loreto is a little more than three feet high, while the Holy Child is not quite a foot and a half in height, carved from the wood of a cedar-tree grown in the Vatican gardens. This is because a terrible accident destroyed the ancient statue in 1921. The original figure was apparently of Egyptian-Jewish inspiration and was made of Cedar of Lebanon. According to tradition it arrived at Loreto together with the house.

In 1797, the Commissaries of the Revolutionary (Communist) French Directory seized upon the sanctuary and carried off all its treasures, including Our Lady of Loreto. They took her to Paris where she was exhibited as a profane curiosity. Napoleon Bonaparte restored the figure to Pope Pius VII, after a period of exposition and ardent veneration in Notre Dame Cathedral, Paris. It was enthroned for some days in the Papal Palace at the Quirinal and solemnly escorted back to Loreto in 1802.

The new figure, made to the personal order of Pope Pius XI, was enthroned in the Sistine Chapel, September 5th to 6th, 1924. There the Holy Child and His Mother were crowned by the Sovereign Pontiff himself with two gold crowns in the presence of several Cardinals. No European coronation could have attracted more loyal or enthusiastic crowds than those which acclaimed the Sovereign Queen of Heaven as she was escorted through the streets of Rome, on September 6th, to the Basilica of St. Mary Major. Eventually, on September 7th, she left for Loreto. The entire route of her progress home was lined with countless members of her loving family. So once again Our beloved Mother is installed in the little Holy House.

On great occasions she is vested with a robe of gold and silk bespangled with diamonds to the value of many hundreds of thousands of pounds—the marriage jewels of the Empress Maria Theresa.

Near her throne is a large silver plaque with a beautiful golden figure of Our Lady standing on a crescent and surrounded by military trophies. This is an ex-voto from the Christian army in Hungary, promised when they seemed to be on the point of being overwhelmed by the Turks.

Fifty silver lamps burn in the Holy House, hanging round the walls, and there are numerous wax tapers in silver sconces.

Many Popes have at different times sought to make it easier for the less credulous of the faithful to accept the tradition of the translation. By order of Benedict XIV, a number of experts dug around the base of the little sanctuary, who proved beyond doubt that the building rested on no foundations at all, but stood directly on the surface of an ancient road. In many places the hand could, and still can, be inserted beneath the walls, which stand with no extraneous support. It has been the privilege of the author to perform this act with his own hands, on December 10th, 1938.

Recently, eminent experts have examined the materials, stones and mortar of the walls and compared them with stones in the remains of the foundations at Nazareth. They were judged to be identical. The stones are announced to be "Jabés", which is found in quarries in Galilee. The mortar used at Loreto and Nazareth, too, is the same, made of lime and vegetable charcoal, common at Nazareth, never used in Italy. The experts were satisfied that the materials used were alien to Italy and that the fabric of the walls had never been pulled down and rebuilt.

Loreto is the premier shrine in Christendom in honour of Our Lady. From it, the Litany so often sung at Benediction takes its name.

There is a connection between Loreto and England —Walsingham. For Walsingham was founded to be forever the memorial of the same mystery of the Annunciation which was first enacted in the Holy House, at Nazareth on March 25th, England's Lady Day. By Henry VIII, Walsingham was swept away. It was the keystone shrine of the Catholic Faith. Loreto, though, has triumphed through time. Not even deliberately aimed enemy bombs could destroy it, any more than Henry VIII could destroy the Old Religion by pulling down Walsingham.

But there, at Loreto, is the actual house wherein Our Lady dwelt and where Our Lord spent the years of His Childhood. It is good to know that this marvellous link in time and history still remains to span the ages and to bring us in truth and spirit the message of the Archangel Gabriel: "Hail, Mary, full of grace, the Lord is with thee!"

## IV: WALSINGHAM

ENGLAND was in no way less devoted to the Blessed Mother of God than the rest of Catholic Europe. Perusal of that splendid work, *Pietas Mariana Britannica,* by Edmund Waterton, F.S.A., published in 1879, leaves no doubt that in every county and diocese, shrines of Our Lady abounded, many being of more than local importance; a number of international repute. To select a list of the more celebrated is difficult, almost invidious. Among them, specially singled out for destruction at the Reformation, were: Canterbury (Our Lady Undercroft), Doncaster, Ely, Evesham, Fountains, Guisborough, Ipswich, Islington, Jesmond, Lincoln, Muswell, Pershore, Walsingham, Westminster (Our Lady of the Pew), Willesden, Worcester, York. At once others cry out for inclusion: Chatham and Dover, Gloucester and Lynn; but space precludes anything like a comprehensive list. Even Waterton, in a large volume, is by no means exhaustive.

Of all these English Mary-shrines, however, there was one of outstanding importance—Walsingham; so well known and beloved that it was popularly averred that the "Milky Way" pointed thither. The tradition of it was so strong that sixty-seven years after its desecration, Cervantes, in Spain, was moved to write that there was an "infinite number of little birds, hopping from branch to branch, all naturally singing 'Walsingham' "—a tune made popular by pilgrims of old.

As with many historic European sanctuaries, large

44

*Present day statue of Our Lady of Loreto, made by order of Pope Pius XI to replace the original burned in 1921*

(Page 37)

*Our Lady of Walsingham enthroned in the
Slipper Chapel*

(Page 44)

gaps in the history of England's chief shrine remain to be filled. English Puritans were no kinder than the Gueux or Huguenots where archives and documents were concerned. Post-reformation disinterest and neglect did more damage than all the iconoclasts together. Charters and deeds bestowing as gifts for all time properties and privileges upon shrines or monasteries were not particularly relished or preserved by Henrican or Elizabethan usurpers, of whom Sir Henry Spelman has left on record so notable a curse.

The earliest record of Walsingham's shrine seems to lie in the confirmation of gift, made about 1169 by the patrons, Robert de Brucurt and Roger, Earl of Clare, to William Turbus, Bishop of Norwich. By that gift, Geoffrey de Faverches, son of Richeldis, a widow, granted: "To God and to Saint Mary, and to Edwy his chaplain, in perpetuity, the chapel which his mother had founded in Walsingham in honour of Mary ever Virgin, together with possession of the Church of All Saints of the same village and all its appurtenances in lands, tithes and rents". To which the patrons, in 1169, added other benefactions.

A house of Augustinian Canons was established. The first prior, apart from Edwy, of whom there is little record, was one Ralph, 1153-1173.

Evidence of the popularity of this Norfolk shrine, established in a remote part of the county, is seen in the foundation, before 1224, of a hospice for poor pilgrims, made by William de Bec, near Billingford, on the Norwich-Walsingham road.

The list of benefactors of the shrine includes an imposing series of names important in English history. Not least was Elizabeth de Burgh, daughter of Gilbert de Clare and Princess Joan, daughter of Edward I. Through her brother's death, at Bannockburn, she inherited the de Clare estates. Her granddaughter married Lionel, son of Edward III, and their descendant became Edward IV. It was of great importance that the principal patrons of Walsingham were of such exalted rank.

Elizabeth de Clare confirmed the sanctuary and its possessions in the guardianship of the Black Canons of St. Augustine. At about that date, the priory held property in eighty-six parishes in Norfolk alone and many rights elsewhere. Many an English monarch paid tribute, and made personal pilgrimage thither, sometimes more than once.

The roads to the great shrine were marked by wayside crosses, probably like those en route to Rocamadour, and by a number of wayside chapels, at which, by custom, pilgrims called on their way.

What was the nature of this all-popular mecca? If major shrines abroad, with their unbroken traditions of veneration, have lost much (and sometimes all) documentation of their origins, is it to be wondered at if Walsingham is compelled to fall back on tradition as to its beginnings?

In the mid-fifteenth century, there was printed by the craftsman Richard Pynson a tract of four pages, dated internally after 1461 and published some few years later. The tract, written in the form of a ballad of twenty-one verses, professes to give an authentic account of the miraculous foundation at Walsingham, and claims to record what was then preserved in older books. Alas that none survives with which to make comparison.

The story thus handed down resolves itself as follows. A widow, Lady of the Manor, Richeldis de Faverches, was accorded a triple vision at Walsingham in 1061. In response to her prayer, that she might be allowed to honour Our Lady with some special work, the Blessed Virgin led her "in spirit" to Nazareth and showed her the little House of the Holy Family, then preserved beneath the Basilica of the Annunciation, commanding her to make another like it, to be set at Walsingham.

It is related that Our Lady gave a threefold reason for her wish. It was to be done: "unto her laud and singular honour," so that: "All who sought her there might find succour"; and in order that there should be found a memorial of the great joy of the Angelic Salutation.

The widow obeyed and called her carpenters to construct accordingly; but there arose a difficulty as to the choice of a site conformable to the Blessed Virgin's wishes. Guidance was sent in a heavy fall of dew which covered the land with a white rime, except two spaces equal in area to the new house.

One of these was close beside a pair of "twin wells", apparently a recognised feature of the place; and it was decided to choose this. But the workmen laboured all day in vain in their efforts to affix the house to the foundations they had laid.

The widow did not despair but saw in this fresh difficulty some design on Our Lady's part, and spent the night in prayer. Next dawn, the workmen found that the house had been lifted "by angels' hands" and set, where it remained for more than four hundred and fifty years, on the other "dry space" two hundred foot and more from the wells. The first site was marked by a chapel dedicated to St. Lawrence. Close beside the other, which was itself in time enshrined in a magnificent Lady Chapel, rose the grand and glorious priory church which was, until 1538, one of the splendours of England.

For the rest, the Pynson ballad tells of the wonders and miracles which were wrought there, in response to prayer, and concludes with a magnificent hymn of praise in honour of England's celestial Queen. England, it is stated, has reason to be glad, even to be compared with the Land of Promise, Sion, because here was built New Nazareth; and a mansion to the honour of the Heavenly Empress, and her most glorious salutation. For this reason, in every realm and region, England is called the "Holy Land, Our Lady's Dowry", and here, at Walsingham, is daily remembered the Angelic "Ave".

It was not to be expected that Henry VIII would spare so wealthy a sanctuary, who even despoiled the Royal Abbey of the Confessor and the resting place of his own parents. So savagely was Walsingham treated that it was laid level with the ground and those who dared to murmur were barbarously executed. So few traces remain that the very site of the Holy House of Walsingham was lost and any future reconstruction becomes problematical. William of Worcester has left guidance in some rather ambiguous measurements, which are probably more accurate than some critics would allow. Erasmus, who slashed violently at abuses which he thought to have cluttered up and obscured the more essential devotion, and who certainly made at least one pilgrimage to our national sanctuary, has left what seems to be a fairly accurate general description in his "Pilgrimage of Pure Devotion". The second part of this so-called satire includes the description of a visit to Canterbury. Insofar as they can be checked, references to the shrine of Our Lady Undercroft are accurate. It is, therefore, likely that references to the Holy House of Walsingham in the same colloquy or dialogue, can be depended on.

According to the Cambridge professor, the little Holy House was sealed over (panelled) with wood, having little light but that of tapers, and glistening within with the reflection of gold, silver and precious stones. Inside, there was an altar, usually with a Canon in attendance, and the figure of Our Lady stood at the right (i.e., Gospel, facing the people) end of the altar, in a dark corner.

These few details can be supplemented by one or two records of gifts or benefactions. There seems to have been a golden, or gilt, altar-piece, portraying the Annunciation. The figures of Our Lady and of St. Gabriel were vested, in accordance with general custom, in precious cloths. The seal of Walsingham Priory, dating back to an early age, portrays a seated figure of the *Sedes Sapientiae* type common in the twelfth century, when Walsingham was endowed, remarkable for the abundance and clarity of its detail. There seems no reason to suppose that this very carefully drawn little figure would represent other than that which the public would associate most prominently with the priory and the shrine. The majority of East Anglian figures of Our Lady—e.g., Lincoln, Ely, and a small wooden figure in the Victoria and Albert Museum—of this period were of the same type, though the details differed. One thing is certain: the figure of Our Lady and Holy Child enthroned, displayed on the Walsingham seal, is one of the most delicate and beautiful medieval representations that have survived.

Walsingham was founded, we are told, to be the shrine *par excellence* of the Mystery of the Incarnation. The seal figure clearly follows the iconography of the oldest, the *Hodegetria,* type of Madonna, exemplified in the eikon preserved in Saint Mary Major's, Rome. There, Our Lady is shown holding her Divine Son on her left arm, Who extends His right hand in blessing across His mother's breast, and Who clasps in His left hand a book—in types still older a scroll of parchment —symbolic of the Word made Flesh. Thus Our Lady is shown as the Seat of Wisdom, extending in her arms the Logos, the Word made Flesh, for the salvation of mankind.

This symbolism agrees exactly with the spirit and purpose of the Holy House, traditional shrine of the Immaculate Conception, and of the Annunciation, and home of the Holy Family during the years of Our Lord's adolescence at Nazareth.

True to this conception, the Walsingham seal shows Our Lady in the direct tradition of the great theological eikons of the Mother of God. She is enthroned as befits the Queen of Angels—Walsingham called her Heavenly Empress. She is crowned as befits the mistress of her English dowry. Her right hand bears the lily-sceptre, symbol of her virginal purity. Her feet, shod, rest upon a footstool, crushing a "toadstone" of uncleanliness. Her head is veiled as in the earliest paintings in the catacombs.

The throne, itself the shrine of the *Mater divinae gratiae,* is adorned with pillars symbolic of the Sacraments of the Church. Curtains on either side have their counterparts in the earliest Byzantine mosaics of the same theme.

Our Lord, with cruciform halo, is seated on Our Lady's left, as in all eikons of Hodegetria type. His posture is the same. His feet are bare, as befitting divinity. His right hand is outstretched in protection and blessing. His left hand clasps and displays for all to see a little Gospel-book, symbol of the Logos.

Apart from the shrine at Nazareth, the Holy House of which was translated to Loreto, where it is yet venerated, the oldest sanctuary of the Annunciation seems, symbolically, to be that on Mount Sinaï, the mountain associated by tradition with the giving of the Law, with the translation of the relics of St. Catherine of Alexandria, and, by early oriental tradition with the burning bush. At an incredibly early date, (c. 385), Silvia made pilgrimage thither and found a church dedicated to the Blessed Mother. This church is so orientated that at sunrise on March 25th, old style, the rays strike directly through an aperture in the wall beneath the altar of the burning bush, and across the silver disc which marks the traditional site of the root itself. The altar is surrounded, modern visitors tell us, with fourteen identical eikons representing the tradition that when Moses looked into the burning bush and beheld God, he saw in fact the image of the Blessed Mother with the Holy Child, the burning bush being thus symbolic of the ineffable and searching purity which is the Incarnation.

Mount Sinaï, the mountain of the Old Law, foreshadows the New. Saint Catherine, the protectress of those who defended Nazareth at the time of the Crusades, and the Holy Places, is laid to rest (traditionally by Angels' hands) upon the holy mountain, her shrine being preserved within the basilica of this proto-shrine of the Annunciation.

What connection is there, then, between old Mount Sinaï and England's New Nazareth, shrine of that great joy which commemorates the birth of the New Law? Simply this: that whereas the domain of Walsingham was regarded as New Nazareth, and "this so holy land", the approach to it was guarded, after the fourteenth century, by a chapel, visited by most if not all pilgrims, dedicated to St. Catherine of Mount Sinaï. More, even as Moses removed his shoes before setting foot on holy ground, pilgrims to Walsingham, we are told, removed their shoes at this spot on the pilgrims' road to England's Holy Land. It was a close analogy and one that does not seem likely to have been merely accidental.

Most of the pilgrims' chapels along the routes to Walsingham were destroyed. This chapel of St. Catherine, a mile outside the village, had the fortune to be preserved if only for mundane and secular uses. At least it does not seem to have been given over for schismatic or heretical worship. It was used as a poorhouse, as a barn, as a cowshed, but never for Protestant worship. And, apart from a chapel at King's Lynn which was the shrine of Our Lady of the Mount, it seems that this symbolic little chapel was the only one with any direct connection with the Holy Pilgrimage to Walsingham to be spared intact.

For some three hundred years, devotion to Our Lady of Walsingham fell into oblivion. The nineteenth century, with its revival of interest in archæology and things antiquarian, brought a new interest. Excavations were made amidst the slender ruins of the priory to seek out the site of the Lady Chapel. Remains were found which tallied closely with all that was known. An old pilgrim's arrow-badge, pointing prophetically, was unearthed. People became slightly Walsingham-conscious, and from a Catholic point of view

Waterton, in his *Pietas Mariana Britannica,* forged ahead. A devoted Catholic, second to none in his love for Our Blessed Lady, he published his exhaustive findings, far and away beyond anything disclosed by the antiquaries; though, undoubtedly, they made his task the easier. Hearts began to yearn for a return; back to Walsingham, back, as closely as possible, to the shrine built of old to commemorate the key Mystery of the Catholic Faith.

Alas, there was no place in Walsingham to which Catholics could turn, and not a single Catholic resident. England's Nazareth formed part of that huge district, the parish of King's Lynn, then larger than some counties. The decision was made to establish, at the parish church of the Annunciation, a shrine of Our Lady of Walsingham, built in replica of the Holy House of Loreto. A figure, copied from that of Our Lady of Cosmedin in Rome, was carved at Oberammergau, blessed by Pope Leo XIII and enshrined in this new sanctuary on August 19th, 1897.

While these plans for a Walsingham shrine at King's Lynn were fructifying, other developments were taking place. An Anglican lady, Miss Charlotte Boyd, was induced to enter into negotiations for the purchase of the dilapidated but still intact chapel of St. Catherine. This saintly woman desired nothing better than to see this chapel restored as a shrine of Our Blessed Lady. Before ever the purchase was complete, she received the gift of Faith and was received into the Catholic Church at the English Convent in Bruges, 1894. She carried on with her purpose, completed the purchase, and in 1895 set on foot to have the chapel perfectly restored. With the result that, in 1897, the day after the inauguration of the shrine at King's Lynn, Walsingham saw its first official Catholic pilgrimage since the Reformation wending its way down the lane to the Slipper Chapel, back in Catholic ownership.

Slipper Chapel? Yes, the chapel of St. Catherine is popularly called that from the tradition that pilgrims here took off their shoes. Probably it has an older significance, for slippers and shoes are not quite synonymous. A slype is a passage-way from the cloisters to the burying-ground in many an ancient monastic place. The word means "a way through", or "something in between". It may have been that this was the slype, or slip chapel, standing as it did between the Holy Land of Walsingham and the outer world.

There is no record whatever of the building of the Slipper Chapel. From the fact that it stands in the parish of Houghton St. Giles, then a cell of the priory of Horsham St. Faith, near Norwich, it is likely that it was served by Benedictines. The date of its building is often given as 1338, though certain architectural details suggest something rather later. It is quite small, measuring 12 feet 5 inches by 28 feet 6 inches. The narrow width and tall walls, with sharp pointed gables and chestnut wood timberings, create a remarkable sense of loftiness. The grand tracery of its east and west windows, strong and rich, the wealth of detail

of the admirable west front, its charming pastoral
situation beside the Stiffkey Brook in so pleasant a
Norfolk vale, all combine to establish in the Slipper
Chapel one of the architectural gems of fourteenth
century England.

Various moves were made to give effect to Miss
Boyd's desire that the Slipper Chapel should be restored
as a shrine. At last, in 1934, some years after her death,
her hopes were fulfilled. Under the direction of the
late Bishop of Northampton, Mgr. Lawrence Youens,
a new statue designed by Professor E. Tristram from
details of the ancient figure, and presented by Miss
Hilda Cary, of Torre Abbey in Devonshire, was
enshrined; and on August 19th, 1934, Cardinal
Bourne, then Archbishop of Westminster, assisted by
many Archbishops and Bishops and some nineteen
thousand pilgrims, led the first great national
pilgrimage back to Walsingham. From that time on,
the "Walsingham Way" between the village and the
Slipper Chapel has been thronged many times.

Confraternities of Our Lady have been founded in
association with many of her shrines. In the same
year, Bishop Youens erected the Guild of Our Lady
of Walsingham, with very simple undertakings, an
important branch of which was established at
Westminster Cathedral, where it thrives. Westminster
then started, in 1935, its first annual pilgrimage, a
custom since adopted by many other dioceses, parishes,
societies and groups. The same summer witnessed the
first walking pilgrimage, re-treading the old pilgrims'
way from London, 117 miles. In 1936 there was the
first of a series of united children's pilgrimages to pray
for their schools. These culminated in 1938, in the
gigantic National Pilgrimage of Catholic Youth, led by
Cardinal Hinsley.

This marked, incidentally, the fourth centenary of
the desecration of Walsingham, an occasion that might

have been doleful except that now it was filled with new hope. It was agreed that as the youth of England had taken the least part in that desecration, they should be given the greatest part in the commemoration. Pontifical High Masses were sung at the Slipper Chapel on both July 2nd and 3rd. On September 8th of the same year, the Bishop had the joy and consolation of being able to consecrate the chapel and an additional chapel of the Holy Ghost, built to provide extra accommodation for the many Masses said there.

Came the war. Walsingham played its part. Many were the prayers addressed to Our Blessed Lady on behalf of those in danger or distress. Catholic men and women of many nations found themselves forced by enemy aggression to take refuge in this country. Free French, Belgians, Dutch, Poles and others found a haven, and a spiritual home from home, in this unpretentious but exquisite shrine of the Mother of us all. Italian prisoners of war came to make thanksgiving for the liberation of their country.

Before they left England, a large number of United States Forces had the privilege of a great thanksgiving function, and they opened the new era of post-war hopes with solemn functions within the grounds of the ancient priory, close beside the twin wells and the actual site of England's Nazareth. English-speaking America can look to Walsingham as being an illustrious part of their common heritage.

And so the tide rolls on. Our Lady has regained a footing in this, the capital of her ancient dowry. The only chapel intact, with any direct connection with the former shrine, is now hers. In the village itself there is a chapel, however small, with daily Mass, and where the Blessed Sacrament is reserved. The present Bishop has announced his intention to build a great pilgrimage church, for which funds are being raised.

1948 marks, so far, the greatest year in this story

of development since the key years, 1894 and 1934.
On July 2nd, fourteen parties of Priests and Laymen
set out from different parts of the country, from places
as far apart as Middlesbrough, Wrexham and
Canterbury, for a fourteen-day journey on foot to
Walsingham, bearing, after the manner of the Vezelay
Centenary Pilgrimage, nine-foot crosses of solid oak.
This was the solemn pilgrimage of Prayer and Penance
which created a profound impression among people of
all classes and beliefs wherever this moving spectacle
was witnessed.

The crosses were timed to arrive at Walsingham by
midnight of July 15th, eve of the feast of Our Lady
of Mount Carmel, to coincide with the national
pilgrimage of the Union of Catholic Mothers on the
feast-day proper. At day-break, the crosses were
borne, one by one, to the Slipper Chapel, where Masses
were being said in continuous succession at a number
of altars.

Special trains and scores of motor coaches brought
supporting pilgrims in their thousands from far and
wide. Pontifical Mass was sung at an open-air altar
near the chapel. After noon began the solemn
procession of these fourteen crosses along the Pilgrims'
Way, into Walsingham, led by His Eminence,
Cardinal Griffin, Archbishop of Westminster, the
Bishop of the diocese, Mgr. Leo Parker, and a
considerable number of prelates.

At the site of the old priory was given the Blessing
of the Sick with the Most Holy Sacrament, followed
by solemn Benediction. This was the occasion when
the Cardinal, fulfilling the request made by Our Lady
at Fatima, dedicated the country to the Immaculate
Heart of Mary.

The story of Walsingham, already ancient four
hundred years ago, is one of the future. Mary inspired
Richeldis to found there a shrine in honour of that

fundamental Mystery of the Annunciation, with the assurance that all who should seek her there devoutly would find her help and succour. The request was obeyed, thereby entitling England to that proud title which is still hers, Our Lady's Dowry.

Sacrilegious attempts were made to snatch that Dowry away. The Dower House was destroyed. But not altogether. A remnant was left and this, aided by the faith of multitudes and strengthened by their prayers and the good works of many, has become like the grain of mustard seed. A new Walsingham has sprung into being, new Walsingham and a new New Nazareth. At a time when the same breed of materialistic atheists who did so much to damage and destroy Our Lady's shrines abroad, but in vain, are making such desperate efforts to stamp out the Catholic Faith, the spearhead of attack seems to be directed against the sanctity and rights of home and family.

Walsingham, shrine of the Annunciation, is, for the same reason, shrine of the Holy Home. As such it provides a focus for countless aspirations and prayers in the thick of this intensive struggle against un-Christian materialism. This is pre-eminently the message of Nazareth and of Loreto.

Mary, at Fatima, promised the world that, in the end, her Immaculate Heart would triumph. Walsingham can play a great part in hastening that supreme victory. It is the privilege of our own age and generation to witness and take part in the rebuilding of a great Marial sanctuary in Great Britain. Walsingham, England's shrine, must take its place once more beside the other citadels of Our Lady with which she has so richly endowed the world.

# V: CHARTRES

MANY people have heard of the lovely cathedral at Chartres. As soon as it is mentioned, they exclaim: "Ah yes! That is the place with the fine stained-glass," for all the world as if the cathedral church had been built especially to display those famous windows.

It is solely to see the glass that quite a number of English visitors journey there, who are apt to be annoyed when their tours of inspection are interrupted by the Divine Office which is daily sung in choir.

No one, however, can study those windows for any length of time and not be impressed, not only with their obviously spiritual portrayal, but with the constant repetition displayed in them of the theme of Our Lady as the Mother of God.

Over and over again, as one walks round the great church, is one confronted by magnificent scenes in which the Holy Mother is the centre, and many of which are known the world over through photographs and pictures. So that, at last, the visitor is quite ready to declare, as if some discovery had just been made, that Chartres Cathedral is indeed a Temple of God and a bejewelled shrine of His Mother; and that, precisely, is what it is.

One is led immediately to find that the cathedral is dedicated to Our Lady and then that it was built to enshrine not just the glass which adorns it, but no less than three famous, distinct shrines of Our Lady in this one church. Of these, that of Our Lady Underground, or Notre Dame de Sous-Terre, claims to be the oldest shrine of Our Lady in the world, having had an astonishing origin in pre-Christian, Druidic times.

The Faith was borne to France, that is to Southern Gaul and the region round Lyons, in the Apostles' lifetime and by certain disciples of St. John, such as St. Pothinus. Chartres, as we learn from Julius Caesar, was the chief seat of Druidic worship in Gaul and in a grotto on the hill where today the cathedral stands was an altar erected to the *Virgo Paritura,* the Virgin who should conceive, to whom the local king and his people dedicated themselves.

Indeed there is eminent authority for believing that in Druidic times they used to offer sacrifice here *Matri futurae Dei nascituri*—to the Mother of the God who was yet to be born.

Thus it was that when the Saints Polentianus and Savinianus reached Chartres with the Gospel they found as it were a shrine of Our Lady already installed and a people prepared to accept their message.

Nor can be it maintained that these facts rest only on tradition. The grotto still forms the crypt of the present cathedral, and has been religiously preserved throughout the ages of development. Modern research, and excavations made necessary during the worst part of the war, led to the discovery of enough traces of undoubted Druidic culture to support the ancient tradition of the place.

In 1020 it was decided to replace the wooden church covering the crypt with a church of stone. The grotto was left intact, as a martyrium surrounded by a processional way, with three side chapels, the whole being roofed with stone and made into a vast crypt beneath the new cathedral.

So celebrated did this shrine become that it attracted attention all over Europe. Hither had already come

the famous Clovis who had been taught the elements
of the Faith here by Solenne, the Bishop.  The earliest
Carolingian kings, Hugues and Pepin, performed acts
of liberality.  Here Louis the Débonnaire and Lothaire
consecrated their arms of war.

Of greater importance still, in 876, Charles the Bald
offered the wonderful relic of Our Lady's veil.  This
treasure had long been preserved at Constantinople
and had been presented to Charlemagne by the
Empress Irene.  The Holy Veil was later removed to
a new shrine, of equal importance to that of Our Lady
in the Crypt, above the High Altar, where it has been
preserved ever since.

Of other royal and famous pilgrims to Our Lady
of Chartres only a few may here be mentioned.  St.
Louis arrived on foot and for his offering caused a
wonderful North Porch to be built to give access to
the sanctuaries.  Every King of France save two, Louis
XV and XVI, made pilgrimage here.

From England, several monarchs paid visits, made
vows or gave rich offerings: Canute, Queen Matilda,
Richard Lion Heart, and Edward III.

Three Popes, Pascal II, Innocent II and Alexander
III journeyed to this proto-shrine of Our Lady, as well
as numerous saints.  Among their number were St.
Anselm and St. Thomas of Canterbury, St. Bernard
and St. Francis de Sales, St. Vincent de Paul and
Benedict Joseph Labre.

The shrine of Our Lady Underground survived intact
throughout the ages until the French Revolution.  This
is the description of the statue given by Pintard in
1681: "The Virgin is seated on a chair, holding her
Son sitting on her knees, who blesses with His right
hand, and in His other holds an orb.  His head is
bare and His hair quite short.  His robe is close-fitting
and girdled with a belt; His face, hands and feet,
which are bare, are of shining grey-ebony colour.  The

VIRGINI PARITVRÆ

*The statue of Our Lady Underground,
Chartres, represents the world's most
ancient shrine to the Mother of God*

(Page 58)

*Our Lady of Einsiedeln reigns in splendour in the Holy Chapel built for her a thousand years ago*

(Page 64)

Virgin is clad in an antique mantle, shaped like a chasuble. Her face is oval, of perfect design and of the same shining black colour. Her crown is plain and only the top is adorned with flowers like small leaves. The chair is one foot in width with four posts, hollowed out at the back and carved. The statue is 29 inches in height.''

Alas, at the Revolution in 1793, Our Lady of Chartres (like Our Lady of Walsingham, earlier in England) was thrown to the flames and destroyed. It is said that all the persons who took part in that sacrilege went mad.

It was some time before any serious effort was made to restore the sanctuary, though the memory of it and devotion to Our Lady of Chartres remained fervent in the hearts of the faithful. At last the order was given to the Parisian sculptor, Fontenelle, who made a new figure according to all the known details—details borne out by certain medieval representations carved on the fabric, or in the stained glass known to be approximate copies. This new figure was enthroned in 1857, since when many National Pilgrimages have been led hither.

Chartres has thus ever been a citadel in the fortress of Devotion to Our Lady.

The special feasts of Our Lady ''Underground'' take place each year on September 8th and 15th and on December 8th. On September 8th children are brought in their thousands to be dedicated to Our Lady. On the 15th there is a glorious procession—one that has to be experienced to appreciate its significance—which winds round the crypt, the largest crypt of any European cathedral.

The second shrine, of Our Lady's Veil, is still preserved with the utmost care in a magnificent golden reliquary in a strong safe by the high altar. From the date when it was given by the Empress Irene to Charlemagne in Byzantium there is no gap in its history. It reached Chartres in 876, the gift of Charles the Bald. In 911, it was hoisted as a battle standard by the townsfolk, when they were being besieged by Rollo and his brigands, who were routed at the sight of it.

For a long time it was thought that this veil, wrapped up in very ancient, fine material, was a tunic or chemise, and was known as such. But at the French Revolution the case was forced open and the veil revealed in its glory. It was about six yards long and woven of the purest and finest silk threads. The insurgents saved it to "prove" the Church wrong: that this holy relic of a shirt was but a veil. But what a veil! Its material and weaving demonstrate it to be very ancient and of oriental, quite possibly Palestinian, origin, cream-white in colour, like ancient ivory.

The veil itself has always been kept wrapped in an outer cloth of unbleached linen, of very ancient, arabic origin. The two together are now preserved in a truly magnificent reliquary, made to commemorate the thousandth anniversary of its donation in 876. The erroneous belief that it was a shirt or "chemise" accounts for the tunic-shaped garment on the cathedral coat-of-arms.

Each year, on August 15th, there is a solemn procession round the city of Chartres in which this priceless relic is carried.

The third shrine at Chartres is that of Our Lady of the Pillar, in the north choir aisle. She is also called the "Black Virgin". In the 16th century this statue was set upon the rood-loft. The city kept such a huge candle burning before it, that it was known as the Tower of Wax. The antiphons of Our Lady were, and still are, solemnly sung at this shrine.

In 1763, the rood-loft was pulled down, and the figure was set upon a marble pillar in a shrine a few yards distant. In 1806 this pillar was replaced by the present one, a column from the old rood-loft used before.

This shrine is today the most popular of the three, partly because it is easiest of access. Lamps are kept burning, and hundreds of votive lights in normal days of plenty. The figure is curiously garbed in rich garments which, however beautiful, conceal the true beauty of the carving. The Blessed Virgin is seated on a plain throne. Her black face speaks of kindness and candour. She has golden hair. With her left hand she holds the Holy Child upon her left knee. In her right hand she holds a pear. The Holy Child faces those who would adore Him and venerate His Mother, extending His right hand in blessing while with His left He clasps an object which is not so much an orb as a globe or ball.

Notre-Dame du Pilier was crowned by Pope Pius IX on 31st May, 1855, and ever since, on this anniversary, the figure is carried in solemn procession.

Chartres, then, still has the original veil of Our Lady, and the original figure of Our Lady of the Pillar. Down below there remains the shrine of the oldest devotion to the Mother of God known in the world. Of three shrines, this is by far the most ancient and of greatest interest to English pilgrims. It is she, Our Lady Underground, who explains the glory of the cathedral and the reason for its coloured glass!

## VI : EINSIEDELN

WE English Catholics tend to feel that our country has been separated from the common Faith of our Continental neighbours for so long that it comes as a pleasant surprise each time we find some fresh evidence of the very close ties that existed between ourselves and our Catholic neighbours in the ages of Faith.

That there should have been some such close contact with Normandy and Northern France, any cursory reading of English History would lead one to expect; non-Catholic history text-books lose no opportunity to point out that the high places in the Church in England were filled with popish foreigners, whether as Bishops or Abbots.

It is, therefore, all the more pleasant to learn that one of the most important Benedictine Abbeys of Europe, that of Einsiedeln, in Switzerland, site of one of the most celebrated sanctuaries of Our Lady, had close ties with our English (Saxon) Royal Family and was for some time actually ruled by an Abbot who renounced the English throne for the monastic life.

Einsiedeln, nowadays, is a pleasant, small market town, not many miles from Zürich, which is crowned and dominated by the great abbey from which it takes its name. Originally there was only one single hermit's cell, founded in 840 by a holy Benedictine monk, St. Meinrad, who had been given permission to seek the solitary life, from his Abbey of Reichenau.

At first he had settled on a small mountain near Altendorf, but soon his popularity as a confessor found him out so, taking his Missal, Rule of St. Benedict, one or two holy books and, above all, a treasured image of Our Lady, he withdrew even further into the wildest part of the surrounding forest. Thus Our Lady of Einsiedeln came to be enshrined in St. Meinrad's tiny oratory where—in very different surroundings—it is still venerated.

Twenty-six years did St. Meinrad live in his seclusion, although he allowed that to be interrupted by the visits of a good many mountain folk for instruction and advice. Wild beasts, too, were not afraid of him and he made friends with many. In particular, two crows made their home near the hermitage and became so tame that they would feed out of the hermit's hand. At last, however, two ruffians, named Richard and Peter, came determined to bludgeon the hermit to death because they imagined some great treasure lay hidden in his cell.

No sooner had they committed this fearful crime when two candles lit of themselves, in honour of the dead saint, and the murderers rushed away terrified without completing their search. As the two men ran, the crows pursued them, pecking at them and flapping with their wings right up to the house where they lived in Zürich.

This story has been reproduced in sculpture and painting in many local churches. The Abbey of Einsiedeln bears two crows on its armorial shield and, until recently, the custom prevailed among the lay-brothers of catching a crow each autumn and caring for it through the bitter winter months until spring, when with some merriment it would be set at liberty.

St. Meinrad died in 863 and was buried at Reichenau, until 1039. In the meantime his hermitage became the scene of great popular devotion, where innumerable favours were granted, it seemed through the intercession of Our Lady whom they besought there.

So impressed was one of these visitors, Benno, a canon of Strasbourg, that he determined to found a community of hermits on this already consecrated spot. For a short time Benno became Bishop of Metz, where he ruled with a stern hand. One day some enemies, who preferred their vices and evil living to the good works of their Bishop, took him and tore out his eyes. Their crime was punished by the Emperor, Henry I, but Benno was glad to take this opportunity of returning to his old beloved hermitage. He died in 940, was buried at the foot of Our Lady's altar, and was succeeded by his especial disciple, Eberhard, a Swabian noble.

It was Eberhard who conceived the idea of turning this group of hermitages into a recognised Benedictine Abbey, and he became the first Abbot. Space does not permit the telling of the history of this important abbey, but the legend of the heavenly consecration of the new abbey church, built to enshrine St. Meinrad's Holy Chapel as a Lady Chapel, is too famous to be ignored.

As soon as the church was ready, it was planned to consecrate it on September 14th, 948, by Conrad, Bishop of Constance, who was accompanied by St. Ulric of Augsburg. The eve of the consecration was observed as a day of vigil and fasting, and, as Conrad and Ulric prayed, they suddenly beheld the church brilliantly lit up, and filled with a heavenly host, with Our Lord Himself in the midst standing at the altar.

Conrad himself wrote down the story and it has been preserved for us to this day as he wrote it. On September 15th, the good Bishop started the ceremonies of Consecration and entered the church for that purpose, but an unknown voice was heard, ringing out among the rafters, in no uncertain tone: *"Cessa,*

*cessa, frater!* *Capellus divinitus consecratus est!"*
"Stop, stop, brother. The chapel has been consecrated
by God."

Sixteen years later Conrad and Ulric both solemnly
deposed to the truth of this narrative before Pope Leo
VIII, who issued a Bull to the whole world, forbidding
any reconstruction of the church and granting large
indulgences to pilgrims there.

St. Eberhard was succeeded by an Englishman as
Abbot, named Gregory. Of him it is recorded that he
was the eldest son of King Edward the Elder, whose
daughter Edith had married the Emperor Otho. With
this strong family tie with the Holy Roman Empire,
the importance of many royal gifts is not to be wondered
at. Among them was the elevation of the
dignity of Abbot of Einsiedeln to a Princedom of the
Empire, and until the end of the eighteenth century
the Abbots of Einsiedeln ranked as Prince-Abbots,
with great powers over the surrounding countryside.

In 1039 the relics of St. Meinrad were brought back
to the Abbey. For the following seven hundred years
the monastery continued its existence with little
disturbance and to the lasting satisfaction and
prosperity of the little town that sprang up around it.
In particular the monks taught the people the art of
carpentry and cabinet making, thus founding an
industry which still flourishes. They also introduced
fairs, to the benefit of all the nearby farmers, and these
fairs, highly picturesque, still serve their useful purpose
in the great square in front of the Abbey.

Although five fires, at various times, destroyed the
enshrining church, it is remarkable that the little Holy
Chapel of St. Meinrad suffered no harm. On entering
the church by the main door it is the first thing which
strikes the eye. In 1467 it was decided to encase the
humble walls with costly marble, which was renewed
in 1617, and later prelates have vied with one another

in ornamenting and enriching this outer casing, so that like the Holy House of Loreto, with which alone it can be compared, it has become a veritable jewel amidst the surrounding glory of the church itself.

The greatest crisis occurred in the revolutionary days of 1798. French troops arrived and on the very day that they seized Einsiedeln, the monks fled with Our Lady's statue to the valley of Alp Thal. From the Curé there, the French demanded the surrender of the figure; but with great bravery he caused it to be smuggled away to a convent of nuns at Bludenz.

This was done by one Placid Keller, disguised as a pedlar, who passed right through the French lines, selling merchandise as he went. At Bludenz, immense demonstrations of devotion were held in the public square. For some years the figure was taken from village to village, never kept so long in any one place that it might be permanently adopted; and then, at long last, back to Bludenz. One of the monks, Conrad, always accompanied Our Lady of Einsiedeln.

In 1803, it proved possible at last to restore the image to its shrine, and it was borne into the Abbey in triumphal procession.

The shrine had suffered fearful material spoliation, and had been stripped of gold and jewels. But devotion had in no way diminished and it was not long before something of the old splendour returned.

Today Einsiedeln is a wonderful centre of devotion. More than a quarter of a million confessions are made there each year. Pilgrims flock from all the surrounding countries and a rule has been made that those who come from the furthest places should be shriven first. It can be gathered that this leads at times to some amusing arguments.

There are some fifty hotels within a few minutes' walk. All of them moderate in price, according to their grade. Masses begin daily in the Holy Chapel at 4-30 a.m., and in the season continue till noon. On Holydays there is a monastic High Mass, and on great feasts the Abbatial Mass is as splendid as any such function in Europe. The Abbey is renowned for its music and singing.

Every day after Vespers, the Choir Monks make a solemn procession out from the enclosure to the Holy Shrine, there to sing a wonderful "Salve Regina", which is impressive for its simplicity and for its lovely music, traditional to Einsiedeln for many centuries. It is this ceremony, perhaps, which will leave the most lasting mark on the pilgrim's memory.

There have been many ties between England and Einsiedeln. It offers a happy halting place for those en route for Rome. It is not to be wondered, therefore, that there is almost always some English-speaking pilgrim in residence in the Abbey, and the number of Masses said for the conversion of our country each year is quite considerable.

It was the author's privilege to assist at no less than four such Masses during a short visit of a single week, quite recently. The progress of Catholic Restoration in England must gain much from the assistance of such Masses at such shrines. Our Lady of the Hermits, Our Lady of Einsiedeln, will pour great grace upon those who intercede for her Dowry in this far-off chosen home of hers.

## VII: MONTSERRAT

S HRINES of Our Blessed Lady may be said to fall
into several distinct categories. Some, like
Lourdes, crown spots chosen through her
Apparitions thereat. Others, like Pompeii, expose for
veneration pictures or statues that attract devotion far
wider than that of merely local congregations. A third
kind, such as that at Chartres, or in Notre Dame, Paris,
has risen to universal eminence through historic
association and antiquity; though it is often hard to
distinguish precisely between the second and third
groups.

There are, however, several sanctuaries of Our Lady
which have claim to belong to all three of these classes,
being of great historic antiquity, widely popular
because of many wonderful favours granted in answer
to prayers at them and chosen, at least according to
tradition, through the apparent intervention of the
Blessed Virgin herself.

Such a shrine is that at Montserrat in Spain, truly
magnificent, fascinating, and one of the most renowned
of all Our Lady's citadels.

Montserrat is the name given to an enormous and
fantastic block of mountains 4,000 feet high which
stands, somewhat aloof, twenty-two miles from
Barcelona. At first sight this sheer mass of rock, seven
miles long, appears inaccessible. In fact several roads
find their way through seemingly impossible gullies up
to a rocky niche that enshrines the sanctuary itself.

The name *Mons Serratus*, ''saw-edged mountain'', is descriptive of the actual massif. Its structure is weird and, at times, terrifying. Vast blocks of rock rise in tiers on all sides; and of all colours, like petrified waves, worn by erosion into crests of extraordinary pattern. But there is found no sense of barren hostility. These are friendly, sheltering rocks and every nook and cranny is fertile, and luxuriant with a vegetation that gives the impression of a tropical countryside.

But it is not just phantasy of nature, or yet the superb panorama which the summit has to display that attracts each year so many thousands of visitors. It is probably true to say that the mountain would have remained unvisited and well-nigh unscaleable had there not been established on it a great shrine of Our Lady. Twelve hundred years ago, when this story began, there dwelt thereon but a few shepherds and hermits; today there is to be found a great abbey, surrounded by a veritable city of pilgrim-hospices and hostelries, reached by well-made roads and by funicular and rack-railways which never lack an abundance of passengers.

The origin of this devotion is lost in antiquity. The earliest written records are dated 932, when Sunyer, Count of Barcelona, confirmed and renewed the gift made by his father, in 888, of Montserrat and its Chapel of St. Mary to the Benedictine Abbey of Ripoli. This gift was again confirmed in 982 by Lothaire, King of France.

There is nothing incredible, that there should have been a shrine of Our Lady here in the ninth century. Spanish devotion to the Blessed Virgin was well advanced two hundred years before.

Constant and unbroken tradition, however, holds that at some time previous to 888, an image of Our Lady was miraculously found among the rocks of Montserrat. It is not without interest or outside the

realms of possibility that ancient chronicles claim that
the figure came from Jerusalem by way of Egypt to
Barcelona, and thence to the mountain to escape from
Saracen profanation.   The original figure of Loreto had
a similar tradition and was of Egyptian origin.   This,
at Montserrat, has strong, oriental, features. Byzantine
craftsmen were so widely employed in the west, though,
that   eastern   characteristics   do   not   of   themselves
determine eastern manufacture.

The legend of the finding is charming, and, to say
the   least,   may   well   contain   elements   of   truth.
Shepherds, watching their flocks by night at the foot
of the mountain, were amazed to behold lights and to
hear singing, as of angels, up on the cliffs on successive
Saturday nights.

The Bishop, who at that time lived at Manresa, was
notified and, with the shepherds as guides, made the
difficult   ascent   to   the   scene.    There   they   found,
enthroned on a ledge in a cavern, a diminutive, wooden
figure of Our Lady and the Holy Child.   This they
venerated and   then   set   about   to   remove   it   to the
cathedral.

A procession was formed but, after a mile or two,
the figure became so heavy (like that of Lujan in
Argentina) that it was decided to accept it as a sign
and to leave it in the chapel of a nearby hermitage.
There it remained, greatly reverenced by the people
of the entire district, until a special church was built to
receive it, on the site of the present Abbey.

The monastery was dependent on Ripoli until 1410,
when Benedict XIII raised it to the status of an
independent abbey.   His Bull was ratified by Popes
Martin V and Eugene IV.   The shrine came to be
regarded as the most celebrated in Spain.   Nor was
the cave, the holy grotto, where the treasured figure
was   found,   forgotten.    A   second   church,   with   a
miniature priory, was built to protect it and special

Masses were said there every Saturday and feast day of Our Lady.

The original Abbey Church underwent many changes. What is certain is that Our Lady was venerated there already in the ninth century. From that date, as the shrine became wider known and played an ever increasing part in people's lives, rebuildings and enlargements were frequent until 1592, when the present glorious basilica was consecrated. The nave is two hundred feet long and more than fifty wide. Twelve side chapels flank it and the sanctuary dominates all, with its truly stupendous high altar and canopy that towers above it, enthroning the ancient figure.

The precious statue is set on a marble throne above, and behind, this high altar. To get near it, pilgrims must ascend by two stairways on either side of the altar, up to the shrine chapel which is known as the "Cambril". This is likened to Our Lady's private apartment; just as Erasmus recorded that Our Lady of Walsingham had her "own privy chamber". Its walls are covered with rare marbles and the panelled ceiling is enriched with a splendid painting of the Discovery of the little Madonna by the Shepherds, by the artist Llimona.

Kneeling at a prayer desk in the "Cambril", one can see the figure, which Spanish people call affectionately "La Morenata"—"Little Black Madonna"—quite clearly. The image is 38 inches high and of whatever wood it is made, is now black with age. The Holy Child is seated centrally on His Mother's knees, with His right hand in blessing. In His left hand, He holds a little fir cone. Both He and His Mother are crowned. Her face, carved with a very dignified regal countenance, is set off by an embroidered veil; and in her right hand she bears a majestic orb. Her robe falls in delicate folds to her ankles—her feet are shod, though Our Lord's are bare.

Normally, the statue is covered with a golden mantle, tunic and veil. Whatever one may think of this custom of vesting statues—it was a normal practice in England before the Reformation—at least one may say that it has been the means of preserving the rich carving and colouring beneath. On rare occasions, when the figure is borne in triumphant procession, it may be seen in its pristine glory.

As one kneels to venerate "La Morenata", it is awe-inspiring to remember that other pilgrims have knelt likewise for more than a thousand years and that many saints are included in their number—SS. Vincent Ferrer, Peter Claver, Francis Borgia, Ignatius Loyola, Joseph Calasanz, Peter Nolasco, John of Matha, Benedict Labre are but a few of the host who have done so.

Adjacent to the "Cambril" is the famous choir school or "Escalonia", one of the happiest features of Montserrat. Here for centuries has been maintained a scola of some forty boys to sing during divine service and serve at the altar. It was founded in the thirteenth century. Boys are admitted at the age of eight and remain until sixteen. They get a sound, happy education—they are full of life and fun and pranks— and many become professional musicians.

The interest of Montserrat is not confined, however, solely to the shrine. Second only in importance is the holy grotto where the figure was found. Perched on the edge of a precipice, this is a charming haven of peace, adorned with a magnificent view. The church was built to enshrine the rock niche, still to be seen inside, behind the main altar. A model of Our Lady rests on the exact spot.

The Abbey is surrounded by a number of mountain peaks, each approached by its own dizzy pathway, each crowned with its own patriarchal hermitage,

thirteen in all. These were occupied, in accordance
with the Rule of St. Benedict, by specially prepared
monks, trained for the particularly solitary life. They
remained in use, or at least some did, until 1822, when
the last of the hermits, Fr. Gaspard Soler, was
murdered. This tragic episode put an end to the
eremetic life of the whole mountain.

Although devotion to Our Lady has continued
unchecked on the mountain for a thousand years, the
Abbey has not always enjoyed unbroken peace. It
was disgracefully sacked by Napoleon—was not that
act the beginning of his downfall? It was looted, and
for a time suppressed, in 1835, but restored in 1842.
Since 1862, the monastery has formed part of the
Cassinese Congregation of the Primitive Benedictine
Observance—the same Congregation to which
Buckfast, Prinknash, Ramsgate and Farnborough
Abbeys belong, as well as Pluscarden in Scotland.

Needless to say, the *Opus Dei* is performed at
Montserrat with true Benedictine splendour.

But even in our own day terror has been enacted
within its walls. Barcelona was a hotbed for the
Communist revolution prior to the World War of 1939.
Who does not remember the terrible days of the
"Spanish Civil War"? Montserrat suffered as bitterly
as any religious house in Spain. Monks were murdered
in cold blood—among them the brother of Dom Anselm
Albareda, O.S.B., Prefect of the Vatican Library, also
a monk of Montserrat.

The figure of Our Lady has survived each of these
upheavals. At each incursion of the godless, friends
forewarned have smuggled her away to safety. On
the last occasion, it was only a replica that the Reds
discovered, and that they hurled to the flames.

Pilgrims approach Montserrat from Barcelona by
way of Monistrol and the rack-railway which takes
them to the square immediately in front of the Abbey.

Here they find the Fountain of the Gate—also called the Fountain of Miracles—which reminds them, with its ever-cool waters, of the abundance of Our Lady's graces that flow for those who seek her in this her chosen sanctuary.

Nearby, too, is the Pilgrimage Office where each pilgrim can arrange with the guest-masters for accommodation in one or other of the eight or nine gigantic hospices according to their means and needs. No one is allowed to stay more than a week.

Some of the hostels are like hotels; all meals are served in large dining-rooms. There are others wherein the rooms are fitted with small kitchens, where pilgrims can cook their own food. The monks provide hospitals and dispensaries for the sick and shops where food may be bought. There is an almonry where the needs of the very poor are relieved. A large army of servants and retainers is employed each year to clean the rooms, wash the linen and attend to the needs of pilgrims. It is a great undertaking.

In Spain, Montserrat has always served as a bulwark against godlessness in all its forms. Today it is a Citadel of Faith to which the whole world may well look as possessing, and presenting, an enduring value which has triumphed over time and all the tyrannies of human government.

MONTSERRAT. *The original statue of Our Lady of Montserrat, and (right) the high altar of the Abbey Church with the statue enthroned*

(Page 70)

HAL. *The beautiful sanctuary of Our Lady of Hal, and (right) the tower crowned with a curious Flemish steeple*

(Page 77)

# VIII: HAL

**F**LANDERS, England's near neighbour, has a history quite as old and rich as our own and in many ways, particularly in Belgium, its culture and mode of government, its people and towns and villages, its farmsteads and countryside resemble those of our country. There is, however, one vast difference. Whereas England, through apostasy, largely lost the Faith, Belgium remained loyal in spite of vicious attacks and brutal onslaughts. Her ancient churches still serve the Faith for which they were built. And, as may well be supposed, the people of Belgium are second to none in the fervour of their devotion to Our Lady.

As in England of old, every Belgian church has its local shrine of the Blessed Mother. Of these more than twenty are important pilgrimage centres, drawing crowds of pilgrims from wide areas. Yet, although so short a distance separates us from them, how many could the average English Catholic name, still less relate anything of their history or message?

Undoubtedly, the most truly national Belgian shrine is that of Hal, a small town a few miles south of Brussels, in the Duchy and Province of Brabant. This sanctuary, more than any other, is Belgium's Walsingham and is in many ways worthy of comparison. It has, too, more than one link with English history.

Certainly the most important event in the annals

of Hal was the gift, in 1267, of the "Black Madonna", by Alice, Princess of Holland and Zeeland. There is an unrefuted tradition that this statue was the finest of four of Our Lady given by St. Elizabeth of Hungary to her daughter, Sophie, who married the Duke of Brabant in 1239. It was her niece who gave this priceless gift to Hal.

At once the fame of this new shrine began to spread, due to the number of graces and favours obtained thereat. As a result, an ever-increasing flood of pilgrims began to surge towards the little town which has continued thither ever since. Within a few years, an important confraternity was established, and plans were made by the townsfolk to raise a magnificent church more worthy of Our Lady, *Regina Coeli,* whose throne was now so firmly established in their midst.

A Register, begun in 1344, claims William II, Duke of Brabant, who laid the foundation stone in 1341, as its earliest signatory but the names that succeed his make it read like a history book. Emperors, kings, princes, nobles, queens and princesses have given their names to this Confraternity, which received recognition and favours from Popes Martin V and Eugene IV. Among the earliest members was King Edward III of England, an interesting proof of the strong ties between Catholic England and the Continent.

Under such august patronage, a new church soared up, to become one of the most splendid of all the Gothic churches of Belgium. A hundred years later, in spite of the ravages of the Black Death, both sanctuary and confraternity had grown to such importance that Pope Eugene IV, in 1438, raised by Papal Bull the church to collegiate rank.

Entire towns vied with each other for the honour of promising annual civic pilgrimages. Forty-five such pledges were made. To this day Brussels, Ghent, Namur, Liege, Bruges and many other places reserve a regular day each year for their municipal pilgrimage.

It would be quite impossible, in one short article, to describe this magnificent sanctuary in detail. The town is dominated by it; and its tower, crowned with its curious Flemish steeple, is visible for many miles around.

Many Belgian churches are larger, but for lavish magnificence this at Hal commands awe and wonderment. The lofty nave and choir, with superb vaulting and exquisite ceilings are open to the eye from end to end. The immense windows, filled with intricate, lace-like tracery, help to create an impression of size and spaciousness which not all the detail and decoration can dwarf or diminish. Wherever the eye turns, there is a wealth of carving and ornament; niches, canopies, corbels, arcading, pinnacles and balustrades; yet never so much that the majestic effect is spoiled. From one end to the other, artists and craftsmen, abetted by liberal benefactors, have conspired and competed to create as superb a palace for Our Lady as human skill could devise.

Originally, Our Lady of Hal had her "own privy chamber", as at Walsingham, in the Lady Chapel— a perfect gem of architecture—on the north side of the chancel; a chapel that is as lovely as anything built in Belgium. But so important has the cultus become in recent years, and so great the number of pilgrims, that it was decided, in 1910, to mark the fifth centenary of the consecration of the church by the erection of a new high altar; and the Shrine of Our Lady was translated thither, to a lofty throne at the east end of the chancel where it is accessible to a far greater number of people.

Surrounding the sanctuary is a corona of nine apsidal chapels—all fourteenth century work—vying with one another in the fascination of the carving and sculpture on their walls, columns and ceilings—biblical scenes, statues of saints and angels, clusters of rich foliage, intertwining grapevines laden with fruit, grotesques of devils, imps and figures of death.

She is seated, is Our Lady of Hal, tall, majestic, slender, queenly; yet as a mother she is feeding her child. Those parts of the statue that are visible are black with age. The rest is hidden by a wealth of regal vestments, the handwork and gifts of queens and princesses. The figure beneath these trappings presents a queer contrast. Of immense antiquity, it seems that the body was at some time bound, round and round, with plaster-stiffened bandages and then covered with silver. This is the suggested explanation of much of the blackness due, it is said, to oxidisation caused by the metal. The Byzantine character of the carving strongly supports the tradition of her near-eastern origin.

Our Lady is represented as the Mother of Christ, but it is as *Regina Coeli* she reigns at Hal; and Queen of Heaven she is: Queen by gift; Queen through the centuries of homage by the faithful; Queen through the abundance of those graces which have flowed from her throne. As Queen she was solemnly crowned in 1874 in the name of Pope Pius IX, although her crown was made four hundred years before.

It must suffice to say that more than a hundred miracles as such have been attested and accredited to Our Lady through her shrine at Hal. Medals bearing her image usually show her statue resting on a pile of cannon balls. These, thirty-two in number, are still to be found preserved in a niche beneath the tower. A commemorative plaque bears the date "9 and 10 July, 1580".

This recalls an episode in the politico-religious wars of the time, when Hal was besieged by William the Silent. It seemed impossible for the town to stand against such overwhelming odds but the people flocked to their Queen in prayer. Hal was victorious, and these are cannon balls which fell harmlessly around the shrine. For this no especial miracle is claimed, though it is remarkable that Hal has come through so many wars with its sanctuary unscathed.

It is worthy of record that on the day of liberation from the Germans in 1945, British soldiers carried Our Lady of Hal on their shoulders through the streets in thanksgiving.

Medals of Our Lady of Hal possess exceptional indulgences, granted by Pope Pius V. When the Gueux, a villainous sect of extreme Protestants, were marching through Flanders, ravaging and destroying all that savoured of Catholicism, Hal became chief centre of resistance. Philip de Croy, the Catholic leader, had resort to the shrine and then affixed a medal to his hat. His example was followed by so many others, that to wear Our Lady of Hal in one's hat became the symbol of loyalty, and as such was specially honoured by the Pope.

But he was by no means the last Pope to favour Hal. On August 15th, 1946, Pope Pius XII raised the old Collegiate Church to the rank of minor basilica, the highest honour that may be conferred on a church outside the city of Rome.

For a time the college of Hal was under Jesuit care. It was they who added the treasury, beside the Lady Chapel. The Jewel House of the Tower of London offers a display hardly more brilliant. There is an immense range of chalices, ciboria, pyxes, reliquaries, crosses, candlesticks of gold, precious stones and silver, the gifts and offerings of many Popes and emperors, kings and nobles, over hundreds of years.

The feature most interesting to an Englishman, however, is a magnificent monstrance presented in his nobler days by our Henry VIII, in 1513, when he personally visited Hal, in thanksgiving for his victories over Louis XII of France. Cardinal Bourne used this same monstrance in 1908, when he carried the Blessed Sacrament at the London Eucharistic Congress.

The crowns of Our Lady and the Holy Child used on all great festivals were made more than four hundred years ago. They are of silver, overlaid with pure gold and richly encrusted with precious stones of untold value. Hal indeed is a palace worthy of the Queen of Heaven—enriched by Popes, emperors and princes and with the heartfelt and fervent prayers and praises of millions of her most devoted subjects—the poor.

These, all the year round, flock to her sanctuary and then make the "Weg-om", or "Grand Tour", a pilgrimage procession which includes visits to fifty-four wayside shrines and chapels along a route encircling the town. All day long in the finer weather little knots of people and, at times, large processions may be seen at their devotions along this pilgrimage way. Once the foreign pilgrim has been put on the right path, he need have no fear of losing the way. There will be plenty of others coming to guide him.

## IX: LE PUY

L E PUY, a city of some twenty-thousand inhabitants, is the chief town of the department of Haute-Loire, and one of the most historic, and astonishing places in the South of France. Centre of ancient, Gallic Velay, it is remarkable for its unspoiled medieval atmosphere and its amazing geographical position. The old town clings to a gigantic lump of volcanic rock which juts out abruptly like the hub of a huge wheel, in the centre of the verdant, prosperous plain which surrounds it. This green belt is encircled in the distance by a grim horizon of weird-shaped mountains.

This rocky hub is crowned with the colossal statue, fifty-five feet tall, of Our Lady of France, which reigns like an apparition over all the adjacent countryside. Within its shadow is the grand old cathedral, inside its own rugged citadel, rising triumphant over the surrounding clutter of red roofs and steep, tortuous alleyways.

In pre-Roman times Le Puy, like Chartres, was a centre of Druid worship. The summit, Mont Anis, was the chosen site of a druidic altar, a monolith reminiscent of Stonehenge. During Roman occupation, the ancient cult was replaced by a temple of Jupiter, but the old altar remained and druidism lingered on.

Legend has it that, soon after the arrival of Christianity, a widow suffering from fever betook herself, according to local custom, to lie on the altar stone, when Our Lady appeared and admonished her to tell the Bishop that she wished to be honoured with a chapel at that spot.

The Bishop was St. George of Velay, an almost legendary figure, accredited as a disciple of St. Peter. His name is preserved locally in the Gate of St. George in the citadel walls. He visited the site and found, it is related, that a fall of snow, although in midsummer, had left outlined the plan of a church. Lacking the means for an immediate building, he fenced the place with a hedge of thorns, only to find next morning that the bushes had burst into flower.

Whatever the truth of this delightful legend, certain deductions may be made. Christian devotion would seem to have been strong in Velay at an early date; the analogy with the legend of the founding of St. Mary Major's in Rome is too striking to be ignored.

Two centuries later Vosy, Bishop of Velay, moved his seat from St. Paulien to Mont Anis, where he was met with another plea for a chapel. A paralytic woman of Ceyssac, similarly cured of fever on the popular rock, was likewise favoured with an apparition of Our Lady, asking for a shrine on the privileged hill.

Work began about 493, Pope Gelasius I sending assistance in the person of a noble Roman, Scutarius, a skilled architect. When the building was almost complete the Bishop set out for Rome to obtain relics for the consecration. Legend relates that on the way he met two old men who told him that his journey was unnecessary, gave him a parcel of relics and bade him return. When the Bishop reached Mont Anis he found the chapel ablaze with lights and filled with music and incense, and that it had already been consecrated, by angels it was believed. Thus tradition gives Le Puy a second link with another of Our Lady's great shrines, that of Einsiedeln, also accredited with heavenly consecration.

Of this first chapel there are few remains, except

some carved stones, carefully preserved in the museum, and the lintel of the Porch of For, a doorway of the present cathedral used subsequently by several Popes. This stone is actually inscribed with Scutarius' name.

By the sixth century, Le Puy was attracting large crowds of pilgrims from a wide area, so that it was necessary to establish a hospice in the city, that still exists. Twice, the all-powerful Charlemagne joined them, once before he set out for Rome for his coronation; again, on his return, wearing the Imperial Crown given him by Pope Leo III. At his command Le Puy was exempted from the tax called Peter's Pence and, by a singular coincidence, Lourdes and its castle was made fief to Our Lady of Puy.

Each one of the princes of the Carlovingian dynasty vied with his predecessor—Louis the Debonair and Lothaire outstanding—in lavishing honours on the shrine; so much that in a Bull of 1051, Pope Leo IX was able to declare that at Le Puy Our Lady received a greater degree of veneration from the French people than at any other sanctuary.

Nor is there, outside Italy, a shrine visited by a greater number of Popes. No less than seven have made the arduous journey; and a number of prelates later raised to the See of Peter. Likewise eighteen kings of France in twenty-five recorded pilgrimages have journeyed thither, and saints innumerable—not least St. Dominic, faced with the huge task of reconverting the Albigensian heretics, St. Louis of France, St. Vincent Ferrer, St. Antony of Padua, St. Hugh, St. Peter the Venerable, St. Francis Regis, St. Joseph Labre.

When Pope Urban II went to Clermont to preach the Crusade, it was from Le Puy, on the Feast of the Assumption, that he dated the Bull addressed to the Princes of Europe, and it was the Bishop of Le Puy, Adhémar, who was his delegate on the Crusade. Two

hundred years later, Duguesclin, fierce enemy of the
Black Prince, was on his way to Mont Anis when he
halted to drive out from Châteauneuf-Randon a party
of English soldiers who made a practice of robbing and
insulting pilgrims.   There he died in 1380.   A few
years later St. Joan of Arc, unable to make the
pilgrimage herself, sent her mother, Isabelle Romée,
to represent her at the Grand Pardon of Le Puy.

One day in 1254, a very illustrious pilgrim climbed
the Holy Mount—St. Louis of France.   During his
period of captivity in Egypt, the Sultan, who had great
admiration for him, allowed him to choose from the
treasury any one object which might especially appeal
to him.   St. Louis chose a cedar-wood figure of Our
Lady and the Holy Child, highly venerated in Islam
because of a strange belief that it had been carved by
none other than the prophet Jeremiah, foreshadowing
the day when all heathen images would be cast down
in the name of the Virgin's Son.   This black statue,
about 27 inches high, represented Our Lady seated on
a kind of stool, holding her Divine Son on her knees.
The entire figure, except face and hands and feet, was
tightly bound in bandages and covered with a robe
over an inner tunic painted red.   Our Lady wore a
crown of copper-gilt, like an old helmet, studded with
pre-Christian cameos.

St. Louis was accompanied by his wife, Marguerite
of Provence, who presented her own crown at the high
altar.   St. Louis then offered this extraordinary image
rescued from the heart of Islam to replace the original
*Notre-Dame du Puy,* venerated on Mont Anis for many
centuries; a figure which, from various representations
on seals, seems to have been not unlike Our Lady of
Walsingham.

Although August 15th is now the occasion of the
great annual procession, the especial devotion to Our
Lady associated with Le Puy is that of the

Annunciation, as it was at Walsingham. Among the great number of extraordinary privileges granted to Mont Anis by various Popes, the most important is that of the Jubilee, or Grand Pardon, granted for each year when Good Friday and March 25th coincide. This Pardon has been celebrated some thirty times since it began, in 992. It was confirmed by Pope Pius XI.

The tenth Pardon was in 1407. The period of grace allowed was still one day only. It was estimated that two hundred thousand pilgrims arrived. To deal with the situation, confessors were placed at every street corner and all along the embattlements of the city walls. The statue was carried in triumph but, in spite of precautions, disaster ensued: some two hundred persons were crushed to death. Still further precautions were taken in 1418, yet thirty more were trampled down and suffocated. At the request of Charles VII, the Pope extended the Jubilee until Low Sunday and in 1429 there was no accident.

1502 marked the fourteenth Jubilee. As it followed so soon after the Universal Jubilee, the Bishop did not expect great numbers. Yet the press was so great that the roads were blocked. Three thousand confessors were insufficient. The Bishop had to appeal for a thousand more. It seemed as if all France, Spain, Italy and England were determined that year to visit Mont Anis. The Jubilee coincided with a heatwave and the solid mass of pilgrims filling the streets besought householders to throw water on their heads, to cool them. Ninety-five were crushed to death at one city gate; seventeen others were killed by a falling wall. In 1622, there were three hundred thousand pilgrims. In 1701 soldiers had to mount guard at the Confessionals. Holy Communion was given daily throughout the Octave, from dawn until after Vespers.

It may well be supposed that Le Puy suffered at the Revolution. With Satanic fury the revolutionists swept into the cathedral which was turned into a Temple of Reason. Our Lady was treated like the Queen. She was dragged to her trial in a manure-cart, and thence, in the same tumbril used for Royalist victims, to the square where she was burned with other ecclesiastical treasures.

Even so, Our Lady triumphed, as she always will. 1796 marked another Jubilee. The Bishop was in exile, but he gained the extension of the privilege for the entire diocese. M. de Rachat, heroic Curé of Tence, took charge and large numbers of the truly faithful were able to make the Pardon.

Towards 1802, it was possible to think of restoration. A local artist, M. Tholance, was commissioned to make a new figure as nearly as possible like the old. He is said to have done so from memory, but in 1777 an artist named Veyrenc made a copy of the St. Louis figure for the Savant, Faujus de Saint-Fond; and at much the same time another, representing the figure vested, seems to have been carved. The former is preserved in the Cathedral treasury. The latter (which in spite of its comparatively small size is heavier than one man can comfortably lift) is most carefully treasured in the medieval Convent of St. Clare, near the Diocesan Seminary.

Yet another figure was carved for the Church of St. Maurice nearby and for various reasons—in particular his collaboration with the anti-God faction during the Revolution—it was decided to remove Tholance's statue and replace it with this other. This, then, was the figure which was reverenced during the ceremonies of the 1853 Jubilee, and crowned on June 8th, 1856, in the name of Pope Pius IX. Various efforts have been made by anti-clerical factions to suppress the annual August procession but thanks to the initiative of Mgr. Rousseau they were revived in 1932 and have since continued.

For a thousand years, Le Puy represented for France what Lourdes, once its fief, does today; and still Mont Anis must be regarded as one of the major sanctuaries of Our Lady at the present time.

The cathedral is still centre of the devotion. Our Lady is enthroned above the high altar, directly beneath the central, romanesque dome. Emile Mâle, in his "Arts and Artists of the Middle Ages", has written: "There is perhaps no cathedral in Europe more extraordinary than that of Le Puy. Here everything speaks of the Orient, that eternal Orient which fascinated the Middle Ages and still holds for us such wonderment. One feels here a nostalgia for the land of light. Its African atmosphere, its southern spirit, gives to this strange cathedral an irresistible charm."

The primitive sanctuary was designed by a Roman. Its present successor, the second church only to be built on the site in thirteen hundred years, was influenced largely by Constantinople. Subsequent additions were made under the influence of the Crusades and inspired by Jerusalem and the Holy Places.

The nave, which consists of a series of cupolas, raised on massive, romanesque arches, was copied from Byzantine basilicas by men more skilled in "Norman" craftsmanship. The very arches, just not quite "round", offer the suggestion of an oriental mosque. The carved capitals are equal to any in France. The porches recall one instantly to Nazareth and the Holy Sepulchre. The Moorish façade is but the shield for a truly magnificent narthex. The mighty flight of stairs from the town below leads straight up to the Stone of Fevers, the ancient Druid altar, now in the narthex, and thence directly into the transepts and the shrine itself.

Of the adjacent and unique sanctuary of St. Michael, perched half a mile away upon another shaft of rock,

this is no place to speak. One cannot, however, pass
by another Marial feature so closely allied to the main
sanctuary, which towers half way between the two . . .
the statue of Our Lady of France. It was a magnificent
idea to raise here a votive offering from the French
nation close by the shrine more closely identified with
national history than any other.

To realise the project, Napoleon III gave 213 cannon
taken from Russia at Sebastopol. With the metal from
these a colossal figure of Our Lady was cast which
was set on the Rocher Corneille, 2484 feet above sea
level. The actual figure is 55 feet tall. Our Lady,
crowned with the stars, standing on a globe, crushes
the serpent beneath her feet and exalts her Divine Son,
who extends His blessing upon all below.

For the rest, it is impossible, in less than a lengthy
tome, to write adequately of the wealth of treasures
here in this stronghold of Marial devotion. The
Baptistery of St. John, the Bell Tower, the Cloisters—
without equal in Europe—the Chapel of Penitents, the
Churches of St. Lawrence and St. Francis Regis, the
Convents of Poor Clares and Carmelites, the College,
the ancient Hospital, thirteen hundred years old, the
Crozatier Museum, the fountains, gates, and city walls,
the Rocher Saint-Michel, third most famous shrine of
the Archangel in the world; all these are features that,
were they but in Venice or Florence, would be the rage
of every art-loving Englishman. As it is they are
hidden and, for many, hardly known. Truly Le Puy
is worthy of recognition and a pilgrimage by all who
love to give their devotion to Our Blessed Lady. Than
Le Puy, there can be few shrines more historic.

# X: ROCAMADOUR

FOR all that Le Puy was such a celebrated shrine, under the patronage of so many Popes, Saints and sovereigns, medieval France possessed yet another sanctuary of Our Lady, at no great distance from Mont Anis, which stood even higher in universal esteem—that of Our Lady of Rocamadour, which ranked in the Middle Ages as one of the four greatest places of pilgrimage in Christendom, equal in merit with the Holy Places of Palestine and Rome, and St. James of Compostella in Spain.

This sanctuary is in a small village in the department of Lot, near St. Denis-près-Martel on the Paris-Toulouse line. Clinging to the side of an abrupt precipice and rising to a giddy height above the canyon-like valley below, its situation is fantastic. The surrounding region is a broad plateau of lime-stone through which various rivers have gouged great ravines many miles long, and hundreds of feet deep, but often less than half a mile wide on top. The surface is almost barren; rainfall soaks quickly through the porous rock into subterranean channels and caverns, not unlike those of Cheddar Gorge, with which the region is honeycombed. Few trees are visible; only the scantiest crops are produced. As a result the population is poor and scattered, often isolated by these impassable ravines. Yet the gorges themselves are rich and fertile; vivid streaks of green winding snake-like through the arid highlands.

Ancient tradition, bitterly assailed in recent years but still more recently justified to great extent by archæologists, claims that a Christian settlement was made in this region by none other than Zaccheus, the Jericho publican with whom Our Lord conversed. (St. Luke xix, 1-10.) The story is that he was driven from Palestine by bitter persecution and, with St. Veronica, his wife, was guided by the Gallic Apostle, St. Martial, to land and settle at Soulac, on the Bay of Biscay. There they founded an oratory of the Blessed Virgin which developed into a popular shrine under the title of Our Lady of Lands End.

When St. Veronica died, Zaccheus migrated to the heart of Gaul where he made a hermitage in a cave in the gorge of the River Alzou, taking the name of Amadour (Lover of God). He died, tradition holds, about the year A.D. 70, and was buried in a rock-hewn sepulchre, oriental-manner, beside his hermitage: hence the name, Roc-Amadour.

Critics who attacked this legend a generation ago asserted that there was no evidence of any shrine here before the twelfth century, and that the identification with Zaccheus of human remains found, in 1116, in the sepulchre was due to a misconception. Profound research, however, on the part of the Savants Abbé Layral and de Valon, has tended to reverse the critical process. There is no doubt whatever that the shrine of Our Lady was popular long before the twelfth century.

Whether Amadour may be identified with Zaccheus is another matter. Certainly there can be no documentary evidence, one way or the other. Rooted tradition is strong evidence, which cannot be invented as easily as some might imagine. If Amadour did not come to this valley, how then does this tradition correspond so accurately with that at Soulac, many miles away? It is less difficult to accept the story than to imagine conspiracy between the "founders"

*Our Lady of Le Puy*

(Page 83)

ROCAMADOUR. *The thousand-year-old*
*statue which was originally covered with*
*plates of silver, and (below) the inner*
*courtyard with its bewildering array of*
*chapels*

(Page 91)

of two shrines far apart and in times when communication was so difficult.

Argument from silence falls rather flat. Is there any impossibility in the suggestion that one of the disciples could have founded a Christian centre in South France within fifty years of the Ascension? Evidence proves that disciples were dispersed at an extremely early date. Many are named in the "Acts of the Apostles" and the Epistles of the New Testament. It is stated clearly that when St. Stephen was martyred disciples were scattered as far as Antioch, Cyprus and Phoenicia. The Phoenicians were great traders. Their markets extended as far as Carthage and Cornwall. There was nothing impossible or even improbable in a Christian disciple finding his way to Southern Gaul.

It is also worthy of remembrance that St. Irenæus, disciple of St. Polycarp (himself taught by St. John), succeeded St. Pothinus as Bishop of Lyons, A.D. 177. St. Irenæus was born in Smyrna, about A.D. 140 and visited Rome, where he may well have seen Christian oratories adorned with paintings of Our Lady. His devotion to the Mother Mediatrix is expressed in his writings. This man was second Bishop of Lyons, not very far from Rocamadour.

Another tradition, which indicates at least the regard for Rocamadour in early ages, is the association of Charlemagne, who is believed to have visited the shrine during his wars with the Saracens in Spain. Closely allied is the story relating to the gift of Durandal, Roland's sword. The hero of the *Chanson de Roland* is said to have cut his way through a defile in the rocks of the Pyrenees, today called "Roland's Pass". He may well, sword in hand, have done so through ranks of the enemy in a militant sense. The historic Roland, Charlemagne's nephew and paladin, led the rearguard of the Emperor's retreating army and was cut off and overwhelmed in the Valley of Roncesvalles. He bequeathed his sword to Our Lady of Rocamadour.

One version of the legend adds that as the paladin lay dying angels bore his Durandal and thrust it up to the hilt into the solid rock beside the shrine. Certainly a very ancient sword might have been seen there of old, but it was destroyed in the French Revolution. A model, in memory of this charming story, may now be found thrust into a cleft in the rock at the door of the Lady Chapel.

Records of bequests provide ample evidence that Rocamadour was well known as a shrine long before the rock-tomb was opened. A pilgrims' hospice dedicated to Notre-Dame de Rocamadour was built at Estella, in Navarre, in 1087. In 1193, after a dispute lasting a century, the Augustinians of Marcilhac ("The Place of St. Martial") renounced all rights at Rocamadour in favour of the Benedictine Abbey of Tulle. This coincided with the great pilgrim-crusader movement from all parts of Europe to Spain, partly to visit the shrine of St. James, partly to assist in pushing back the Saracens. All looked to Our Lady of Rocamadour as Patroness; all made a point of visiting her shrine.

Hospices, hospitals, priories and abbeys along the route to Compostella were dedicated to her. Great impetus was given to the movement by the Abbey of Cluny. Out of gratitude, Spanish sovereigns handed out largesse. Monks from Rocamadour were directed to the service of the faithful fighting in Spain. The foundation of the basilica and hospice at Estella, in Navarre, by the King of Aragon, is a typical example. The church was dedicated to Our Lady of Rocamadour and served by monks from the shrine, who built a replica shrine at Estella, which came to be of considerable importance, too.

The Abbots of Tulle—who became Bishops of Tulle later on—built up strong fortifications round the sanctuary, necessary in those dangerous times and parts. A veritable castle-stronghold came into being, and there as barons they reigned on equal terms with the powers around them.

There is only one monastery in Europe which resembles Rocamadour in this matter of defences—the castle-abbey of St. Michael's Mount, in Normandy. But here, by the Alzou, are lacking the cloisters which even the Mount managed to find place for.

Under normal conditions of medieval warfare this fortified valley must have been impregnable; the castle-shrine doubly so. From the plateau one single path wound down towards the bottom of the gorge. The approach was guarded by a fortress at the top and by other gateways. From the lowest point the path began the ascent to the castle proper through several defences and then up a steep stairway, sole means of access, of 216 steps.

Pilgrims climb these on their knees—hence the present-day name of Holy Stairs. At the top there is a sharp bend followed by a second, if shorter, flight which passes through a heavy archway directly under the main castle into the innermost courtyard of the churches.

Here was the Baron-Abbot's residence, the monks' accommodation and rooms for more celebrated guests. Others were given hospitality in hospices outside.

The outermost gate was shut regularly from dusk till dawn. Beyond it was the large Hospice of St. John. Parts of the gateway remain, together with ruins of the hospice and more of the church, which now serves as the parish church. The cemetery, still in use, where many a pilgrim found his last rest, has yielded up a number of Merovingian tombs, proving that there was a Christian settlement here much earlier than those critics would like us to believe.

From this point, *Hospitalet,* the pilgrim gains his first and most striking view of the shrine and village. This seems to have been carved out of the sheer precipice, from the green river-bed to the summit, five hundred feet above. The lower buildings comprise one narrow street with its present-day shops and hotels. A second tier is occupied by the castle, basilica, Lady Chapel and monastic buildings. The summit is crowned with the château, the Bishop's residence, heavily guarded with embattled walls and surmounted by a modern bell-tower with a chime of bells.

Until one enters the courtyard, the impression gained is that of a spectacular, almost theatrical, medieval village, overshadowed by its frowning castle. Except for a few souvenir shops there is little to betray the nearby existence of a great shrine. Actually the wayside is marked with numerous reminders of medieval piety, wayside shrines and stone crosses with altars at their bases, all of which play a traditional part during the great Pardons.

Once inside the courtyard, a different scene greets the eye. The pilgrim is surrounded by an unexpected array of churches and chapels, for the most part many hundreds of years old.

The basilica which towers directly ahead is surely one of the strangest-looking churches designed. In style and plan it looks like a great banqueting hall, gigantic pillars down its centre, worthy of the Tower of London. But church it is and always has been. Huguenots and Revolutionaries between them spared few of its treasures but the walls exhibit paintings of many celebrated pilgrims—Charlemagne and Roland; St. Louis and Blanche, his mother; John, King of Bohemia and, by no means least, Henry II, King of

England. As befitted the ruler of wide French territories, he had great regard for the chief shrine of Our Lady in his Province of Guyenne and made more than one pilgrimage thither with his illustrious, if vindictive, Queen, Eleanor of Aquitaine. Later he was imitated by his rebellious second son, Henry Fitzhenry, who seems to have come more to plunder than pray. Few if any material benefits of these English royal pilgrimages remain.

Immediately adjacent to the basilica but in a distinct chapel is the world-famous shrine and the statue of Our Lady that has been venerated for perhaps a thousand years.

Externally the chapel is beautiful, lofty, gracious, strong, embellished with a dignified amount of late Gothic decoration, quite unlike the severe baronial basilica. The door commemorates Bishop de Bar who restored the chapel in 1479, after a severe fall of rock that well-nigh obliterated it but marvellously spared the actual shrine.

The interior offers a sharp contrast to the brilliance of the courtyard—it is dark and bewildering. The end by the door has been cut into the living rock, black with the soot from thousands of votive candles. The walls, pillars and ceilings, every conceivable corner, are smothered with ex-votos, lamps, banners, orders, decorations, medals, pictures, crutches, hernia-belts, leg-irons, children's toys and shoes and so forth, and hearts innumerable in silver and gold.

Conspicuous is a large ship, gift of the historic Valon family which recalls the prodigious number of favours granted to mariners. There can be few Lady-shrines in Europe further from the sea. It is a great tribute to the popularity of the devotion that so many sailors, French, Spanish and Basque, retain such ardent regard for the Holy Virgin of Rocamadour.

Innermost is the massive modern high altar, of

bronze and enamels, thrown into prominence by the solid, black wall behind it. The bronze-work encases another stone altar which is very old and which is called "St. Martial's". Unfortunately no photograph was taken of it before it was hidden but, whatever the truth of its origin, enough is known of it to say that it proves that a Christian altar was here used long before the crusades. It is comparable with the one called "St. Peter's" in the Loreto Holy House.

The place of honour above the Blessed Sacrament is reserved for Our Lady. As usual the figure is vested in gorgeous robes, crowned with a diadem of gold and gems. It is of wood, probably cedar, black with age and with oxidisation, for at one time it was covered with silver. Our Lady is seated, dressed in a simple robe, with no mantle, fastened at the neck and at the waist by a girdle. Her head is covered with a short veil on which rests a mutilated crown. The Holy Child sits on His Mother's left knee, dressed in a simple robe like hers. In His left hand He holds a Gospel-book; His right is extended in blessing. The back of the seat provides a cavity for some relic.

No two critics are agreed as to its age or provenance. The statue can be compared with others at Beaulieu and St. Foy in the district, and with another at Walcourt in Belgium, all of which retain their silver covering. That at Hal, of similar workmanship, has lost its cases but shows the same traces of oxidisation. The date of all these cannot be much later than the eleventh century—it is generally agreed that the Rocamadour figure is a century or two earlier.

Yet another treasure hangs in the roof, and is best seen from the gallery. It is a bell of wrought iron that is at least fifteen hundred years old. This, too, is accredited to St. Amadour. Quite as remarkable is the tradition that it "rings of its own accord" from time to time to announce some miracle granted in response to prayer at the shrine. This last happened, it is said, in 1924.

Interest, too, attaches to the iron manacles which hang near the shrine, given in gratitude by prisoners rescued or escaped from the Saracens, aided sometimes by Guilds of Ransom dedicated to Our Lady.

But these two chapels do not complete the list of wonders here to be found. There must be included at least a reference to the Crypt of St. Amadour; his traditional, rock-hewn, hebraic sepulchre; the extraordinary eagle's-nest chapel of St. Michael perched high on the rock; the parochial chapel of St. John where hang the parish bells; the Bishop's banqueting hall; the modern hospice; the charming mountainous path with the Stations of the Cross; the ramparts of the château, where the chaplains live, with the magnificent panorama. All these are features unique to Rocamadour but beyond our present scope to describe.

By Bulls of various Popes, Martin V in 1428 in particular, Rocamadour has, like Le Puy, the privilege of celebrating a great Pardon, whenever Corpus Christi falls on the Feast of St. John the Baptist. This happens but rarely, but every year witnesses an incredible influx of pilgrims, arriving in crowds, usually at dawn, with hymns and ejaculations, flooding up the holy stairs, packing into the courtyard, cramming the miraculous chapel to bursting point.

September 8th—15th is the period of the Annual Novena or Retreat; another season of great crowds. Scores of additional confessors are brought in. Holy Communion is given at all hours of the morning. Preachings and devotions fill the day. The fervour of these thousands reassures one that after so many centuries of devotion, the Shrine of Our Lady of Rocamadour is still vital and a living force in the lives of many; just as it was to the crusaders on their way to fight, and maybe to die, in Saracen Spain.

# XI: AVIOTH

IN all the Meuse region of France, there is no sanctuary of Our Blessed Lady more astonishing, or less known in England, than that of Avioth, well off the main road, several miles from Montmedy. Nor is there one which has better preserved its ancient character.

Here is a primitive Madonna of the twelfth century, still venerated on the very spot where first began this devotion; enthroned in a grand basilica, a veritable gem of architecture, which was built in the ages of Faith to enshrine her.

The very modest hamlet which sprawls round this church seems to exist only to enhance by its humbleness the triumphant glory of the shrine; by its poverty, the wealth that past and present ages have outpoured in honour of the Mother of God.

The setting for this jewel is a region of frontiers and boundary-lines: on one hand the Meuse, on the other the Ardennes; on one side the Belgian, on another the Luxemburg frontiers. Before the Treaty of the Pyrenees, in 1659, this was part of the Compté of Chiny, powerful centre of religious, and in particular of Cistercian, life. Then, for nearly two centuries, it was part of the Grand Duchy of Luxemburg and like it, for a thousand years and more, it was included in the parent diocese of Trier until the French Revolution.

Documents relating to the origins of the shrine are scanty. The ravagings of constant wars did not make for the safe-keeping of parchments and suchlike. The "Brief Account of Avioth", by Jean Delhôtel, Curé of the parish in 1668, dates back only to the seventeenth century.

By his own account, he wrote down the traditions of the place handed down to the grandparents of people then living by their grandfathers before them. He records the story just as it was given him, just as so many another old tradition has been preserved.

According to the Curé, the local inhabitants discovered, one day in the twelfth century, a figure of Our Lady deposited beneath a thorn bush. This they bore to the local parish church, believing the image to have been brought, if not actually carved, by angel's hands. But, on the morrow, they found that it had been removed back to the spot where first it had been found. This was taken to be a sure indication that Our Lady desired nothing better than to be venerated in that place. Whereupon these faithful souls set to work to build a modest oratory.

Thither a stream of pilgrims began to flow, never to dry up; first from places near at hand, soon from cities far afield; all drawn by the news of the favours granted by the Queen of Heaven. Before many years had elapsed, it proved possible to replace the oratory with a church of stone which, in course of time, gave place to the present basilica.

From whatever sources Father Jean may have drawn his story, much of it is borne out by the internal evidence of the fabric of the church which is one of the marvels of northern France, and by the characteristics of the statue itself.

The legend is similar to many another associated with figures of Our Lady discovered in thorn bushes. Our Lady of Avioth, without attaining quite the majesty which marks, for example, its near neighbour at Iré-les-Près, is certainly of the twelfth century and bears close comparison with another of the same epoch at Signeulx in the Grand Duchy.

Were they both carved by "angels" whom various historians suppose to have been monks? Certainly the white monks, or Cistercians, were the "angels" of the nearby great abbey of Orval and had close relations with Avioth. They were fully competent to produce such a work of art.

Others have thought to see in Our Lady of Avioth traces of Byzantine influence, from which some conjecture she was brought hither and "lost" beneath the thorn-bush by some returning crusader. Against this one must remember that, after the fierce eikon controversy, the Byzantine East, which painted a profusion of holy pictures, absolutely repudiated statuary which triumphed in the West.

Truth be told—and does it matter very much?— the story of the origin of Avioth is lost in a remote past and it is unlikely that the early history may ever be verified. Suffice it that here is venerated a figure of Our Lady probably eight hundred years old. That is marvellous, but it is by no means all the wonder of the place.

The church which replaced the primitive oratory would seem to have been built before 1131, in the time of Pope Innocent II. There seems to be no reason to doubt that, or the tradition that St. Bernard was among the earliest pilgrims. He was in the neighbourhood in 1132, when a colony of his monks came to revive the monastic life at Orval; and in 1147, when he travelled from Verdun to Trier with Pope Eugene III.

Tradition favours the earlier date as the occasion when St. Bernard himself gave at Avioth the order, or at least pious request, which was instantly obeyed, that here in front of the shrine should be sung the *Salve Regina*: "*daily and reverently by a warden and scola, immediately after the Mass of the Day; and that the said warden be engaged for the purpose at the expense of the church"*.

It is known that this famous anthem, so well known to all Catholics, was particularly dear to St. Bernard, great apostle of Our Lady. The *Salve Regina* was probably composed by Hermann Contract, a monk of Reichenau, who died in 1054. St. Bernard, undoubtedly the greatest medieval contributor to devotion to Our Lady, strongly advocated its use. Whatever the tradition of its introduction at Avioth, the *Salve Regina* continues to resound each day in the basilica, and the singing of it is a chief feature of all pilgrimages.

The stone church of St. Bernard's time gave way to another still larger, made possible partly by the generosity of pilgrims, partly by the rich gifts of the nobility, the Counts of Chiny and the nearby Sires of Rodemack and Breux. The new church was begun in the fourteenth century and took some fifty years to build. In its east and western parts, it incorporated the obvious remains of the twelfth century building.

This basilica with its twin spires, its lofty arcading and clerestory, its luxurious façade and almost overpowering portals, the enormous wealth of its ornate Gothic sculpture, is one of the wonders of France. It is curious that so few guide books make mention of it, that so few tourists have ever learned of its survival. Perhaps that is because it is hidden away, hard to get at, far from any station or motor bus. Yet one's first "discovery" is a breath-taking experience and it is hard to believe that the outside world knows and cares so little for something so rarely lovely.

Lest one be thought guilty of grave exaggeration, a line or two quoted from a recent book by one of the most accurate French historians of the region may not be out of place: "The church at Avioth . . . is a work truly French, comparable to the cathedral at

Rheims, with its two portals, one of which possesses
an elaborate tympanum, its arcading, its triforium, its
splendid rose-window, and the great windows of its
apse. The choir presents a unique ensemble, where
all the furnishing and decoration date back to the
Middle Ages—the high altar, the imposing carved
Sacrament House, the throne for Our Lady, the carved
armorial bearings, the wall paintings, the statues of
the Apostles and the glass.''

Added to which, of course, the *original* figure of
Our Lady is enthroned on the pedestal built especially
for her six hundred years ago. What other church in
France has more to offer? The glass, alas, was
sadly shattered by German bombardment in June
1940, and has yet to be restored. But the rest remains.

Our Lady reigns on a lofty pedestal on the north
side of the apse, on the gospel side of the fourteenth
century high altar. Experts who have examined the
figure do not hesitate to attribute it to the twelfth
century. Originally black—that is blackened with time
—it was carved in oak and represents Our Lady seated
in majesty. The throne has two uprights on each
side, in one piece with the actual figure. Our Lady
is vested in a long, ample robe and with a mantle over
her left shoulder, which leaves her right arm uncovered.
Her hair falls in long tresses down her back. Her
features are calm and strong.

At some time, the original figure of the Holy Child
and Our Lady's right hand have been lost. They were
replaced at a later date unknown. The whole figure
has a height of thirty-five inches. It was repainted
early this century.

Beneath the statue, in the thickness of the pedestal,
is a relic-aumbry with its original bronze doors. This
was probably meant to enshrine a precious treasure,
a tiny fragment of ''Our Lady's Girdle'', with a
tradition similar to other pieces preserved and

venerated at Maastricht in Holland, Tongres in Belgium, and at Angers in the west of France. Its blessing was eagerly sought by brides and expectant mothers.

Overhead soars a superb canopy to a height of twenty feet, somewhat after the manner of that above Our Lady's shrine in the Slipper Chapel at Walsingham. That is of wood, this of stone but carved so exquisitely that it might well have been of the softer medium.

For the rest, the basilica is indeed a true palace of Our Lady. Wherever one looks, inside or out, one is reminded by some motive, some carving, some design, that this is her church. Near the shrine is a lovely picture, rather faded, of the Virgin Mother, surrounded by a halo of light, before whom kneels the two saints, John, Evangelist and Baptist, and two angels offering incense. Immediately beneath is the kneeling figure of a priest, in surplice and biretta, addressing a Latin prayer to Our Lady: "Hail! Splendour of Heaven! Enlighten from on high a soul plunged into shadows."

Until lately, the main apsidal window showed a sumptuous scene of Our Lady's coronation. Other windows told of the chief episodes in her life. The central panel of the fifteenth century stone pulpit shows the Queen of Heaven, crowned by angels. The main theme of the carvings of the west portal is the Last Judgment. By way of mediation, the Chief Mysteries of the Holy Rosary are set between the sinners and their Judge. Above all is yet another Coronation of the Queen. Even the gables provide space for more portrayals of Our Lady in glory.

All this is evidence of the devotion given at Avioth to the Blessed Mother. It is a just reflection of the profound importance of the shrine as a place of pilgrimage. In addition to brides and mothers, all manner of afflicted persons have sought Our Lady's aid. Their number was, and is, without reckoning.

Curé Delhôtel put on record no less than one hundred and thirty-one cures during his pastorate and several during that of his predecessor.

Our Lady of Avioth was especially invoked by prisoners of war, who, on their release from captivity, gave fetters and chains in thanksgiving. One may still see the rings from which these were hung. The ex-votos themselves were pillaged during one of several wars in the seventeenth century.

Demoniacs and persons thought to be possessed, and all manner of nervous cases were brought thither. Tradition affirms that a certain room near the church was set apart for them. For others, the blind, the sick and the halt, a special hospice was built about the year 1442.

From 1446, the church maintained eleven altars, fully endowed for as many Chaplains to say Mass. In addition to these chantry priests, a College of four priests, with the Curé, existed to sing the public Masses and the Divine Office as well as the daily *Salve Regina*. There were several local sodalities, but two Confraternities were outstanding; that of the Scapular of Our Lady of Mount Carmel, erected for the Belgian Province of the Order in 1679, and of the Holy Rosary, begun in 1638 and enriched by Pope Alexander VII (1656) with numerous indulgences. July 16th, Feast of Our Lady of Mount Carmel, still remains as one of the chief days in the calendar of Avioth.

The most refreshing feature in the history of this shrine is its unbroken continuity. The Thirty Years War was the harshest period. Swedish and Croat soldiers, 1637-42, made themselves particularly unpleasant and while the interior was respected, they did some damage to the exterior carvings of the basilica. Twice, for short periods, it was thought necessary to take Our Lady to safety in the strong castle of Montmedy.

Even the French Revolution, so fatal to other shrines, did less harm than the Prussians of Brunswick who broke into the church by force of arms in 1792. They murdered a priest saying Mass at the high altar and beheaded a figure of Our Lady in an outside shrine. But Our Lady of Avioth remained undisturbed.

Once the prohibitions of the Revolution had passed away, the cult of Our Lady was restored with energy. Renewed vigour was given especially in 1850 by the Abbé Jacquemain and the establishment of a college of priests missioners, as at Le Laus, La Salette and elsewhere.

One feature of Avioth remains to be examined. Outside the great Pilgrims' porch is an elaborate and highly ornate structure, the *Recevresse,* of the same date as the interior work, but the origin of which has never been precisely determined. It was, and is, undoubtedly a second shrine of Our Lady, not impossibly to mark the site of the thorn tree and/or the first oratory.

To it was carried the figure of Our Lady on great occasions, of which July 16th each year is still one. This chapel is built like an enormous, crochetted pinnacle, open on one side at the base. It contains an altar and a niche with a figure of Our Lady presented in 1805 to replace the one that was beheaded. So unique, architecturally, is this "Recevresse" that did Avioth possess no other treasure it would still be fortunate.

A convent of Bernardine nuns is normally attached to the basilica. The late war destroyed their house which has yet to be rebuilt. They have their stalls behind the high altar and their sweet singing of the Divine Office adds to the delight of Avioth.

Throughout the year there comes a continuous stream of pilgrims, little "organised", almost always on foot. July 16th, however, is the greatest annual

**117**

feast. Then the historic figure is borne in triumph to the Recevresse and Mass is sung by the Bishop before a gathering so large that it could never hope to gain access to the inner shrine, even if it waited all day.

In 1934, by special authority of the Holy See, a new Office of Our Lady of Avioth was sung for the first time by Cardinal Suhard in the presence of all those bishops whose dioceses today include parts of the old Grand Duchy. For it must not be forgotten that though present-day Luxemburg possesses its own most wonderful shrine, Avioth, in the days before the partition, was the chief national sanctuary; and it is as Queen of Luxemburg that the majority of pilgrims still acclaim Our Lady of Avioth in this very historic sanctuary.

*AVIOTH.    Our Lady of Avioth venerated for 800 years, and (below) the statue in its centuries-old shrine*

(Page 100)

LUXEMBURG. *Our Lady of Luxemburg, and (below) the Cathedral, shrine church of Our Lady Consoler of the Afflicted*

(Page 109)

# XII: LUXEMBURG

THERE is always something fascinating about those tiny European States which have managed to retain their independence in spite of the violent upheavals which have so sadly shaken their greater neighbours. Such are San Marino, professedly the oldest independent state in Europe; Monaco; Andorra; Liechtenstein; and, by no means least, the Grand Duchy of Luxemburg.

This little country is sandwiched between Belgium, France and Germany, with an area and population almost identical in size with those of Northamptonshire. The Capital, from which the Duchy takes its name, is one of the most picturesquely situated cities of Europe, lodged on a plateau which ends in three sides in almost precipitous cliffs, several hundred feet high, formed by a sharp loop of the Alzette river.

The very name, Luxemburg, is derived from German meaning "the strong little castle".

The city had its origin in such a stronghold built on this almost impregnable spur of rock and by its position helped its rulers to maintain their independence and importance. The House of Luxemburg was particularly distinguished in the 14th and 15th centuries, producing a series of Emperors of the Holy Roman Empire, including that Charles IV who published the Golden Bull, and his sons Wenceslas I and Sigismund, who called the Church Council of Constance which solved the fearful triple schism in the Papacy. He it was who founded the Houses of Saxony and Hohenzollern which endured to our own times.

Throughout the eighteenth century the Duchy was hotly disputed by France and Austria, until 1814 when it became a major fortress of the German Confederation. Finally, in 1867, by order of the London Conference, the Grand Duchy was made a perpetually neutral, independent state.

An important episode in the history of Luxemburg, always fervently Catholic, was the foundation in 1607 of a College of Jesuit Fathers, on the site of a much older convent of Penitents of St. Mary Magdalene. The Duchy was then still included in the ancient, apostolic Diocese of Trier and the coadjutor Bishop of Trier laid the foundation stone in 1613 for a great new projected church. It took eight years to complete and was consecrated to the Immaculate Conception.

Fortunately the records of the building operations have been preserved. They make interesting reading. We are told that the plan was drawn by a skilled architect, Frère Jean du Blocq: the masonry was under a master-builder, Ulrich Job of Lucerne; the stone was brought from various local quarries; some 67,500 bricks were needed in the first year: they were hand-made by Matthew Copin and Antony Sudan.

Alabaster for pillars and jasper for altars were brought from Homburg and Namur; flagstones for the choir from Huy. The roof-timbers were cut from oaks in the Eisch Valley and were erected by one Master Maurice and his men. Twenty-four thousand tiles were used: they came from Salm and were hung by John Leyendecker and his sons. Master Caspar, blacksmith, forged great iron crosses to be set over the roof of the choir and on top of the bell-towers. Andrew Newbecker and Peter Nelis did the rest of the carpentry. Stained glass came from the studios and kilns of Michael and Paul of Luxemburg. All carved work was the responsibility of the sculptor Daniel, who worked from the designs of Martin the Artist.

Workers, townsfolk, soldiers and even women daily took part in the task of building. The brunt of the cost was borne by the entire community. Thus, well on into the seventeenth century, Luxemburg retained much of the medieval spirit and system. It is good to think that the actual names of these craftsmen and tradesmen have been preserved and honoured. How astonished many would have been had they been told so!

Such was the splendid church raised to the glory of God and in Our Lady's honour, on the "best site possible" (we are told) in this devoted city. The Jesuit Fathers were ever great lovers of the Holy Mother of God and, wherever they went, promoted devotion to her in solemn obligation. It was not long, then, before their teaching in Luxemburg bore fruit.

In response to an overwhelming demand, Father James Brocquart, S.J., decided to build, on the outskirts of the city, close to the ramparts, a small and curiously planned shrine-chapel of Our Lady, Consolation of the Afflicted, to which the townsfolk might make frequent pilgrimage. Therein was enthroned a truly delightful figure of Our Lady, carved in lime-wood. Its origin, of the same epoch, is unknown, but the closeness of its resemblance to the miraculous statue of Our Lady of Montaigu is too striking to be ignored.

The figure is 38 inches tall. As Mother, Our Lady holds the Holy Child on her left arm. There is tremendous dignity of expression in her face, dignity and royal majesty. Her hair flows in riplets over her shoulders. In spite of three hundred years of veneration, the richness of the colouring and the brilliance of the gilding have hardly been diminished. As Virgin Immaculate she is crowned, and with her right heel crushes the serpent. A large crescent moon, doubly symbolic at a time when fierce conflict still raged (as it ought to, now) between the Cross and the Mohammedan crescent, curbs upward at Our Lady's feet, recalling Holy Scripture . . . "and the moon under her feet, and on her head a crown of twelve stars''. (*Apoc.* xii, 1.)

From its position this shrine-chapel was usually known as the Chapel of the Glacis and was highly popular as a centre of devotion. Immediately began a sequence of remarkable answers to prayer. Numerous extraordinary favours were granted. The founder of the shrine, himself smitten by the plague, was wonderfully cured. In 1627, a suffocated baby revived during the singing of the Litany of Our Lady. Hearing was given to a child born deaf. A long series of cases of persons afflicted, blind, paralysed and dumb, some thirty-three instances in all, had been as wonderfully healed before October 12th, 1640. Many other claims of cures were recorded and authenticated by the Bishops of Trier, between 1640 and 1647.

Then, in 1666, the city, moved by so much favour, declared by Official Decree that henceforth it placed itself under the Patronage of Our Lady, Consolation of the Afflicted. There was swift response. Next year the Duchy was dragged into the conflict between France and Spain. The city was besieged, but an attempt to mine the walls was discovered, through Our Lady's intervention it was believed. In thanksgiving, a gold key was presented, which may still be seen, suspended by a cord from Our Lady's right wrist. A second French attack was foiled by an unexpected torrent of water which rushed suddenly down the gorge of the Alzette river.

Thus it was that the States General, moved by this evidence of invisible protection, resolved to follow Luxemburg's example and consecrate the entire Duchy, and the important County of Chiny too, to *Consolatrix Afflictorum.* Proclamation was made in the towns and villages, and with grand unanimity the populace flocked to the capital. At the ceremony of dedication, some 40,000 Communions were given.

Other evidence of the depth of this devotion is to be found in the figures for the celebrations, in 1781, of the Jubilee. Then there were 100,000 pilgrims and 55,000 Communions; 2,400 Masses were said at the shrine during the Octave.

A few years later the storm of the French Revolution broke and hurled itself upon the Grand Duchy. On June 5th, 1795, the city fell; all the churches were desecrated but the Chapel of Our Lady was destroyed. The beloved statue, however, was spared. It was smuggled to safety and hidden somewhere in the vaults of the great Jesuit church. Henceforth, once the storm was quelled, that church—by then, alas, deprived of the services of its founders—was to become the home and centre of the devotion.

Not even the dismemberment of the Duchy, part being ceded to France and part to Belgium, seriously interrupted the pilgrimage. All who considered themselves Luxembourgeois, no matter on which side of the frontier they lived, continued to look to their Mother in her citadel and to regard her as their especial Patroness, no matter what government was set over them.

To conjure up a realistic impression of the vitality of the devotion it is necessary to visit Luxemburg during what is called the Great Octave. In 1666, the statue was carried from its Chapel to the Jesuit church for the great Consecration. For a full Octave, Masses were sung for the special intentions of the various guilds and fraternities. Then the figure was borne back in state.

For several years this Octave was repeated in October, but since 1680 it has been transferred to the latter part of Paschaltide. Since 1920, the Octave has been doubled, to include the fifteen days between the third and fifth Sundays after Easter. Extraordinary privileges have been granted by the Holy See from time to time, confirmed and increased as recently as 1933. A special Mass and Office—with particularly fine antiphons—was approved for use throughout the Duchy by Pope Pius IX in 1854.

Normally, throughout the year, Our Lady of Luxemburg (her official title is still *Consolatrix Afflictorum*) is enthroned behind the magnificent high altar. During the "Octave" a special votive altar of hand-wrought iron is set up between the choir and the body of the church. This, too, has a history. It was made as an ex-voto offering of the Duchy for the first centenary of the election of Our Lady as their Patron.

This "Iron Altar" consists of a great screen of fine iron grill-work, extending the width of the sanctuary, linking two side altars to a central altar, with tabernacle, wrought-iron reredos and a fairy-landish canopy of the same material. It is the great masterpiece of Pierre Petit, mastersmith, who was trained at the Cistercian Abbey of Orval. The Jesuit Fathers did not see the installation for they were expelled from Luxemburg in 1773, on the suppression of the Order.

During the "Octave" all is banked with flowers; the altars are vested in rich frontals, and Our Lady is enthroned in a central position. In these modern days there has been added the custom, which some may regret, of outlining and illuminating the whole framework with electric lights. A great number of votive offerings hang from the iron background, gold, silver and bronze; legs, arms, hearts and eyes, according to the thanksgiving made for favours granted. A number of silver lamps likewise hang around this curious shrine.

Nowhere may the custom of dressing a venerated statue of Our Lady in royal robes be seen to greater effect than here. Our Lady possesses a wardrobe and jewel-case, containing the gifts and handiwork of queens, princesses and royal duchesses which might well be envied by many an empress. This custom calls to mind the words of Psalm 44, line 10: "The daughters of kings have delighted Thee in Thy glory: the queen stood on Thy right hand in gilded clothes, surrounded with variety". There is kept in the sacristy a large array of magnificent vestments, crowns, sceptres, orbs, brooches and necklaces studded with gems, chaplets and medals of pearls and gold.

In particular some of the lace veils are worthy of remark. They are the priceless offerings of one of the most famous lace-making districts of Europe. Here one sees the vivid evidence of centuries of love and devotion towards their Mother of a people who are genuinely and whole-heartedly Catholic. One looks and marvels and then turns away feeling a little ashamed at the poverty of one's own devotion.

Surely, too, the great procession in honour of Our Lady each year at the close of the "Octave" is one of the most magnificent in Europe? This last day begins with a series of Low Masses, at all altars, starting at 4 a.m. There is Pontifical Mass at 9 a.m., followed by the renewal of the Consecration made three hundred years ago. Holy Communion is given at two altars, without interruption from the earliest Mass until noon.

The Procession begins at 2 p.m. Typical of all was that in 1939. It consisted of seventy-nine distinct units, including many of the ancient guilds which still continue. A section of the official "Order" reads thus:

45. The Guild of Artisans of Luxemburg.
46. The Association of Carpenters.
47. The Association of Slaters.
48. The Guild of Stall-keepers of the Market.
49. The Society of the Holy Family, with its statue and Choral Society . . . and so on.

Each and every section of society is represented and present. Twenty or more choirs take part and as many bands and philharmonic societies. Sixty-one on the list is "The Miraculous Statue of the Consolation of

The Afflicted, carried on a magnificent daïs". Seventieth is "The Most Holy Sacrament (carried by the Bishop) on a superb platform". Finally, seventy-third, is the note, delightful in its simplicity: "Le peuple qui prie"—"The people, who pray".

After the French Revolution, and with the recognition of Luxemburg as an independent state, the old ties with Trier were severed and a new diocese was created. A new honour was thus accorded to the church of Our Lady's present-day shrine. It was promoted to Cathedral rank. Already the old church had proved entirely inadequate for the great press of pilgrims which thronged it. Now the situation was impossible. To pull down the old was, however, unthinkable. Instead it was enlarged.

The old church was entirely incorporated as a nave. Eastward, a large central construction was added, opening onto an impressive and dignified sanctuary. This work began in 1935 and included a large crypt and pilgrims' porch of truly grand dimensions. The architect was Hubert Schumacher, a worthy successor of Frère Jean, three hundred years earlier.

No stone of the old work was sacrificed needlessly. Every detail of the new was given consideration and care. The result is a truly remarkable combination of new and old with which the severest critic will find it difficult to find fault. Space precludes any description; but mention must be made at least of the stained glass windows which adorn all the new parts. The general theme is that of Mary, Queen; Queen of Patriarchs; of Apostles; of Martyrs; of Confessors; of Virgins; of Prophets; and of all the Mysteries of the Holy Rosary. The artist was Louis Barillet of Paris and it is hardly an exaggeration to say that the result he has achieved compares with the glory of Chartres on a somewhat smaller scale. Our Lady of Luxemburg rejoices indeed in a truly sumptuous shrine.

## XIII: FOURVIERE

ONE needs only a slight knowledge of English history to remember how close were the ties which linked England and Scotland in medieval days with the countries of the continent and with France in particular. Long before the Conquest there were bonds of marriage between our respective rulers, exchanges in trade between our merchants, and an immense amount of good culture common to us all. The Conqueror of 1066 was a Norman and the very name Anjou reminds us that for centuries English kings ruled tracts of France as large as England.

It is a curious defect of Protestantism to be unable to recognise that the ties between the Church in these realms and the Church abroad were equally close. Non-Catholic history books make much of the "foreign-ness" of the bishops imposed by the Church on England, but forget how many bishops abroad were English. The Church was the great international link between nations, supplying a common bond in language, devotion and spiritual leadership. A thrilling example of this is to be found in the history of the great French national shrine of Our Lady, Notre-Dame de Fourvière at Lyons, where there have been continuous links between France and Catholic England since the days of St. Thomas of Canterbury.

Lyons was early noted for devotion to Our Lady. St. Pothinus, Apostle of Gaul, is said to have enshrined a picture of Our Lady in the underground oratory which now lies beneath the city church of St. Nazaire. As at Rome, large numbers of Christians suffered under Roman persecution, many dying in the Old Forum (called Fourvière today) on the Hill of Blood.

In the ninth century, one of the Roman ruins was transformed into a chapel of Our Lady of Good Counsel and by degrees this outstripped the older Lady Chapel as a popular place of pilgrimage. In 1168, the Canons of the Cathedral started to build a larger church over the Fourvière shrine. The new Archbishop, Guichard, was an intimate friend of St. Thomas à Becket, and it was to him that our English primate turned when he fled from England after his quarrel with Henry II. One day, as the two Archbishops were walking through Lyons, St. Thomas noticed the uprising walls of this new church and enquired as to its dedication. The architect gave a curious answer: "To the very next martyr who sheds his blood for the Church. Who knows, your Grace, but that your enemies in England may gain you that honour!"

Lyons gave as great an honour to the exiled Archbishop as London Catholics would today to Archbishop Stepinac could he but be delivered from bondage. St. Thomas was made a Canon of Lyons and given a Manor, the income from which provided revenue for Archbishops of Canterbury for hundreds of years. Two years later, 1170, St. Thomas was murdered; and in 1173 he was canonised. True to their promise, the Canons of Lyons dedicated the shrine church of Fourvière to him, the first church among hundreds to have that honour.

Almost immediately, King Louis VII of France received a great favour through the intercession of the new martyr. His eldest son, at the point of death, was cured when St. Thomas appeared to him in a dream. In thanksgiving King Louis made a pilgrimage to Canterbury and then to the new church at Lyons, where he caused an ex-voto tablet to be set up before the shrine of Our Lady of Fourvière.

Thus it came to pass that through this devotion to the English Martyr Primate, intercession for England became regularly associated with one of the historic sanctuaries of Our Lady abroad. More and more did pilgrims flock up the hill to Fourvière. In 1466, King Louis XI founded a daily Mass in perpetuity, to be followed always by the *Salve Regina* solemnly sung.

Again and again, vast pilgrimages besought Our Lady, especially in the terrible years of famine, 1504, 1534, 1556. In the last year the worst famine recorded in France was turned suddenly into a new spring (in late autumn); trees blossomed afresh and bore fresh crops of fruit; apples, plums and nuts as well.

French gratitude was no less fickle than ours in Mary's Dowry. For a time Lyons became a stronghold of Geneva Calvinists, and terrible acts of sacrilege and blasphemy were endured. Fourvière was pillaged. Years later the Canons returned, to find St. Thomas' walls blackened by fire; but Our Lady of Fourvière had been hidden and spared.

Then a new series of disasters befell the city. Again and again Lyons was stricken with the plague. At last, in 1643, it was determined to dedicate the city to Our Lady of Fourvière. Instantly all trace of pestilence vanished and, until 1792, twenty-five Masses were said daily at the shrine in thanksgiving.

Then began the French Revolution. One shudders to relate the blasphemies enacted beside Fourvière. An ass, decked in sacred vestments, was made to trample on a crucifix and Gospel book, and to drink out of a chalice. Even worse profanities were planned but God intervened with a tempest so sudden and so fierce that all those assembled fled in terror. In the dark years of the guillotine which followed, parties of pilgrims visited the shrine at night at peril of their lives. Then came a new dawn. In 1805, Pope Pius VII personally presided at the re-opening of the Fourvière Sanctuary and himself gave Holy Communion to many of the people present.

Other dangers threatened this ancient shrine. Shortly before the Battle of Waterloo, Napoleon ordered Marshal Suchet to fortify the hillside to make Fourvière impregnable. Workmen stood awaiting the marshal's order to destroy the sanctuary. Instead, he who had already refused to plunder the shrine of Our Lady of the Pillar in Spain, stood and gazed at this church, for he had been born under its shadow. "My mother brought me here as a child to pray. Please take this offering and say several Masses for my intention." Thus again was Fourvière spared, and so it happened that in the terrible cholera years which came later, Lyons was passed by. Likewise, during the Communard Massacres of 1830 and 1848, Lyons suffered less than many cities. One revolutionary was heard to remark in disgust, "We shall never succeed in *this* place as long as that *montagnarde* (mountain lady) remains up there".

In thanksgiving for such mercies the Lyonnese built a tall tower to the church, surmounted by a great figure of Our Lady in gilded bronze. By 1865, the approaches had been turned into leafy avenues, bordered by the Stations of the Cross, and 16,000 Masses were being said at Fourvière each year.

Five years later, France staggered under the Prussian invasion of 1870. Again was Lyons menaced. Bishop Ginoulhiac, so closely associated with Our Lady of La Salette, had just become Archbishop and himself placed a monster pledge, signed by thousands, promising to build a superb basilica, above the ancient altar of Our Lady.

There was no question of pulling down the old church. That had been saved forever by the visit of the Curé of Ars, who had come in pilgrimage with his entire parish. Pierre Bossau, an architect trained in Rome and a native of Lyons, was blessed specially for the new work by the holy Curé. The vast new basilica, Mary's Mount Thabor, and symbolic of Our Lady as Tower of David, was raised close beside the old shrine which was left almost untouched.

The completed building stands today for all the world to see, in a situation as grand and commanding as that of the Sacred Heart Basilica of Montmartre, Paris. It crowns and triumphs over the city. Though it took twenty-two years to build, the interior is hardly complete even today. It was consecrated to Our Lady as the ex-voto offering of the French nation by Cardinal Couillé in 1896.

The exterior is splendid, giving at one and the same time an idea of strength and endurance and yet of lightness and delicacy. Four towers guard the angles of the huge rectangular building. The eastern apse is surmounted by a cupola, crowned with a gleaming figure of St. Michael. The façade is composed of gigantic monoliths, each weighing many tons. They are surmounted, above the west door, by Our Lady, at whose feet crouches the rugged Lion of Lyons, the city's symbol. Two wide flights of steps lead down to a huge crypt, or lower church, larger than many a cathedral, dedicated to St. Joseph. But the main flight leads to the upper church.

It is when the visitor first enters this that he holds his breath in astonishment. The combined impression of soaring loftiness, untrammelled spaciousness and overwhelming richness is not thus available in any other church in France. The apparent height of the golden ceiling from the richly inlaid floor is incredible.

At the east end, beneath a tall baldachino, reigns an immaculate white marble figure of Our Lady of Fourvière, compellingly lovely in its sheer simplicity.

If the external appearance suggests the Tower of David, within it is the Tower of Ivory, fitting shrine of the Heavenly Empress. In various ways every architectural detail is made to represent either one of the titles of the Litany of Loreto, or some scene in the Life of Our Lady. Few are omitted, little forgotten. The ceiling is uplifted by angels bearing scrolls with the words of the *Magnificat;* the coloured windows display all her titles of royalty. One is led by the artist, with absorbing single-mindedness, from one plane to another in the history of the Co-redemptrix of mankind, until finally one reaches the Chapel of the Immaculate Conception, her highest title of honour, the perfection of all created things.

Side by side with all this splendour, knit to the modern by many centuries of fervent devotion, the old shrine of Fourvière stands, equal tribute to Our Lady's triumph over ages of cruelty, unrest, persecution, famine, war; and staunch, historic witness of her unfailing favours and her people's persistent devotion. Blackened by the years of many centuries Our Lady of St. Thomas' Church of Fourvière, richly adorned in gold, still reigns above the altar of the ancient church where she was beloved of the Curé of Ars and where constant prayers are said for the restoration of the Faith to the realm for which once, in Canterbury Cathedral, St. Thomas, our blissful martyr, died.

# XIV: MADONNA DELLA QUERCIA, VITERBO

ONE custom, still widely prevalent abroad but not yet revived to any marked degree in England, is that of erect ng wayside shrines of Our Blessed Lady, whether at street-corners or at convenient spots along the highways, for the comfort and inspiration of passers-by.

It is interesting to reflect that quite a number of the more celebrated shrines of Our Lady had their origins in such simple, charitable offerings which were the direct evidence of deep-rooted love of, and devotion to, the Holy Mother and her Son.

Another kindred practice, almost as common, was to enshrine some picture or image of Our Lady beside some familiar landmark in more remote regions, to increase and focus the devotion of shepherds and farm-workers too far from their parochial churches to be able regularly to assist in the various acts of public worship.

To such shrines, often crude but always devotional, herdsmen and field-workers would turn when the echoes of the Angelus bells reached them from valleys below.

It was just such a shrine that a farmer named Battista Juzzante set up in 1417, beside the high-road running through his vineyards on the outskirts of the famous hill-city of Viterbo, a city connected in history with so many of the popes of the 12th and 13th centuries. This he did for the benefit of workers tending his vines, but also to benefit numerous passers-by and to gain their prayers as well.

The shrine was simple. It consisted of a quite beautiful painting of Our Blessed Lady on a flat, earthen tile, fixed to the trunk of a grand old oak tree, chosen because it was more likely to survive storms and because it was so outstanding.

It was some time before this little shrine had any marked effect on the neighbourhood. By degrees, however, it became increasingly popular. Nearly fifty years later, a hermit who lived in a cave on a crag in the nearby Ciminian Forest, a Sienese named Pier Dominico Alberti, formed the habit of coming almost daily to pray there. One day, according to the story, he decided to enshrine the picture in the oratory of his hermitage. Next morning, he was astonished to find that it had been taken back, by means unknown, to the oak tree.

Likewise a devout widow in Viterbo had a similar experience. From henceforth both, and the hermit especially, became ardent apostles of the new devotion, of "Our Lady della Quercia"—of the oak tree—by which title she has ever since been known.

It is related at Walsingham that a certain knight, hard pressed by his enemies, invoked Our Lady of Walsingham and as instantly found himself on the safe side of a little gateway, known to posterity as the "Knight's Gate". A similar story is recorded at Viterbo. A citizen, forced to flee for his life from a rival faction, found himself, on the 8th July, 1467, without hope of escape on the road beside the oak tree. He was instantly delivered in response to his prayer, and lost no time in making known his wonderful escape to his friends.

Thus it was that the new shrine became popular, and to it, that same month, was brought solemn invocation

*The altar which enshrines the ancient statue of Our Lady of Good Counsel in the church at Fourviere dedicated to St. Thomas of Canterbury*

(Page 117)

The "Little Temple" in the church at Viterbo which
enshrines the original picture of Our Lady and the
remains of the oak tree trunk

(Page 123)

against a fearful pestilence which that summer devastated so large a part of Central Italy. Before the end of the month, the plague had ceased within the city. On the first Sunday of August, it is recorded, forty thousand townsfolk, headed by the Bishop and the city magistrates, made an immense procession nearly three miles long out to the shrine. For the first time, it seems, Mass was said at an altar in the shade of the tree.

In Siena, too, the new devotion soon took root. The people were terrified by a series of sharp earthquakes which rocked their houses and cracked the cathedral walls. Pier Dominico exhorted them to repent and to turn to the Madonna della Quercia. Their prayers were answered and, in thanksgiving, they presented a silver plaque with an inscription recording their city's official gratitude.

The fame of the Viterbo sanctuary was thus assured and spread throughout the length of Italy so that it became a shrine second only to Loreto in popularity.

In the autumn of 1467, it was decided to erect a chapel above the altar which had been first used that August Sunday. Its care was committed to the Priors of the Dominican, Franciscan, Augustinian and Servite houses in Viterbo. By the following year, a more permanent plan had to be made and eventually the Master General of the Dominicans was selected and agreed to take charge. A bull to this effect was granted by Pope Paul II; and, in July 1470, work began on a spacious church, adequate for the needs of pilgrims and for the protection of the shrine.

As in the case of Montaigu, it seems that the great tree did not survive the eager devotion of pilgrims, who hacked off large pieces of bark, limbs even, as pious souvenirs. What remained of the trunk, therefore, was encased in a superb marble "tempietto", or "little temple", behind the high altar of the new building. This was designed by the artist Andrea Bregno (1421-1506); though it was Bramante who designed the cloisters; Andrea della Robbia, the reliefs in the lunettes of the entrance; and the wooden ceiling was by Antonio da Sangallo the Younger. Ghirlandaio (1449-1494) added the frescoes which adorn the sides and back of the actual shrine. It is eloquent of the fame of the sanctuary that so many illustrious artists combined in its erection and decoration.

The plaque of Our Lady is visible within an arch in the centre of Bregno's masterpiece, hardly changed after four hundred years. Our Lady is shown dressed in a rose coloured robe, with a cloak of azure blue. The Holy Child, in a yellow tunic, is clasped in her left arm, holding in His right hand a little swallow. With His left hand He clutches at His mother's breast.

Our Lady della Quercia has twice been crowned by decree of the Vatican Chapter and the devotion is honoured with a special Mass and Office throughout the diocese of Viterbo.

The Dominicans, alas, no longer have guardianship of the shrine, from which they were expelled during the troubles of the past century. The shrine and the magnificent church above it were, however, spared and today the adjacent buildings serve as a diocesan seminary. The pilgrimage is still one of great popularity.

The list of famous pilgrims is as imposing as the history of the shrine. Popes Paul III and St. Pius V were fervent visitors. The former made his pilgrimage annually. The latter gave orders for special devotions to be offered without ceasing, and in his name, for the victory of the Christian allies at Lepanto. One of the patriots in that vital engagement, upon which the fate of Christianity in Europe may well have depended, received a remarkable answer to his own prayers for the intercession of Our Lady of the Oak.

His name was Tomaso Roberti and he had suffered such severe wounds that he was left for dead on the battlefield. Upon his invocation of Our Lady della Quercia, he felt himself raised, his wounds staunched and healed. He was able to participate in the victory and in person to give thanks at Viterbo. He left a small statue of himself as a votive offering. An immense number of his fellow-combatants likewise left tokens of gratitude for their own safety.

Other famous pilgrims include St. Philip Neri, St. Camillus of Lellis, St. Paul of the Cross, St. John Leonard of Lucca, Blessed Lucy of Narni, St. Hyacinth Marescotti (who, after she became enclosed, continued to send pilgrims, especially children, as her deputies), Blessed Columba of Rieti.

It was here, in the Friary attached to the shrine, that Père Lacordaire was inspired to raise up the new body of Blackfriars who were to refound the Order of Preachers in France. Here he and his companions welded themselves together in their novitiate. One of them, the renowned Père Hyacinth Besson, who was a skilled artist, made a careful copy of Our Lady della Quercia which was solemnly placed above the altar of their first restored house in France, at Nancy.

Père Lacordaire was preaching one day in the church of the actual shrine, upon the importance of putting trust in Our Lady. "Look around you," he cried to his hearers. "Look at this church, these houses and cloisters. Who built them? I will answer you; that *piece of tile* has done all this!" And he pointed to the piece of tile bearing Our Lady's image, enshrined behind the altar.

As with Our Lady of Montserrat, of Montaigu, and so many other of her titles, a number of churches were built under her patronage and with the dedication "della Quercia". Whether there was any direct connection between the devotions or not, it is impossible to say; but the church of St. Martin-at-Oak (Oak Street), Norwich, preserves the tradition of the local devotion to a plaque of Our Lady, called "Our Lady of the Oak", hung on a tree in the churchyard. The present oak tree is said to be the fifth one planted in the same spot.

The devotion of the Roman people themselves is marked by the presence in Rome, in the Piazza Farnese, of the Church of San Niccolò, rededicated to the Madonna della Quercia, wherein a copy of the original picture was hung, fastened upon a silver oak branch.

# XV: MONTAIGU

NOT far from Louvain in Belgium, and in the diocese of Malines, a spur of hills rises so abruptly from the surrounding lowlands that the highest point has been named Scherpenheuvel, Sharp Hill, in Flemish, or Montaigu in French, from the Latin *Mons Acutus*. This, many centuries ago, was crested by a mighty, solitary oak tree visible over a wide area.

Dating, perhaps, from the Druids, this tree seems to have been a centre of superstitious practices; countryfolk are slow to abandon old customs. To correct these, or to give them truer meaning, a wooden figure of Our Lady was affixed to the tree in a natural niche during the fourteenth century. This came to be venerated by its neighbours as a favourite, but quite local shrine to which those in need or distress had recourse.

One day, a shepherd found that the wind had blown down the statue, which he picked up with intent to take it home with him. He became transfixed to the ground and unable to move except to restore the little statue to its niche. The shrine thus gained a wider celebrity, so much, in fact, that a personage so distinguished as Alexander Farnese, victor in the Battle of Lepanto, and Governor of the Netherlands, made a pilgrimage to Montaigu before he began the siege of nearby Sichem.

In 1579 the statuette disappeared. It was probably destroyed by that band of heretics, the Gueux, who

were marching through the Netherlands, looting and
destroying all they could lay hands on that represented
the Catholic Faith.   But even though the figure was
missing, devotion to Our Lady continued unabated at
the shrine for several years and it is recorded that
many graces and favours were granted there during
those years.

It was in 1586 that a resident of Sichem, devoted to
Our Lady of Montaigu, well familiar with the lost
figure, paid a visit to a widow in the town of Diest, six
miles away.   He found that she had acquired and set
in a place of honour in her house, a statuette so like
the other that he was convinced it was the same, as,
indeed, many others thought.   But, whether so or not,
the widow gladly offered it to fill the vacant niche in
the oak tree.   From that date, 1587, the modern
history of the devotion began.

In 1602, Abbé Van Thienwinckel took a further
step.   A little wooden chapel was built under the
shadow of the tree and the figure of Our Lady was
enshrined within.   Instantly there began a series of
wonderful responses to prayer.   By the end of that
year the stream of pilgrims flocking there had become
considerable.   Then occurred the most celebrated of
all the recorded prodigies associated with the shrine.

Early in January, 1603, three counsellors, returning
home from a parish meeting, stopped at the chapel
to pay their respects.   Each one, independently,
observed drops of blood trickling from the statue's lips.
Careful scrutiny revealed no evidence that the statue
had been painted, or that natural moisture was
exuding.   The men were well-known, pious, and
responsible.   Magistrates who held an official enquiry
could only accept such testimony.   Then a commission
sat to sift all the many reports of miracles and favours
associated with the shrine.

Evidence was given by a number of the older

inhabitants and recorded by the respected historian, Numan. It was observed that since the replacing of a statue at the oak tree more than two hundred cures had occurred.

As a result, application was made to Pope Pius V, who was quick to recognise the strategic importance of Montaigu and who granted numerous indulgences to those who visited the shrine. The royal governors, Archduke Albert and the Infanta Isabella, took the place under their direct patronage. A larger and better chapel was at once built but this was destroyed almost immediately by another band of heretics who were roaming through the country, smashing everything which represented Catholicism. The figure was rescued in time, however, and hidden until danger had passed.

To make amends for such sacrilege Albert and Isabella launched forth on a truly magnificent scheme. Just as Our Lady of Loreto was protected in a mighty stronghold, with bastions and battlements, so it was planned that Our Lady of Montaigu should reign in a great fortress or citadel which should act as a tower of strength for the Faith, to dominate the Netherlands against invasion by Protestant doctrines.

The area round the oak tree was laid out as a large park within a seven-sided enclosure of walls, each point being strengthened with a bastion. The oak tree itself, killed because so many pilgrims had hacked away bark for souvenirs, was removed. On its site was erected the high altar of the new, heptagonal basilica.

The wood of the oak was cut up into small pieces and carved by a local craftsman into statuettes, similar to the figure of Our Lady of Montaigu. These were presented as a mark of esteem, either to local magnates and patrons of the new shrine, or to friends of the Archduchess. Wherever they went, these figures were enshrined with honour, and it seemed as if Our Lady of Montaigu sent her favour with them.

Thus shrines in her name were established throughout Western Europe, several score in number, each becoming in itself a centre of renewed love and honour for Our Lady. One became the first celebrated shrine in the Church of Our Lady of Victories, Paris. It was indeed the forerunner of the tremendous devotion which led to the founding there of the Universal Archconfraternity. Another was presented to some English Carmelite nuns who had just established a house at Antwerp. In due course, these nuns brought it with them to Lanherne, in Cornwall, under the title of Our Lady of the Oak of Sichem; where it is still venerated in England's oldest Carmel.

The task of designing the "fortress" and basilica at Montaigu was entrusted to the greatest European architect of his day, Cobergher, who raised a triumphant church, with a dome that can be likened only to that of St. Peter's, Rome.

The basilica is a rotunda. The high altar stands in the centre of a circle of six chapels. Each of these seven altars represents one of the seven Mysteries in the life of the Mother of God and is given for a reredos a splendid picture depicting each subject, painted by the Flemish master, Van Loon. Towering above the altar piece of the high altar, where Our Lady of Montaigu is enshrined, is a marble oak tree, in memory of the great oak which was the origin of the shrine.

Each step in the development of this huge undertaking was personally directed by the royal governors. They themselves laid the foundation stone in 1609, in the presence of the Cardinal Archbishop of Malines. They provided, without regard to expense, the most lavish set of altar equipment that graced any church in the Holy Roman Empire. Gold from Mexico, silver from Columbia, gems from the treasure-ships of the Spanish Main, costly silks and embroideries from the East, all manner of wealth was heaped upon their beloved sanctuary. Isabella herself set to work and embroidered with her own fingers a gorgeous set of altar frontals, High Mass vestments, and robes for the venerated statue.

It was not until 1627 that this superb enterprise was completed. In that year it was consecrated and placed under the care of the Oratorians of St. Philip Neri who were created guardians of the shrine by decree of Pope Urban VIII, and served there until the French Revolution.

As at Hal, a Confraternity was established at Montaigu. Most fortunately the first register of membership has survived the fury of later wars and destructions, and recently came back into the ownership of the basilica. It is a sumptuous volume, hand illuminated, on vellum; page after page bearing the coats of arms of the illustrious signatories, and their respective autographs. No single volume elsewhere in the world contains such an array of eminent and historic signatures.

The treasury, which is on occasion open to the public, is a veritable museum of art, with this difference, that here every object shewn, regardless of its value or antiquity, is faithfully used in the service of God and to the honour of His Mother. A full catalogue would (and does) occupy a large volume. The privileged visitor can only marvel that such a wealth of treasure has survived revolutions, wars and invasions intact. Most notable are the gold crowns, presented in 1603 by the city of Brussels; a gold cup and altar frontal, by the Princess Dorothy of Lorraine; a set of massive silver candlesticks, by the city of Antwerp; all of which date back to the first humble chapel. Some of the vestments, too, were presented by the Archduchess at the same time.

There is a monstrance presented by the Empress Marie-Thérèse; a processional cross in silver dating from the thirteenth century, given by Pope Adrian VI; a chasuble that was worn by St. Thomas of Canterbury; a set of lamps, of solid silver, given by Archduke Albert; and literally dozens of silver candlesticks—all in one set, of one design, for the seven altars.

Our Lady of Montaigu is very simple and very small. The figure was polychromed in the eighteenth century and is usually hidden by heavy copes and a blaze of jewellery. She is exquisitely carved. Standing, Our Lady is shown in a long robe of brocade, with a cord girdle round her waist, and sleeves down to her wrists. Her hair flows in natural waves over her shoulders. The Holy Child, as a delightful bambino, rests poised upon her left arm, extending His right hand in blessing, holding a small orb in the other. In her left hand, Our Lady holds a massive sceptre which terminates in a large star. A cloak of material similar to her dress hangs from her shoulders and is caught round in front of her girdle. The dress is typical of a fifteenth century European princess, but the statue is carved by an artist of the same school which produced Our Lady of Brewood in Staffordshire. Although the pose is different, there are certain marked similarities in detail.

Montaigu is almost unknown to the majority of Catholics in England. This is more than a pity because it is comparatively easy of access, situated in a charming small town with a useful train service and several moderate-priced hostels and inns for pilgrims' accommodation; and because it is so truly magnificent both in conception and detail. One fears to find a small figure, decked in gaudy robes, in some out of the way church. One discovers a delicious work of art, gloriously enshrined in a basilica built to represent the spirit of devotion to Our Lady and its rightful place in the heart of Christendom.

Indirectly, England owes a debt of gratitude to Our Lady of Montaigu for the courage and consolation she gave to many of our brave and constant recusant forefathers; some of them actual martyrs. Many were the religious houses established in Flanders for those who could not practise their faith in England. All such looked to Montaigu for hope and help. Soldiers from these islands who enlisted in the religious wars of the seventeenth century—in particular Irish mercenaries—were regularly brought here on pilgrimage before their battles or during convalescence after wounds.

According to Numan, Father Walter Talbot, a Jesuit Chaplain, frequently led Irish recruits here on pilgrimage, about 1587. There is a tradition that one of the English Franciscan martyrs, exiled from his homeland, made just such a pilgrimage to intercede for permission to return on the mission—a prayer which was granted with the glorious addition of a martyr's crown.

Our Lady of Montaigu is, in fact, a strong link in the historic chain of English devotion to Our Lady. When no shrine remained in this her Dowry, English hearts turned to Montaigu.

# XVI: LUJAN, A SOUTH AMERICAN SHRINE

**D**EVOTION to Our Blessed Lady spread, naturally, to every corner of the globe where there was a Catholic to take and maintain it. Shrines of Our Lady, sanctuaries of power, are to be found not exclusively in Europe. Nor is it to be expected that the Virgin Most Renowned, *Consolatrix Afflictorum,* should restrict the abundance of her aid to those who seek her in the sanctuaries of this old-world continent that has so often proved fickle in its devotion to the Mother of God.

The opening up of South America in the sixteenth century, following the discoveries of Cabral and Magellan, of Cortez and Pizzaro, brought into reality a vast new field where the Faith might take root and increase.

Few Catholics in England realise the tremendous, dynamic importance of modern South America, as far as Catholicism is concerned. Brazil, with its thirty millions of Catholics; Argentina, with its great cities of hundreds of thousands of inhabitants; and all those other nations of the Southern American continent may well prove to be the chief human bulwark of the Faith in future ages.

It is good, then, to know that Our Lady has not omitted to provide this glorious new world with a number of her chosen sanctuaries, each being every whit as fascinating and inspiring as those more familiar to us because nearer home. Quito, in Ecuador, Guadalupe, in Mexico, are perhaps not unknown in England. But who has heard of Córdoba, Catamarca, Itatí, or Sumampa; all popular, authentic shrines of Our Lady in Argentina, some of them three hundred years old?

Of all the shrines of the Blessed Virgin in South America, perhaps the most historic, most famous, is that of Our Lady of Lujan (pronounced Luhán), a city about forty miles west of Buenos Aires. The story of its foundation and later development is as thrilling as any in this series; and bears every mark that here indeed may be found a true, chosen, sanctuary of Our Lady, of the same calibre as those at Genazzano or Montserrat.

In 1630, there lived at Cordoba, in the far interior of Argentina, a Portuguese settler who was so grieved at the lack of religious influences in his district that he sent to Brazil, which was in those days slightly more civilised, on the coast, for a statue of Our Lady. A friend, not knowing what type or style to choose, packed and sent two locally-made figures, one a Madonna with Holy Child, the other a representation of the Virgin Immaculate, to make the hazardous journey inland, in a caravan of carts and pack-horses banded together against the savage attacks of hostile Indians.

On the way from Buenos Aires, camp was made near the lonely ranch of one Don Rosendo de Oramus. Next dawn the waggon carrying the two figures "refused" to budge an inch; nor would it, in spite of every effort on the part of the drivers and of ranchers called to help; until the figure of Our Lady of the Immaculate Conception was lifted from it.

The other statue, of Madonna and Holy Child, continued its journey in due course to Sumampa where it is still venerated under the title of Our Lady of

Consolation. The first figure, however, was solemnly borne to the ranch and enthroned in the best room, which became henceforth, for the next forty years, a popular local shrine.

Accompanying the caravan thus far was a small eight year old negro slave from Angola, in Africa, who had been sold to and brought up by his Portuguese master to have an intense love for the Faith. This child was so captivated by the strange episode that he begged, and was allowed by Don Rosendo, to remain behind as a humble little servant of the Mother of God in her new sanctuary.

For many years he worked as sacristan, looked upon by all as an example in charity, devoted in his service to any sick or afflicted, nursing the dying and tending the little chapel of Our Lady. Whenever Manuel, as he was named, was given an alms he saved it for Our Lady's "purse", amassing in this way no less than fourteen thousand pesos before he died; a very large sum in those days.

Good Don Rosendo de Oramus died in 1670. As his ranch was so remote, and in constant danger of attack from Indians, a pious lady, Doña Ana de Mattos, obtained permission to move the shrine to a chapel on her own ranch, fifteen miles away, on the other side of the River Lujan. Manuel was left behind. The story which follows has its exact counterpart in the history of the oak tree shrine of Viterbo. This is doubly interesting because it is not likely that any of the principals in this Argentinian episode had any knowledge of the older story.

Next morning, it was discovered that the image had vanished although the chapel was still securely locked, and it was found again set on its former pedestal. A second time the figure was replaced in the new chapel but although this time careful watch was kept it returned as mysteriously to the former site. As no natural explanation could be found for these strange occurrences—it was proved impossible for Manuel to have been involved—Doña Ana turned for advice to the Bishop and the Governor of the Province; both of whom came to hold a careful enquiry.

Strict examination of all concerned ensued. While no verdict of miraculous intervention seems to have been given, the fact remains that both ecclesiastical and civil authorities were thus made officially aware of the remarkable nature of this particular shrine and of the multitude of graces and favours which may be said to have sprung therefrom. It was agreed, however, that the original site was in real danger from Indians, so the Bishop and Governor bore the sacred image in solemn state back to Doña Ana's home, themselves on foot, taking Manuel with them to be sacristan.

At length it became essential to build a proper church. The foundation stone was laid in 1677 by Fra Gabriel, a Carmelite Friar, and Our Lady of Lujan was solemnly translated there in 1685. A new chaplain was appointed: Dom Pedro de Montalbo who believed he had been cured of a serious illness through Our Lady's intercession. He died in 1701, leaving her all his possessions. From that date onwards, the Feast of the Immaculate Conception was observed with great splendour each year at Lujan.

The humble Manuel died, too, in the odour of sanctity, and was laid to rest in a tomb at the feet of his beloved Mother. It is recorded that Our Lady revealed to him the date of his death and promised him eternal bliss.

So famous did the shrine now become that a township sprang up around it, which was accorded a privileged charter by the King of Spain, in 1755.

In the meantime, in 1730, a second church was needed but before ever it was completed it was found

inadequate and, in 1754, yet a third church was begun
which was opened with many solemn functions in 1763.
In the following hundred years Carmelites,
Dominicans, Franciscans, Jesuits and Mercedarians
all played some part in the progress of the sanctuary.
Thus, through the religious orders, it obtained world-
wide reputation.

Therefore, in 1886, Pope Leo XIII determined to
honour Our Lady of Lujan with solemn encoronation.
On September 30th, he blessed the crown, made of
pure gold, set with 365 diamonds, rubies, emeralds and
sapphires, 132 pearls and a number of precious
enamels. The coronation took place on May 8th, 1887,
at the hands of a Papal Legate.

Since 1872, the shrine had been in the custody of
the Lazarist Fathers and it was they who conceived
the idea, strongly supported by the Archbishop, of
raising a superb basilica as a national monument that
should compare with any cathedral in the world. By
1904 this new and final sanctuary was sufficiently ready
to receive the sacred image which was solemnly
translated with the utmost splendour. But it was not
until 1910 that this gigantic church could be
consecrated.

The basilica is little smaller than the famous Spanish
cathedral of Toledo, larger than that of Burgos, and
compares favourably with York Minster, which is
longer but not so wide.

Among the Popes who have enriched the sanctuary
are Clement XI and XIV, Pius VI and IX, and Leo
XIII. Pope Pius IX, when accompanying the
Apostolic Nuncio to Chile in 1824, visited the shrine
in person as Father John Mastai Ferretti.

Our Lady of Lujan is enshrined under an enormous
canopy in the centre of the Camarin behind the high
altar. The figure, made of baked clay, is small, as
was Our Lady of Walsingham, and like so many other

*The miraculous statue of Our Lady of Montaigu enshrined over the high altar*

(Page 129)

*The ancient statue of Our Lady of Lujan*

(Page 136)

famous Madonnas of the world's great shrines. She is twenty-three inches high, though with crown and pedestal she measures thirty-two inches. Her face is oval, with large, open, clear blue eyes. Her hands are joined on her breast in an attitude of prayer. A crescent moon, encrusted with gems, glistens beneath her feet, and a solid gold aureole, of fifteen rays, shines all round her.

So well preserved is this ancient figure, it is hard to believe that it is made of such fragile material or that it has survived three hundred years of such hazardous existence.

As with all major shrines of Our Lady, it is utterly impossible to describe or assess the great number of favours bestowed by the Blessed Mother upon her clients at this shrine. The first recorded wonderful healing is that of Father Pedro de Montalbo, about 1677; though others are known to have occurred before then. Another cure, regarded as miraculous, was that of Father Bernabé de Gutiérrez, of a malignant tumour in his throat in 1710. In this case oil from the lamp of Our Lady's Shrine was applied. A similar practice, to be found still at Le Laus in France, is referred to in a later chapter.

On August 28th, 1780, the inhabitants of Lujan were put into panic by the news of what they had long dreaded; that a huge army of ferocious Indians was sweeping the plains, massacring all in their path and advancing rapidly on the town. Utterly defenceless, the people fled to the shrine and in a body put their whole trust in their especial Protectress. Suddenly, even as they prayed, a dense and unexpected fog rolled up and enveloped the town so that the savage hordes lost their way and passed by in another direction. In this way was Lujan mercifully saved by Our Blessed Lady and her shrine was preserved for our own age and generation to revere.

Much information about this wonderful shrine may be gained by reference to an excellent booklet by a Passionist Father, entitled *"Our Lady of Lujan"*, and published, in 1918, by the Catholic Truth Society, Calle Estados Unidos, 3150, Buenos Aires.

It comes as a welcome reminder that many aspects of the history of the New World are not so recent. Lujan, which has a history as fascinating as that of many a European sanctuary, had its origin long before the Fire of London and testifies to a devotion to Our Blessed Lady which Europe as a whole would do well to emulate.

# XVII: OUR LADY OF GOOD COUNSEL

ABOUT thirty miles south-east of Rome, in the Diocese of Palestrina, is the busy little town of Genazzano, crowning a hill-top less outstanding, perhaps, than many in Tuscany but still formidable enough in the days when steep approaches lent strength to fortresses.

Genazzano became wedded to devotion to Our Lady at an early date. In the fifth century, Pope Sixtus III gave a large part of the township to provide endowment for the shrine of Our Lady at St. Mary Major's in Rome. A church dedicated to Our Lady of Good Counsel was built in that quarter of Genazzano in the same century. In 1356, this ancient church, which was neither large nor beautiful, but which seems to have been decrepit and ill kempt, was given into the care of the friars of the Order of St. Augustine.

They still had custody of it in 1467, when a local widow, Petruccia de Geneo, determined to rebuild it on a more worthy scale. She undertook this task in spite of the mockery of many of her neighbours and, although her own means were slender, because she felt inspired to do so by Our Lady herself. In this her friends charged her with presumption and when, through lack of funds and lack of the support which they might have given, building had to cease, the people gathered round the unfinished walls of the church, calling them "Petruccia's Folly"

But the widow persisted, even to the selling of her last possessions, declaring: "The work will be completed, and that before I die. Our Lady and St. Augustine will see to it right soon. And what a great lady will come to take possession of it."

There is a rule of the Church, made in defence against superstitious abuses, which forbids the heeding of dreams and such-like revelations unless supported by external or other independent testimony. On these grounds, when funds finally dried up, Petruccia was forbidden to make any appeal and on St. Mark's Day, 1467, it seemed to all the scoffing townsfolk as if the widow's folly had reached its limit.

For many centuries it had been the custom of the town to keep St. Mark's Day with a grand public fiesta. As usual on that day, the streets were thronged with holidaymakers. The market square was filled with gaily decorated booths, surrounded by clusters of eager purchasers.

Towards evening, when the fun of the fair was at its height, a number of people standing in the main square saw a fleecy cloud float across the clear sky, descend and affix itself, after the manner of a swarm of bees, to the face of one of the walls of Petruccia's unfinished church. All these witnesses turned in astonishment, to behold the cloud divide and display in its midst a beautiful small picture of the Madonna and Child. This was set against the wall on a narrow ledge, a few feet from the ground, where no picture had been before. At the same moment, it is recorded, all the church bells of the town began to ring, causing wonder, and some alarm, among the people.

Petruccia, who had at that moment been saying her prayers in another place, came running forth and threw herself upon her knees, crying with joy and proclaiming that this indeed was the Great Lady come to take possession of her house, as she had foretold.

Immediately people in outlying villages, attracted and alarmed by the unexpected ringing of bells, flocked to the town and with one accord they and the townsfolk began to pour out their praises and prayers in front of this wonderful picture of Our Lady, and as instantly began a marvellous shower of graces and favours. So great was the number of these apparent miracles that with a prudence almost unprecedented at that date a special notary was appointed to make a register of the principal cases.

This record is still preserved. It dates from April 27th, and continues till August 14th, 1467, and contains the description of one hundred and seventy-one reputed miracles, sufficient in the eyes of the most sceptical of critics at the time to establish the right to call this a "Miraculous Madonna".

The townsfolk were at a loss to explain the origin of the picture. From the manner of its arrival they were led to call it the "Madonna of Paradise", brought hither by angels' hands.

A few days later, however, two strangers arrived, attracted by the repute of the picture; one of them an Albanian, the other a Slav, both of whom averred to have seen the same picture a few weeks previously in a church on a hillside just outside Scutari, in Albania. And so devoted were these two that, before the week was out, they and a number of their Albanian friends, refugees from the Turks who ravaged their country, had taken up residence in Genazzano, to be near to their especially beloved Madonna.

In the meantime, report of these strange events was taken to the authorities of the Church in Rome and, in July, Pope Paul II sent two bishops as Commissioners to examine the circumstances of this new shrine and devotion. These were Bishop Gaucer of Gap in the Dauphiny, a French bishop known to the Bishop of the Diocese, and Nicholas de Crucibus, Bishop of Lesina, a Dalmatian Diocese, who was familiar with Scutari.

The details of the findings of this Commission are preserved in their original texts which are supported by other contemporary records and writings in the

Papal Archives. We even know how much were the expenses of the Commission—nearly twenty-three florins, worth a good deal more then than today.

It was found that the painting was executed not upon wood, or canvas, or metal, but upon a thin layer of plaster of porcelain texture and thickness—the thickness of an egg-shell. This no human skill could have detached whole and uncracked from another wall, still less have transported it and placed it in its new position. For this wafer-like sheet of plaster was standing upright and with no support of any kind except the narrow ledge whereon it rested.

For five hundred years this extraordinary phenomenon has remained unchanged. Although "enshrined" in marvellous golden framework, and adorned with a king's ransom of precious stones, at no place is this fragile painting supported, except the base, and none of the adornments is allowed to touch it at any point. It was found possible by the Commission, and it is still possible, to pass a thread of wire round and behind the picture from top to bottom.

These careful investigations convinced the Commissioners, and Pope Paul himself, that this was none other than the picture of Our Lady of Good Counsel that had been venerated for centuries in Scutari. It was proved that the church from which it was believed to have been borne retained the empty space of exact area and dimensions where the picture had formerly been set.

At Loreto much of the contemporary evidence concerning the translation of the Holy House from Nazareth has been lost, or preserved only in secondary form. But at Genazzano many of those factors which are produced by sceptics as reason for their scoffing are lacking. Or, rather, the reverse; all the contemporary, painstaking and authentic evidence for the wonder of Genazzano has been preserved.

In 1630, Pope Urban VIII, who set his face against the recognition of any unsubstantiated "miraculous" legend, was so convinced of the truth and reality of the Genazzano tradition that he made pilgrimage there in person to pray for the cessation of a plague which was then scourging Italy.

In 1777, the Sacred Congregation of Rites added its token of recognition by approving a proper Office, commemorating the history of this shrine, to be used by all the Augustinian Order who, to this day, have the cherished honour of serving "Our Lady of Good Counsel".

It was through the proximity of the English College in Rome, who possess a country villa in the close neighbourhood of Genazzano, that devotion to Our Lady of Good Counsel spread fervently to this country. Not least devoted was Cardinal Acton, who gave thanksgiving in 1845 for preservation from a dreadful accident, when he and several of the students and his chaplain were plunged over a bank in their carriage, to a depth of twenty feet, unscathed. The Cardinal had a copy of the painting made, with the greatest accuracy possible, which he kept in his own oratory and which was later given to the church of Our Lady of the Angels, Stoke-on-Trent.

The recent catastrophe of war which swept Italy has left yet another remarkable piece of witness of the durability of the paradoxically fragile picture. Determined to check the Allied advance, the Germans stopped at bombing no shrine however sacred. The dome above the Holy House of Loreto was thus destroyed, and the Holy House itself saved only through the vigilance and quick action of a number of Polish soldiers.

At Genazzano, a bomb came crashing through the roof of the chancel of the little basilica, Petruccia's own church in fact, which was completed soon after the events of 1467. The bomb exploded with full force in the sanctuary, doing fearful damage. The high altar was obliterated. But the portrait of Our Lady of Good Counsel, a few yards away, survived intact and apparently unshaken, although the plaster on surrounding walls, covered with later-date paintings and frescoes, crumbled and fell.

The golden shrine and gorgeous trappings of the Lady Chapel will, for centuries to come, show the scars and shrapnel marks of the late war. But Our Lady of Good Counsel reigns on, serene and inviting, at home to all who may seek her there.

Of late, English devotion has somewhat slackened through lack of information perhaps, rather than lack of interest. More modern shrines of Our Blessed Lady have commanded so much attention. But Our Lady of Good Counsel gives title to at least one of our important English Catholic societies which does valiant work in giving legal advice to the poor who may stand in need of it—the Society of Our Lady of Good Counsel, specially designated to watch over Catholic interests where all points of law are concerned.

In London, undoubtedly the finest shrine to her honour is that in the Oratory Church. It is in the Chapel of St. Wilfrid, though the picture (surrounded by numerous votive offerings) hangs rather high compared with the original, which is about shoulder high.

Another excellent reproduction is enshrined in the Priory Church of St. Augustine in Hammersmith. But it is doubtful if any reproduction can now be purchased at our Catholic repositories. May one be led to hope that this lack will soon be remedied, and that a new flame of devotion to Our Lady of Good Counsel may be kindled in this land which owes so very much to the gracious Mother of God, the Seat of Wisdom.

# XVIII:   OUR LADY OF PERPETUAL SUCCOUR

IN the mid-fifteenth century, a wonderful picture of Our Blessed Lady, in the Byzantine style, was highly reverenced in a church on the island of Crete. It had been painted, possibly by the master Andreas Rico de Candia, after the model of an older eikon, and was regarded with much devotion because of numerous favours granted in response to prayers at that particular shrine.

One day, however, towards the close of the century, the picture was stolen by a merchant who took it to Rome, where he was taken ill and died.   On his deathbed this man confessed his theft to the Roman friend in whose house he was lying and begged him to present the eikon to some suitable church as soon as possible.   But the Roman's wife persuaded her husband to keep it himself and, in spite of several warnings in dreams, the picture hung in the bedroom for some time.

Then the Roman was smitten with some fell disease and died, too.   Soon afterwards, his six-year-old daughter had a vision in which, it was said, Our Lady told her to go to her mother and grandfather and say: "Holy Mary of Perpetual Succour bids you forthwith to remove her picture from your house, otherwise you shall die".

A neighbour then intervened who expostulated that the Blessed Virgin in heaven would hardly bother about a mere picture which, if cut up, would burn like any other kindling.   But this neighbour also was taken very ill and would have died had she not had the sense to go and kneel in front of that "mere picture" and promise a votive offering.

Soon the child received a second vision and was told to tell her mother to place the painting in a certain church of St. Matthew, part way between the Basilicas of St. Mary Major and St. John Lateran. At that time this church was in the care of some Augustinian Friars who gave heed to the strange story.

An old chronicle, which hung for many years beside this new shrine, related that the picture was carried thither in solemn procession through the streets of Rome, and concluded: "In this manner, the picture of the most glorious Virgin Mary was enshrined in the church of St. Matthew the Apostle, on the 27th of March, 1499, in the seventh year of the Pontificate of our most Holy Father and Lord in Christ, the Lord Pope Alexander VI".

Immediately, Our Lady of Perpetual Succour vouchsafed a miracle in Rome: a man who had long been paralysed was cured at the moment the procession passed by where he lay, in much the same way as in recent times cures have been reported at the passing by of statues of Our Lady of Fatima.

For three hundred years, the picture hung in St. Matthew's, highly venerated, and known under various titles. That of "Our Lady of St. Matthew" was frequently used but, by degrees, the name given in the vision to the little girl prevailed. So many favours were granted to those who here besought Our Lady's aid that it was natural to acclaim her "Our Lady of Never-failing Help" and "Our Lady of Ever-enduring Succour".

Among the host of pilgrims thus attracted were King James III of England (the "Old Pretender"), Queen Casimir of Poland and a large number of famous people since canonised.

During the wars of 1798, Marshal Berthier, under

orders from Bonaparte, broke into Rome and bore into fatal exile that aged devotee of Our Lady, Pope Pius VI. Berthier's successor, Massena, under pretext of "strengthening the city defences", destroyed some thirty churches, St. Matthew's included. The Friars had time to remove Our Lady of Perpetual Succour which for several years found a refuge in the Church of St. Eusebius until, in 1819, Pope Pius VII gave the Friars the use of St. Mary in Posterula, where a famous picture of Our Lady of Grace was already enshrined.

The Madonna of St. Matthew was hung, probably as a temporary measure, in a side chapel; but, whatever plans were formulated, no further action was taken, for there, in an obscure corner, Our Lady of Perpetual Succour hung, ignored and neglected, for sixty-seven years.

But not entirely forgotten. One aged lay-brother, Augustine Orsini, often served Mass at that altar and often impressed the story of the wonderful picture upon another, very youthful, server, Michael Marchi.

In due course, in 1853, Pope Pius IX requested the Redemptorists to found a house in Rome. They chose a property on the Via Merula, which lay between the Lateran and St. Mary Major's. There, one day in 1862, while the Fathers were at recreation, Fr. Edward Schwindenhammer mentioned that he had discovered from an ancient reference that their new church stood on the spot where once had been venerated a wonderful picture, "Our Lady of Perpetual Succour". "No one," he concluded wistfully, "seems to know what became of it."

At these words, another Father intervened. It was that same Michael Marchi who knew its exact whereabouts. He repeated all that he had been told by Brother Augustine. As instantly was borne a widespread desire, fanned to eagerness by the unexpected coincidence of a sermon preached at the church of

Gesu, by a Jesuit, Fr. Blosi, on the same topic—to see
the shrine restored. The Redemptorist General, Fr.
Nicholas Mauron, gained a private audience with the
Pope, who listened eagerly to the whole story. This
interest was explained when the Sovereign Pontiff
related how he himself, as a little boy, had been taken
to St. Matthew's to visit the miraculous picture.

The Pope took up his pen and wrote: "December
11th, 1865. The Cardinal Prefect of the Propaganda
is to send for the Superior of the Community of St. Mary
in Posterula and tell him it is Our desire that the picture
of the Most Blessed Virgin Mary be re-enshrined
between St. Mary Major's and St. John Lateran, with
the obligation on the Superior of the Redemptorists
to replace it with some other suitable picture. Pius,
P.P. IX."

No difficulty was encountered. With the greatest
goodwill, the Augustinians agreed to the scheme and,
as soon as preparations were complete at the
Redemptorist Church of St. Alphonsus in the Via
Merula, Our Lady's triumphal return to her chosen
site began on April 26th, 1866, in a procession with
all the pomp and splendour that Rome can provide
for such an occasion.

Two cures were reported during this translation: a
girl recovered the full use of a paralysed leg; a small
boy was as suddenly cured of meningitis.

On June 23rd, 1867, the cultus of Our Lady of
Perpetual Succour was accorded that important sign
of the Church's favour, an official coronation in the
name of the Pope. The act was performed by the
Latin Patriarch of Constantinople, a fact significant in
view of the popularity of this eikon among Eastern
Rite Christians. A year later, the first confraternity
under that title was started in Limerick, an honour to
Ireland. Soon, so many other confraternities sprang
up over Europe that, in 1876, it was decided to bind

all together into one Archconfraternity of Our Lady of Perpetual Succour and St. Alphonsus, which today numbers at least five million members. Doubtless the Fathers of any Redemptorist House would be glad to give further information.

The Byzantine schools of eikon-painters did not aim at producing "artistically beautiful" pictures although they did in fact achieve many such. Stern reality, not sentimentalism, was their guide, and stress was laid on inner meaning rather than on elegance or "prettiness". With an infinite number of variations, the earlier eikons followed certain accepted themes. Of these, the most important was incorporated in the *Hodegetria* eikon, a celebrated picture believed, like that in St. Mary Major's, to have been the handiwork of St. Luke, which was sent to Byzantium from the Holy Land at an early date. A vast number of such pictures, and indeed of early carvings, of Our Blessed Lady correspond in symbolic detail and theological message to the *Hodegetria* eikon. This, then, is the important link between the painting in St. Mary Major's, Rome, and all true "Seat of Wisdom" figures as exemplified by Our Lady of Walsingham and of Mount Carmel.

A second group, hardly less important, is that of "Our Lady of Tenderness", or *Eleousa*. Whereas in the former the Holy Child reigns princely on His Mother's left knee, and extends His right hand across her breast, in the "Tenderness" group He looks up at His Mother from her right arm, clasping her neck, pressing His cheek against hers. The eikon of Our Lady of Vladimir is the most famous example, now, alas, "elevated" to the status of a museum piece in Moscow.

Our Lady of Perpetual Succour combines features of both groups, those of the *Hodegetria* predominating. There are, however, remarkable changes. On either side of the Madonna's head are the Archangels, St. Michael and St. Gabriel, bearing emblems of the Passion; the former the spear and the sponge upon the reed; the latter the cross and holy nails. The Holy Child, upon His Mother's left arm, looks back with a glance akin to fear, as if dreading to behold the awful signs; and in His distress He seizes firmly upon Our Lady's right hand, while He kicks off the sandal from His right foot.

All other iconographic details of Our Lady and the Holy Child are faithfully presented; the colour and arrangement of the robes; the patterns of the haloes; the features of Our Lady's face. The Holy Mother wears a red robe with a rich, blue mantle lined with green. On her brow are an eight-pointed star and an elaborate cross in gold. The Holy Child wears a green tunic, girt with a red sash, and a purple-yellowish cloak is wrapped around Him. Crowns were added at a much later date, but the richness of the picture is much enhanced by gold work, both in the robes and the background.

This particular mode of eikon, representing the Suffering Mother, formed a third group, as widely spread through the east as the others. From its theme of suffering, eikons of this type are called *Strasdnaia,* forming thus the prototype of later pictures of Our Lady of Sorrows.

"Our Lady of Perpetual Succour" is unique, perhaps, in the fact that it is regarded with veneration alike in the east and west, by Catholics and by Greek schismatics with their 125,000,000 adherents. It becomes, therefore, a natural, accepted meeting-place for prayers from both sides for Unity. Hope of such unity is based largely upon devotion to the Mother of God. The Greek Church holds her in profound veneration. So do we Catholics, in union with the Holy See.

# XIX: OUR LADY OF ABERDEEN

HALFWAY down the Rue Neuve, the Bond Street of Brussels, stands the church of Our Lady of Finistère. Within, in a separate chapel, is enshrined an ancient figure of the Blessed Virgin which attracts such a large number of faithful clients of Mary that this church may in many ways be regarded as the Belgian counterpart of the world famous Our Lady of Victories in Paris.

The title of this Brussels shrine is *Our Lady of Good Success,* but the interest of English speaking Catholics is greatly increased by the knowledge that it is also the same as Our Lady of Aberdeen, brought hence to safety from her Scottish citadel at the Reformation.

The early history of the statue is wrapped in mystery, though its original home and title are undoubted. As there were several shrines of Our Lady in Aberdeen and no certainty which one was specially distinguished with the city's title, it is hard to tell from which the statue was rescued.

In all probability, however, considering its style, period of craftsmanship, and the known facts of the history of the Aberdeen sanctuaries, the figure was first presented to be enthroned near the high altar of Aberdeen Cathedral in 1436. About sixty years later, a new statue of solid silver (a *pieta* group) was presented which became an object of much veneration, with a weekly Mass "of the Compassion of Our Lady".

The redundant statue then seems to have been moved to a new shrine in a chapel built on, or close to, the Bridge of Dee. Other accounts suggest that the Bishop, Gavin Dunbar, later moved it back again to a new Lady Chapel which he added to the end of an aisle of the Cathedral.

At any rate, it was as Our Lady of Aberdeen that the figure was taken to Flanders, at the time of the Scottish Reformation, and this is how its rescue came about. When the Cathedral was desecrated by the Calvinists, it was hidden away by a Catholic family; but in due course fell into Protestant hands. The family who took possession received a number of graces and blessings, which, it is related, they attributed to the presence of this holy image in their house. Thus they were reconciled to the Church.

After a time another Scottish Catholic, William Laing, styled "Procurator" to the King of Spain, obtained possession of the figure. At last, in 1623, he put it into the hands of a Spanish captain about to sail for Flanders, with strict instructions that he was to deliver the statue to no less a person than the Archduchess Isabella, who was so devoted to the cause of Our Lady, and who, as we have seen, had taken the chief part in the building of the sanctuary of Montaigu.

Several chroniclers have recorded the story of the arrival of Our Lady of Aberdeen in Brussels. That written down about 1631 by Father Gilbert Blackall, Priest of the Scots Mission, who said Mass in the new Brussels shrine, is of great interest. He wrote: "And that same day that the shippe in which it did arrive at Ostend, the Infanta (Isabella) did winne a battaile against the Hollanders, the people thinking that Our Ladye, for the civil reception of her statu, did obteane that victorye to the Princesse, who did send for the statu to be brought to Bruselle, wher the princesse,

*The miraculous picture of Our Lady of Good Counsel*

(Page 143)

*Our Lady of Perpetual Succour as enshrined
in St. Alphonsus in Rome*

(Page 149)

with a solemne procession, did receave it at the porte of the towne, and place it in this chapelle, where it is much honored, and the chapelle dedicated to our Ladye of *bonne successe*, which befor was pouer and desolat, now is riche and wel frequented.''

Father Blackall then denies as a fable a story that the figure had been miraculously rescued from the waves of the sea; a story associated more accurately with another Spanish shrine, that of Our Lady of Cobre, in Cuba, then Spanish territory, still the most important shrine of Our Lady in the West Indies.

The chaplain who bore the statue from Ostend to Brussels was one Father de los Rois, an Augustinian Canon, in the suite of the Infanta, and it was transferred to the newly-built church of that Order in Brussels, in 1626. The translation took place May 3rd, with the utmost pomp. All the clergy, nobility and magistracy of the city were present, and Pope Urban VIII granted a plenary indulgence to all who should assist at the ceremony.

The procession was enlivened by the ringing of bells and the thunder of guns as they fired salvos in homage. The statue appeared decked in the crown jewels, adorned with a robe of sheer gold. The Infanta followed on foot and when she reached the Augustinian church Mass was sung for the *good success* of Her Royal Highness, which established the title of the new shrine.

The festivities which followed lasted for ten days and included the founding of the Confraternity of Our Lady of Good Success. It is worth recalling that this was twelve years prior to the Consecration of France to Our Lady by Louis XIII, in 1638, and just previous to the building of the church of Our Lady of Victories in Paris, in 1629, by that same monarch, which became, under Father des Genettes, the seat of the Universal Archconfraternity of the Immaculate Heart of Mary, in 1837. The Finistère Church in Brussels is so very much the Belgian counterpart of the Parisian sanctuary that the two societies are worthy of close comparison. The Infanta was the first to be enrolled in the Belgian Confraternity. Mary de Medicis, wife of Henry IV, inscribed her own name on the Rolls, kneeling before the statue as she did so.

Our Lady *from* Aberdeen reigned in her new shrine for 150 years, until the revolutionary troubles swept through France to Belgium. The Augustinians lost everything but, once again, Our Lady's image was saved. Singularly enough it was placed into British hands for safekeeping; an English Catholic named Morris kept the figure secure until 1805, when it was restored to its former shrine.

Nine years later, however, a Protestant sect obtained a decree giving them the use of the old Augustinian church; so, for a last time, Our Lady of Aberdeen was moved to a new home, to a niche in St. Joseph's Chapel in the parish church of Our Lady of Finistère, in which parish the Augustinian church had stood.

In 1852, M. Van Genechten, curé of the parish, obtained authority from the Archbishop of Malines to restore the old confraternity, her Royal Highness the Duchess of Brabant becoming honorary provost.

At this point the author may be allowed to introduce a personal note, a reminiscence of his own first visit to this historic shrine. It was a pouring wet day and, owing to a mistake, he set out in a totally wrong direction to find it. After an hour of fruitless search and being soaked to the skin, he decided to abandon his mission and take what seemed to be a short cut back to his hotel. On the way, he was forced by a particularly vicious downpour to take shelter in the welcoming porch of a church, only to find that without intention or expectation on his part he was taking refuge at the shrine of Our Lady of Good Success.

The church is typical of eighteenth century renaissance architecture, with a strong classic façade, from which a large, well-sculptured figure of Our Lady Immaculate reigns over the hosts of busy passers-by.

Within the main church, a small, smiling figure of Our Lady of Finistère stands above a side altar. One has to find one's way into a separate and distict chapel on the south side to discover Our Lady from Scotland. This chapel is dark and comparatively small, but one's senses immediately become aware of that indefinable sense of intimacy and security which may be experienced at so many of Our Lady's chosen shrines.

Light enters only through a glass louvre in the roof, but the sanctuary is bright with a myriad votive lamps and candles flickering and glimmering by the altar rails. At all hours of the day, from the first Mass at dawn until late at night, the chapel is apt to be thronged, so that one has to wait one's turn to get anywhere near the altar. Long before one can visit the ancient figure, one receives the impression of a vast number of ex-voto plaques and offerings, covering the walls from floor to ceiling.

Our Lady of Good Success is set high on a pedestal behind a surprisingly simple marble altar. It is a standing figure, with Our Lord reclining, rather than sitting upright, on the right arm (not left, as many descriptions would have it) of His Mother, who wears a robe as exquisite for the manner in which its folds are carved as for the richness of the blue with which it was coloured. A large rosary and a still larger key, the key to good success, giving, it is said, Our Lady the freedom of the City of Brussels, are suspended from Our Lady's right wrist; with her left hand she supports the right foot of her Infant Son.

The quality of design and workmanship is the highest: the statue is the work of a truly great if unknown artist. Combining sweet, simple charm with the dignity of majesty, it has no rival in Belgium.

There have, from time to time, been moves and suggestions that Our Lady of Good Success be given back to Aberdeen. One wonders as to the wisdom of that. For less than two centuries she was venerated there. During that time, if deductions are correct, she was moved from place to place and finally desecrated —saved only by chance, and the fidelity of one or two.

On her arrival in Belgium, already the home of a hundred other Marial Shrines, she was acclaimed and given royal honours. There she now reigns, surrounded by multitudes of those who are glad she is there. Our Lady of Aberdeen has been taken to their hearts and become theirs by adoption. Scotland is not forgotten. Countless prayers and Masses are offered by friends of the northern kingdom, and who can tell but more may be done for the conversion of Scotland by those prayers than by her return to the city which once rejected her.

## XX: LE LAUS

ONE of the most fascinating sanctuaries of Our Blessed Lady, blessed with a series of authentic apparitions, yet hardly known outside France, is that of Le Laus (pronounced Low), a tiny hamlet tucked away in a remote fold of the French Alps.

At the outset of this work, the author was condemned to a period of bed and, to wile away the time, he read some chapters of a very old, out-of-print book, (*Celebrated Sanctuaries of the Madonna,* by Rev. J. Spencer Northcote, D.D., President of Oscott College, Longmans, Green and Co., 1868) which is still one of the standard works in English on certain of Our Lady's Shrines. As he read, he became more and more astonished that he had hitherto heard only the vaguest details of such an amazing place and story. Curiously enough, although that day no such plan was even contemplated, within a fortnight arrangements had been made which made it possible for him to visit this very sanctuary of Our Lady, a few months after the ending of the war.

To reach Le Laus the pilgrim has to journey in a crowded motor-bus for some sixty miles from Grenoble along the reverse of the route which Napoleon followed when he landed from Elba: one of the most exciting motor routes in France—winding through great mountain ranges, along the edges of terrific precipices, across mighty chasms, then deep down into one of them and up the other side in dizzy fashion.

At last one reaches Gap, a homely little cathedral town, the nearest market to the shrine. Many pilgrims walk across the mountains from this place but the author had rare luck to catch—and get into—the tiny motor-carrier which takes the mail to Le Laus; and so he completed the journey in easy time for lunch, which he badly needed, having started at half-past four in the morning!

Even so, as the mail-bus threaded its way up the valleys from Gap, there had been time to become more and more impressed at the signs of the sanctity of the place he was approaching. Chapels, wayside shrines, and crosses are set on all sides to commemorate some event in the life of the poor shepherdess to whom it owes its celebrity; and the last mile of abrupt ascent to the basilica itself is marked by a series of Stations of the Cross as fine as their setting on the mountainside is dramatic.

This is the story of Le Laus and its shrine. On the Feast of St. Michael, 1647, Benoîte Rencurel was born at St. Etienne, another hamlet nearby. Her parents were humble mountain-folk who found it difficult to bring up their large family. In her twelfth year Benoîte was sent to serve as shepherdess for a neighbouring farmer—to mind his sheep as they grazed upon the various common pastures in the district.

One day in May, 1664, Benoîte led the sheep to a favourite spot on the mountain of St. Maurice, near an old ruined chapel. Here she sat down to eat her lunch and say her rosary. While she did so a very old man, dressed in a red robe, approached and asked what she did there. With naïve simplicity, Benoîte replied that she watched her sheep, was praying to the Good God, and that she was feeling very thirsty!

"Yet there is water beside you," said the old man, pointing to a spring of clear water which she had never before seen, but which is still there and produces excellent water.

The girl thanked her visitor and asked him to share her bread; who replied that he was St. Maurice and that he desired her to take her flock to a small valley nearer St. Etienne where a great grace would be granted to her.

Hither Benoîte led her sheep the next day and, towards evening, standing on a rock known as *Les Fours,* she saw a Lady and Child of singular beauty. The Lady did not speak but Benoîte was entirely happy just to gaze upon her.   For two months these visions continued with frequency, and rumour of them spread. At last a magistrate of the district, M. Grimaud, questioned the shepherdess, advised her to make a good Confession and Communion and then on the next possible occasion to ask this Lady her name.

Benoîte did as she was told, and the Lady replied: "I am Mary, the Mother of Jesus.   It is the will of my Son that I should be honoured in this Parish, though not on this spot.   You will therefore ask the priest to come here with his people in procession".

The good priest made careful enquiry, decided to obey, and, on August 29th, 1664, led a solemn procession to *Les Fours* where Our Lady had appeared at least thirty times.   A chapel now marks the spot.

A month later, on September 29th, Our Lady appeared again, this time at another pasturage, at Pindreau, a little eminence on the road to Le Laus. Here Benoîte was startled by a light shining brighter than the sun, in the midst of which appeared the Mother of God alone.   "Go," she commanded, "to Le Laus. There you will find a little chapel where delicious perfumes abound.   There you will often find and see me."

The scene of this Apparition at Pindreau is also

marked with a chapel and a magnificent group of statuary in bronze.

Now Benoîte was led to find in the tiny hamlet of Le Laus the ruined chapel Our Lady described, and here it was revealed that before long this poor ruined wayside chapel would be enshrined in a large church, richly adorned and served by many priests; that many sinners would be converted there and that the money for the church would come from the poor.

Our Lady said: *"I have requested Le Laus from my Divine Son for the Conversion of Sinners and He has given it to me. This church will be built in His Honour and mine. Many sinners will be converted here."*

The news of this spread, causing great crowds of people to gather at the little oratory of Le Laus. The chapel soon became too small. Extra priests had to be called in, who said Mass at open-air altars, and heard the hundreds of confessions outside among the rocks. Whole parishes walked here for many miles; on one single day thirty-five such processions arrived. Many favours and graces were granted until at last, in the absence of the Archbishop of Embrun, the Vicar General, Mgr. Lambert, ordered an enquiry, and in September, 1665, a Commission of twenty-two ecclesiastics arrived to investigate.

Benoîte Rencurel was subjected to many severe examinations. She was attacked with questions, arguments, and ridicule, but her simplicity and honesty stood the test. Finally, on the last day of the enquiry, while the Vicar General was saying Mass, served by the Grand Vicar of Gap, he was privileged to behold what has since been accepted as a first class miracle. A widow-woman, Catherine Vial, well known to have been a cripple for many years, whose limbs were withered and helpless, was suddenly restored to full health and strength on the ninth day of the novena she was making, at the very door of the chapel where Mgr. Lambert was saying Mass.   At the general cry, "A Miracle!   A Miracle!" he turned to see her rise from her stretcher and walk unaided into the church.

A fresh enquiry was at once made into this prodigy. Two doctors concerned, both Calvinists, attested that they had known Catherine Vial well for some long time, that her disease had been incurable by human means, avowed themselves convinced by what they had seen, and ready to abjure their heresy.   The *procès-verbal* was drawn up, the miracle was approved, and the *Te Deum* was officially sung at Le Laus in thanksgiving.

Now Mgr. Lambert gave permission for a church to be built over the original chapel: but there was no money.   Then a poor woman, dressed all in rags, presented a *louis d'or*, a gold coin in those days worth a considerable sum, enough to start the work.   Day by day always just enough for the work in hand came in.   It was literally the pence of the poor that built the Sanctuary as Our Lady prophesied.

Pilgrims aided the rising work with their labour.   It became the custom for each pilgrim to fetch a stone from the nearby quarry.   Within a year, there was enough material, and in less than four years the church was completed.   The west front, and lovely portico, was the gift of the Archbishop of Embrun, at that time Papal Nuncio in Spain, as a votive offering in thanksgiving for recovery from a serious illness.

Then began years of great testing for Le Laus.   Both Archbishop and Vicar General died.   The Chapter of Embrun, fearing lest this new devotion should curtail devotion to Our Lady of Embrun, banned the pilgrimage, closed the church and threatened to excommunicate any priest who said Mass there.   Of course they had not authority to do that, and as soon as a new Archbishop and Vicar General were appointed, a fresh enquiry was held.

The result was a declaration that the Pilgrimage of Our Lady of Le Laus was the work of God and that Benoîte was above suspicion in the matter. The new Archbishop, Mgr. de Genlis, visited the sanctuary in person and when he beheld the vast crowds of pilgrims and penitents exclaimed: *"Vere Dominus est in loco isto"*—indeed is God in this place.

Two more dangers threatened the sanctuary. In 1692 the Duke of Savoy invaded the country. Benoîte was forced to flee to Marseilles and the church was pillaged and smashed, though the original figure of Our Lady was saved. When restoration was begun, it was with the pence of the poor again, and after a time the church was better than before.

Then a new college of priests were appointed who proved to be Jansenists. They caused all the oratories round about to be destroyed, publicly preached against the popular devotion to Our Lady, banned Benoîte from the Sacraments, put her under confinement and allowed her to hear Mass only once a week.

At last, in 1712, the Archbishop intervened, dismissed the Jansenists and erected a Congregation of Missionary Priests to care for the sanctuary. Thus Benoîte Rencurel was able to die truly at peace and in the knowledge that the work entrusted to her by Our Lady was complete. Her body lies buried in a vault in front of the high altar at Le Laus, under this inscription:

> *The Tomb of Sister Benoîte,*
> *Died in the odour of sanctity 28 December, 1718.*

The title "sister" was bestowed on her, as she was an associate of the third Order of St. Dominic. Since then the devotion to Our Lady of Le Laus has continued uninterrupted. Not even the French Revolution could suppress it.

In 1716, with the approval of Benoîte, a new statue of Our Lady was carved and placed behind the high altar. The original figure of Our Lady of Good Meeting (Bon-Rencontre) was enshrined in another Chapel immediately behind the high altar where it is still greatly venerated. On May 23rd, 1855, His Holiness Pope Pius IX had the new, and now recognised, statue of Our Lady of Le Laus crowned, even as Our Lady of Fatima was crowned, by a Papal Legate. The church was declared a minor basilica, by a Bull of Pope Leo XIII.

The surrounding sanctuary is literally encrusted with votive offerings of all kinds, marble tablets of thanks, gold and silver ex-voto hearts, pictures depicting favours granted and records of cures innumerable. Next door, and connected by an archway, is the priests' house and a large pilgrims' hospice, capable of accommodating many hundreds. It is never shut, year in or out.

Those familiar with Lourdes will find that Le Laus presents a marked contrast. The village consists of only a few houses clustered together, a post office, and a single shop. The grounds around the basilica, the open-air altars, the processional routes, and the adjacent shrines and chapels have retained a natural, rugged simplicity which is charming. In one place only, run by the nuns who care for the pilgrims, can one buy souvenirs!

At Le Laus itself there is no miraculous well or fountain. But Our Lady left a strange bequest. She promised that healing properties would attach to the oil of the lamp which burns before her shrine. The same lamp still hangs before her altar and, from time to time, oil is taken from it and drops of it are sent to the sick and afflicted. Many thanksgivings have been made for "cures" and favours granted after its use.

Benoîte Rencurel was declared Venerable by Pope Pius IX in 1871. Three minutes' walk from the hospice takes one to the primitive, unaltered room which formed her home from 1672 until her death. There is no window except a grille in the door. The furniture is just as it was left by the voyante; rough plank-bed, cupboard, table and chair of plain wood, no luxuries of any kind. As at Lourdes, where the home of the Soubirous family illustrates the homelife of St. Bernadette so vividly, so here at Le Laus there could be no memorial more eloquent of the mortified life of that venerable servant of God, Benoîte Rencurel.

# XXI: OUR LADY OF VICTORIES

ONE of the key centres of modern devotion to Our Blessed Lady is undoubtedly that which is known all the world over as Our Lady of Victories, Paris. Its history is quite as impressive as the burning devotion to the Mother of God which emanates therefrom and, for its own interest, is well worth a survey.

In the days when Paris was still a compact city, a zone of fields and market gardens lay between it and what was then the village of Montmartre, where now the mighty basilica of the Sacred Heart towers above a somewhat squalid congestion of houses and tenements. Here, by the wayside, and amidst fields, Queen Marguerite of Valois founded, in 1590, a little votive church of Our Lady, to be served by some discalced Augustinian friars who were nicknamed "Petits Pères", or "Little Fathers", from the small size of their church and house.

In 1619, an important acquisition was made. Father Angel of St. Claire, Chaplain to the Archduchess of the Netherlands, joined the Community and brought with him a figure of Our Lady of Montaigu, made from the actual wood of the oak tree in Brabant whereon Our Lady was believed to have appeared. From that moment the Friars' work began to flourish. A marked number of favours began to flow from the new sanctuary and people began to flock there.

A fervent apostle of Our Lady of Montaigu was one of the friars, Brother Fiacre, whose reputation for sanctity brought the city and the royal court to beg his prayers. To him, it is recorded, Our Lady appeared several times in his cell.

Ten years later found the Little Fathers' house and church too small. They appealed to the King, Louis XIII, to provide them with a new establishment. This he promised on condition that the new church was dedicated to Our Lady of Victories, in thanksgiving for all her favours and, in particular, for a victory over the Protestants at La Rochelle. The King laid the foundation stone himself; a grand Lady Altar, with a white marble figure of Our Lady of Victories was erected, and Our Lady of Montaigu was enshrined in another side chapel.

Added impetus was given to devotion to Our Lady by a strange event in Brother Fiacre's life. On pilgrimage to the Holy House of Loreto, his ship was forced to shelter in the sea port of Savona, where the Brother found the people celebrating the anniversary of an Apparition of Our Lady on a nearby mountain, to Antony Botta (in 1536). Thus he was inspired to introduce into France this devotion to Our Lady of Mercy, *Refugium Peccatorum*. A fine statue of Our Lady of Savona, Refuge of Sinners, was ordered and paid for by the Queen Mother, in 1674. Thus Our Lady, Refuge of Sinners, took the parish under the protection which it was to need so vitally during the next hundred and fifty years.

In 1791, the religious were expelled by the revolutionaries and the Church was shut. Our Lady of Savona was replaced by Diana and all the bestiality of revolutionary infidelity was performed with frenzy in the sanctuary. Before the church could be reclaimed, it was used for schismatic worship and then as the Stock Exchange; but at last, in 1809, it was united to the local parish of St. Augustine, and struggled on until Father Charles du Friche des Genettes was appointed Curé, in 1832.

Father des Genettes had, until recently, been parish priest of the Rue du Bac area. Even if he did not actually know Saint Catherine Labouré, he was well aware of the subject of Our Lady's Apparitions in the convent chapel in the Rue du Bac and of the wonderful story of the Miraculous Medal. For several years he laboured in his new sphere. To his distress he found that the whole district had completely abandoned the faith. Hardly anyone practised their religion. In spite of his perseverance so little attention was paid to the good priest's teaching, he began to feel it his duty to resign as a failure.

On Sunday, December 3rd, 1836, Father des Genettes began to say Mass in an almost empty church when he was seized with a distraction so frightful—his anxiety that he must resign—that by the time he reached the Canon he cried out in his distress. At that moment he heard a calm, distinct voice announce most solemnly: "Consecrate your parish to the Most Holy and Immaculate Heart of Mary".

After Mass the priest retired to the sacristy where he fought a great battle; unwilling to believe that he had become a *visionnaire* yet unable to deny his senses of what he had as certainly heard. At last he triumphed, as he thought, over his foolishness and knelt down to begin his thanksgiving when again he heard clearly and unmistakably, the same words: "Consecrate your parish to the Most Holy and Immaculate Heart of Mary"

He could doubt no longer. Forthwith he took up his pen and composed the Rules for a Confraternity of Our Lady which the Bishop approved that same week. On the following Sunday, the third in Advent, he announced his project to the ten people at Mass.

That evening, he proposed, there should be Vespers of Our Lady, when full details about the Confraternity would be given.

At seven o'clock, when the Curé entered the church, he found it full, with well over four hundred people, a large number of them being men. At Benediction they sang the Litany of Loreto. When the petition *Refugium Peccatorum* was reached the entire congregation felt moved, spontaneously, without previous plan or announcement, to repeat the phrase three times and then to cry out: *"Parce Domine"*. It was indeed a dramatic moment. Our Lady of Savona had come back into her own.

On January 12th, 1837, the Confraternity published its rules. Today it numbers 1,593,933 members. At once conversions began. Sunday by Sunday was adopted the custom of praying for particular cases, for special intentions. On a recent August Sunday the intentions reached the gigantic figure of 65,851! As instantly favours began to pour out for those who sought Our Lady's graces, as they did of old, in the days when first the shrines of Montaigu and Mercy had been established in the district. Today the walls of the church are encrusted with nearly 90,000 ex-voto offerings in thanksgiving.

On June 24th, 1838, Pope Gregory XVI decreed that the Confraternity become the (Universal) Arch-confraternity of the Holy and Immaculate Heart of Mary for the conversion of Sinners. In 1941, there were 20,777 affiliated societies throughout the world.

On 11th March, 1855, at the end of an octave of prayer and thanksgiving for the Dogmatisation of the Immaculate Conception the previous December, the statue of the Immaculate Heart of Mary was seen to move. Pius IX, after searching enquiry as to the facts concerning the phenomena which recurred again and again, came to regard these occurrences as

*Our Lady of Good Success, Brussels—once Our
Lady of Aberdeen*

(Page 155)

Our Lady of Laus crowned by Pope
Pius IX in 1855

(Page 161)

and (below) the crowned statue of Our
Lady of Victories in Paris

(Page 169)

indications from Heaven of approval of his great Act and ordered the statue to be crowned, June 1st, 1856.

In 1871, after the Siege of Paris, the horrors of the Commune were again enacted. The Shrine was profaned; the crowns given by Pius IX were stolen and the tomb of the founder was broken open, though no one dared to violate the actual statue of Our Lady of Victories. The present crowns were provided by public subscription in 1876.

Recognition of the magnificent work of this sanctuary in the cause of the Faith, and of the abundance of favours bestowed by Our Lady of Victories upon those who seek her there in this favoured shrine was further granted in 1927 by Pope Pius XI, when he raised the church to the dignity of a minor basilica.

In view of recent interest in the fiftieth anniversary of the death of St. Therese of the Child Jesus, it is opportune to record the story of her own visit to this wonderful sanctuary on November 4th, 1887, after being cured in 1883.

"Having arrived in Paris," she wrote, "Papa took us to see the sights. For me there was only one—Our Lady of Victories. What I felt in her sanctuary I cannot say. The graces she granted me resembled those of my First Communion. I was filled with peace and joy. It was there that my Mother, the Virgin Mary, told me distinctly that it was indeed she who cured me. With what fervour did I beg her always to keep me and to bring about my dream, to enfold me ever beneath the shadow of the cloak of her Virginity. I besought her again to keep all occasions of sin away from me."

It is good to know what so glorious a Saint felt and wrote about this particular shrine, which meant so much to her. By no means was she the only Saint attracted thereto. Blessed Theophane Venard, for whom St. Theresa had especial devotion, and who was martyred in Tonkin in 1881, often prayed here and many another martyr of the Foreign Mission field. St. John Bosco said Mass at the shrine altar on April 28th, 1883. A pilgrim then present remarked: "This is the Mass for the conversion of sinners and a Saint is going to say it."

From England a number of the early converts of the Oxford Movement came in thanksgiving and to pray for their fellows up to then unmoved. Some of them—Father Ignatius Spencer, the Passionist, included—have left ex-voto plaques in remembrance. And hardly a day goes by but Holy Mass is offered here, at Our Lady of Victories in Paris, that England may be brought back to the Faith. This is indeed a shrine of Our Lady worthy of more recognition among Catholics in this country.

# XXII: POMPEII

THE name Pompeii conjures up in most people's minds the picture of a large and prosperous city of ancient Roman times that was destroyed in A.D. 79 by a fierce eruption of Vesuvius.

But it was not until some centuries later that the Faith penetrated that region. In the course of time, however, the subsequent inhabitants built a church, about a mile from the ruined, buried city, which became a Benedictine Abbey. This in turn was relinquished by the monks, to become a powerful parish church of the Diocese of Nola, with the unusual privilege of *patronage,* the right of nominating the parish priest, which was reserved until recent times to the parishioners themselves.

In 1659 the Valley of Pompeii was ravaged by an epidemic of malaria which decimated the population. The district was deserted by its entire populace except a few struggling small-holders and a number of bandits who preyed upon the countryside, adding to its disrepute.

The ancient church was pulled down in 1740 and a small chapel was built opposite the local inn, "The Prince of the Valley", a tavern that belonged to the Counts of Fusco. And here one simple parish priest essayed to serve the small handful of people left in what once had been a great parish. It is hard to describe the abandonment of the region less than seventy-five years ago. Scourged with malaria, riddled with superstition and fear of the evil-eye, pillaged by cruel brigands and torn with the vendetta, the Valley of Pompeii was summed up in the official records of the time as being "a most dangerous resort of bold and infamous robbers".

It was on such soil that Our Lady chose to establish one of her sanctuaries that has since become world-famous and beloved of Popes, thereat to grant favours that Commissions of the Church have since pronounced miraculous.

In October, 1872, there came to the district one Bartolo Long, husband of the Countess of Fusco of those days; to attend to his wife's property. Although educated in a Christian School, Bartolo Long had allowed himself to get mixed up with spiritualism and was at that time enduring a struggle to retain his grip on the Faith. Even so he was shocked at the spiritual poverty of the Valley and at the desolation he found around him.

The crisis of his life occurred on October 9th. Walking through the most desolate part of the parish, at a moment when his own doubts were most persistent, he suddenly realised that a distinct voice was speaking to him:

> *"If you seek salvation, promulgate the Rosary.*
> *This is Mary's own promise."*

Bartolo Long himself has recorded his reply. He answered: "If it is true that thou didst promise St. Dominic that whosoever should promulgate thy Rosary should be saved, then shall I be saved, for I will not leave this valley until I have propagated thy Rosary".

Instantly the noonday Angelus rang out from a distant church tower. Bartolo fell on his knees to confirm his pledge.

Bartolo decided that his first step should be the foundation of a Rosary Confraternity and he planned a festival to take place a year hence in honour of the Rosary, that might attract many people to make a start. This first effort was a fiasco. Thunder and rain frustrated it and the special preacher found the people understood only their local dialect.

A fresh attempt was made in 1874 and at last, after a most successful anniversary in 1875, the Bishop of Nola was won over to approve and even to champion the work of a man whom he might well have considered to be an interfering crank. He visited the humble chapel and, impressed by what he found, turned to those around him and declared: "You wish to raise an altar here in honour of the Rosary? I propose we raise not an altar but a church!" Then, pointing to a field opposite, he added: "That is where a basilica will be raised for Pompeii".

The Bishop was truly a prophet. Before fifteen years had elapsed, the church had acquired universal fame and received solemn consecration at the hands of a Papal Legate. Today a basilica stands in the field as foretold, built at the orders of Pope Pius XI.

In order to encourage the simple peasants in their daily recitation of the Rosary, Bartolo determined to purchase a picture to be exposed for their veneration at the end of a three day mission. On the third day he was told that the picture he had chosen would not suffice, being but an oleograph on paper. Canon Law required a painting in oils upon canvas or wood. So, with haste, he travelled to Naples only to find that the cheapest available new picture cost four hundred francs, a price beyond his pocket. He was therefore constrained by a friend, rather than disappoint the people of Pompeii, to accept the gift of a second-hand oil-painting that had been bought in a junk shop for three francs.

Thus did Bartolo describe it: "Not only was it worm-eaten, but the face of the Madonna was that of a coarse, rough country-woman . . . a piece of canvas was missing j 1st above her head . . . her mantle was cracked. Nothing can be said of the hideousness of the other figures. St. Dominic looked like a street idiot. To Our Lady's left was a St. Rose. This latter I had changed later into a St. Catherine of Siena . . . I hesitated whether to refuse the gift or to accept. I had promised a picture unconditionally for that evening. I took it."

Too large to carry by hand, the painting was wrapped in a sheet and given to a carrier who plied between Naples and Pompeii, to be delivered at the chapel that evening. In due course the man arrived at the chapel door, bringing it thither all unwittingly, not knowing what manner of picture it was, on top of a cart-load of manure which he had to leave at a nearby field. Thus did Our Lady of Pompeii arrive at her chosen sanctuary, to be the focus of homage from countless thousands.

This was in November, 1875. In January, 1876, the picture was somewhat restored to be ready for the canonical foundation of the Confraternity, on February 13th. It was also considerably "improved" in 1879, by Maldarelli, a Neapolitan artist of some repute, who did his best with what he considered a hopeless task.

Today the picture is enshrined in a frame of gold and encrusted with diamonds and gems which hide all but the faces of the Saints and the Holy Child. And daily it is besieged by vast pilgrimages and crowds of the faithful, beseeching Our Lady for her graces and favour.

What was the cause of this amazing, popular, devotion towards such a singularly unlikely shrine?

While steps were still being taken to establish the

Confraternity, an extraordinary event took place in Naples which soon reached the ears of the Cardinal Archbishop. Clorinda Lucarelli, a child of twelve, had for some months been the victim of fearful epilepsy, from which no cure seemed possible. Indeed, imminent death seemed a mercy. But her aunt and guardian heard of the plans to found the Confraternity at Pompeii and vowed to assist in the building of the proposed church if the child got well. Wonderful to relate, on the very day the picture was re-exposed for veneration, Clorinda was restored to complete and lasting health. Two eminent professors who had examined her previously certified, on oath, that the cure was not due to any medical intervention.

Immediately after, under extraordinary circumstances, the relatives of a young woman, Concetta Vasterilla, who was dying in agony, were led to make similar promises to Our Lady of Pompeii. As swiftly, complete recovery ensued and a second miracle was acclaimed.

It was decided to lay the cornerstone of the new church on May 8th of that same year (1876). Yet another wonder was to be recorded before then. Father Anthony Varone, dying of a fearful, gangrenous malady, had been given the last Sacraments. He was persuaded by the Countess of Fusco to put his faith directly in Our Lady of Pompeii. That same evening all his ill symptoms vanished. Even his finger-nails began to grow afresh. Next morning he arose and said Mass. The following Feast of the Holy Rosary, he sang the Mass at Pompeii and publicly acknowledged his cure from the pulpit.

A month after the cornerstone was laid, a fourth miracle was allowed. Madame Giovannina Muta lay in the last stages of consumption, beyond the aid of medicine. She, too, was persuaded to make promises to Our Lady of Pompeii. On June 8th, Madame Muta, in her bed, seemed to see an exact replica of Our Lady in the Pompeian picture, which she had never visited; except that Our Lady gazed upon her and then threw towards her a kind of white ribbon on which was the message: "The Virgin of Pompeii grants your request, Giovannina Muta". As this vision faded new life throbbed through the no-longer-sick woman's veins, and she was entirely cured.

To recall here all the other marvellous favours granted by Our Lady of Pompeii would be quite impossible. The church was finished and then enlarged; and in May 1891, it was consecrated by Cardinal La Valletta, as Papal Legate for Pope Leo XIII, who warmly espoused the cause of Pompeii. Close beside it was built a large orphanage and also a spacious hospice for the pilgrims who resorted to the shrine.

The whole property was taken under the direct protection of the Holy See and, in 1906, Bartolo Long made over all his rights in the Valley in favour of Pope Pius X, who vied with Pope Leo XIII in pouring honours and gifts to enrich this sanctuary.

Under the Lateran Treaty, the church, by then raised to basilica rank, became directly subject to the Vatican City State. In 1934, at the express command of Pope Pius XI, a great new basilica was begun. This was not completed until 1939, when it was opened in the name of Pope Pius XII by Cardinal Maglione, Secretary of State to His Holiness.

At a time when Our Lady was appealing to the world from Fatima to make use of her Rosary, there, at Pompeii, was growing to perfection a great shrine of the Holy Rosary, in 1917-1923, to tide Italy over one of her gravest political crises. Likewise the opening of the new basilica gave fresh impetus, in 1939, to endure throughout the late war to the present day.

Mighty things are thus raised from the humble and small, and the proud are cast down. There, at Pompeii Our Lady showed her preference for no grand statue, no precious painting, but for a cheap, discarded, "vulgar", three-franc picture in what many artists call "the worst possible taste". This is what has been accepted and has become the focus of devotion, in what is undoubtedly one of the most popular sanctuaries of Our Lady in Christendom.

And this is a story not of events in some far-off century but of our own age and generation. The whole episode has taken place within the lifetime of many people still living.

## XXIII: THE MIRACULOUS MEDAL

OUR LADY'S Apparitions have so often occurred in wild or lonely places like Fatima, or La Salette, that it comes as a surprise to discover that on several occasions she has appeared in the middle of quite busy cities. But of all the unlikely places chosen by the Mother of God for three of her celebrated appearances, the narrow, noisy Rue du Bac in Paris, over-shadowed by a huge department store, would seem to be most surprising. This is the story of that remarkable series of events.

On May 2nd, 1806, there was born on a farm at Fain-les-Moutiers (Côte d'Or), near Dijon, Zoé Labouré, one of the youngest of seventeen children. Her parents were people of great faith who had struggled through the fierce, anti-Catholic years of the French Revolution without sacrificing a jot or tittle of their religion.

Pierre, Zoé's father, kept his farm well and prospered. His wife had died when Zoé was ten, and but ten of the children survived. Most of them left home and did well for themselves, in the army or in business. Auguste stayed to look after the farm, with Zoé and her sister Antoinette, where they were very happy. Marie Louise, the eldest girl, became a Sister of Charity.

It seems odd nowadays to think that Zoé never went to school. She could read and write only enough to help with the house-keeping. In those days, country people did not set nearly so much store on "book-learning" as we do. In any case, the years of Zoé's childhood were fraught with danger. Born in 1804, she was eleven at the time of the Battle of Waterloo. Living in the midst of a province overrun with soldiers, first Napoleon's armies, then those of the Allies, prudent parents preferred to keep their young daughters safely at home.

Without the "distraction of books", but surrounded by all the tragedy of war, Zoé grew up thoughtful, and prepared to receive and accept the solemn messages which were to be given to her. When she was twelve she chose Our Lady to be "her only mother" instead of her own who had died. At fourteen she began to have ideas about the religious life. She started to fast every Friday and Saturday and to hear Mass daily in the chapel of the Sisters of Charity not far from her home.

One may visit the picturesque village which Zoé knew so well as a child. The farm buildings, her home, even her cradle, are wonderfully unspoiled; a compact little block, with low, arched entrance, dairies, cowsheds and the massive square pigeon-house; though no descendant of any of the eight hundred white doves she loved to tend remains there.

Across the road is the quaint, steepled, village church. The Labouré family pew is marked; and the altar and altar-rails, where Zoé so often received Holy Communion, remain in their rustic simplicity. The tiny chancel, with a delightful fourteenth century east-window, can have changed but little since she knelt there with her brothers and sisters, Sunday by Sunday, for the Parish Mass.

It was in 1818 that Marie Louise had become a nun but M. Labouré had other ideas for Zoé. He positively refused to allow her to do the same; and as she for her part declined a good offer of marriage which he had arranged for her, he packed off Zoé to help a brother who kept a restaurant in Paris—hoping to distract her from her "convent ideas". But there Zoé was so miserable and out of place that she was sent instead to help a sister-in-law who ran a boarding-school at Châtillon-sur-Seine.

There Mrs. Hubert Labouré adopted Zoé's cause, persuaded the father to give his consent, herself advanced the small sum of money then required as a "dowry" by the community, and saw her enter as a postulant at the house of the Sisters of Charity at Châtillon-sur-Seine. This old house, where the future Saint passed the first months of her religious life, was destroyed by German bombardment in 1940. On April 21st, 1830, as Sister Catherine Labouré, Zoé left for Paris to begin her novitiate at the Mother House, at "140, Rue du Bac".

Standard Guide Books give only the briefest note on this historic convent. Whereas "The Blue Guide" gives two pages to Lourdes, it dismisses this wonderful house in three lines: "No. 140 is the Hôtel de Châtillon, built by Mansart, with two handsome portals, and now occupied by the Soeurs de Charité". Little do they know of the interior, or of what passed behind those "portals".

Within a few weeks of her arrival, Catherine began her series of rare, mystical experiences. On the night of July 18th, 1830, at about half-past eleven, she was wakened by her guardian angel, in the form of a child, about four or five years old, dressed in white. It was the Eve of the Feast of St. Vincent de Paul.

"Come to the chapel," said the angel. "The Holy Virgin is waiting for you."

Sister Catherine sat up in bed, astonished and a little troubled. "How can I!" she replied. "How can I get up and cross the dormitory without awaking my companions?"

The child reassured her: "Be at ease. It is half-past eleven and everyone is asleep. I will come with you."

So Catherine dressed, followed the child and reached the chapel without difficulty. To her added amazement it was all lit up, "as if for Midnight Mass".

The child led the novice to the altar-rails, where she was prompted to kneel. "Here is the Holy Virgin," he announced. Suddenly there was a rustling, as of a silk dress, and a Lady of incomparable beauty stepped forward and took her seat on the chair normally reserved for the Director of the Seminary.

She was dressed in an ivory robe and blue mantle, and a white veil fell over her shoulders. With pure simplicity, Catherine stepped forward, fell on her knees and rested her clasped hands upon the knees of the Blessed Virgin.

"At that moment," she declared afterwards, "I felt the sweetest emotion of my life, impossible to describe. I cannot say how long I remained like that. All I know is that after speaking to me for a long time the Holy Virgin left, disappearing like a cloud that has evaporated."

When Our Lady had withdrawn, the child led Catherine back to her dormitory and she got back into bed as the clock outside was striking two.

Much of that celestial conversation was secret and, except to her confessor, was never revealed by Sister Catherine. Just as there were secrets at La Salette so, too, there is a "Secret of the Rue du Bac" which has been guarded quite as jealously.

But a good deal of the conversation is known from an actual record, carefully preserved in Catherine's handwriting. It began: "My child, God wishes you to undertake a mission. For it you will have much to suffer, but you will overcome that by recalling that you do so for the Glory of God . . ."

Then Our Lady warned Catherine of certain coming events. "Times are very evil. Among the troubles that will beset France, the Throne will be upset. The entire world will be distressed with afflictions. *But do you come to the foot of this altar"*—here she pointed with her right hand—*"and there graces will be showered upon all who ask for them with faith and fervour*. They will be bestowed upon the great and upon the small."

Our Lady then made certain declarations concerning the future welfare and progress of that community in particular, adding "I love it very much".

"But grave troubles are coming. There will be great danger. Do not fear. God and Saint Vincent will protect the Community. I myself shall be with you . . .

"At one moment, when the danger is acute, everyone will believe all to be lost. You will recall my visit and the protection of God . . .

"But it will not be the same for others, or for the clergy of Paris. There will indeed be victims. The Archbishop will die . . . the Cross will be trampled on, blood will run in the streets . . . the world will be plunged into sadness." And then she revealed that these last events would take place "in 40 years", i.e., in or about 1870.

Sister Catherine was forbidden to tell anyone of her experience save only her confessor, Father Aladel. He was gravely perplexed, but was inclined to dismiss the whole story as being the product of the overwrought mind of an unsettled novice. He paid little or no attention to it.

Father Aladel was, therefore, startled when, a few days later, revolution suddenly broke out in Paris, scenes of terror were enacted throughout France, churches and crucifixes were profaned, convents were pillaged, priests were ill-treated and the Archbishop of Paris was forced to hide. Astonishing, too, that as

Sister Catherine had predicted, the Convent in the Rue
du Bac was never touched although it shook with gun-
fire and was surrounded by delirious mobs.

The fulfilment of such predictions, of which the
young novice could have had no possible human
inkling, and so rapidly, made the good priest thoughtful
and he reconsidered the whole matter. Sister Catherine
continued placid as before.

At half-past-five on Saturday, November 27th, the
Sisters were gathered in the Chapel for the evening
meditation. There was absolute silence. Suddenly
Catherine seemed to hear the distant rustle of silk.
Turning towards the sound she saw Our Lady, "so
lovely that no words could describe her beauty". She
was dressed in a robe of shining white; her head was
covered with a white veil that hung to her feet on
either side. Her feet rested on a globe. Her hands,
raised breast-high, clasped in a very light manner
another globe surmounted by a small cross.

The Holy Virgin's eyes were turned towards heaven;
her face shone; her lips moved in prayer as she offered
the globe to Our Lord. Soon, the globe disappeared
and the Blessed Virgin's hands were stretched out.
Her fingers were covered with rings and precious stones,
reflecting rays of light on every side, of such
brilliance that they hid her feet and her dress.

"As I was absorbed in this contemplation," told
Sister Catherine, "the Holy Virgin lowered her eyes
on me and her voice penetrated my heart:

" 'My child, the globe you saw represented the entire
world, France in particular, and especially every
single person.'

"Here," Catherine continued, "I do not know
how to express what I saw, but the Holy Virgin added:
'This is the symbol of the graces which I bestow upon
all who ask of me'.

"Then there was formed round about the Virgin

an oval tableau, on which was written in golden letters:

*"O Marie, conçue sans péché, priez pour nous qui avons recours à vous.* 'O Mary, conceived without sin, pray for us who have recourse to thee'."

After a moment, this vision altered and, instead, Catherine saw a letter M surmounted by a cross, standing on a bar beneath which were two hearts, the Sacred Hearts of Jesus and Mary.

Then she heard a voice say: "Make a medal after this model. Those who carry it with piety will receive great graces; above all, those who carry it round their necks; graces abundant for those who have confidence."

Catherine Labouré likewise reported this vision to Father Aladel and told him: "The Holy Virgin wishes a medal to be struck with this image". But even so, the priest did not seem to receive the novice any more kindly than before, and she went back to her occupations as if nothing had happened.

The date, November 27th, 1830, of this vision of the Miraculous Medal was declared authentic by Catherine Labouré herself at two canonical enquiries. A third Apparition, however, took place some days later, in December, at the same time, and under the same conditions as the second, but with this difference that Our Lady appeared above the tabernacle. She was dressed exactly as before. Again the details were revealed, the promise of graces were extended, and Catherine was requested to have the medal struck. Once more she obeyed and brought the matter to the priest. But even so he was not convinced and nothing was done at the time.

In January 1831, Sister Catherine took the habit, and was sent from the Rue du Bac to the Hospice of Enghien, in the Faubourg Saint-Antoine, to look after a number of old-age pensioners. This was to be her home for forty-six years, though she returned to the

*Our Lady of Pompeii*
(Page 175)

*The body of Saint Catherine Labouré enshrined below the altar of Our Lady of the Globe in the convent of the Rue du Bac, Paris*

(Page 182)

Chapel at the Mother House from time to time to visit her confessor. On two such occasions, in March and September 1831, she was favoured with yet other visions of the Medal.

Finally, at the last of these Apparitions, Our Lady seems to have reiterated her request and to have added some displeasure that it had not already been obeyed.

This announcement roused Father Aladel. Far from being inactive, he had really been paying close attention, studying the young Sister's character and statements. At the first convenient opportunity he took the matter to Mgr. de Quélen, the Archbishop of Paris, who, after careful enquiry and thought, decided that though it would be premature to give recognition to the Apparitions, the medal should be struck. Some of the first copies were taken to the Archbishop.

From that moment wonderful favours were granted to those who wore or carried it. The first recorded instance was that of an apostate prelate, Mgr. de Pradt, Archbishop of Malines, who had fallen away during the Revolution, and since refused to submit to the Pope. Now his death was imminent. Although hitherto he had refused every overture, this time Archbishop Quélen went armed with one of the new medals. Mgr. de Pradt immediately humbled himself, retracted all his errors, begged pardon from the Pope, and was reconciled to the Church. He received the Sacraments and died in excellent disposition, literally in the arms of the Archbishop of Paris.

Although the official title of the medal is "the medal of the Immaculate Conception", this episode and many another like it soon caused it to be called the Miraculous Medal, the name by which it is most popularly known.

Two years after the medal was struck, the Archbishop was so impressed by the number of graces and conversions which accompanied its use that he ordered a Canonical enquiry into the subject of the Rue du Bac

Apparitions as bearing on "the origin and effect of the medal of the Holy Virgin, called Miraculous". Nineteen sessions were held and the report of the Promoter upheld the reality of the Apparitions to Catherine Labouré and the veracity of the miracles obtained through the use of the medal. In his Pastoral, the Archbishop exhorted the faithful always to carry a copy of the medal and frequently to recite the prayer inscribed on it.

The devotion of the Miraculous Medal spread with great rapidity through all the Christian world. The Holy See has instituted November 27th for the celebration of the feast, with a special Office and Mass, of the Manifestation of the Immaculate Virgin under the title of the Miraculous Medal.

In 1870, forty years after the first Apparition, the dread crises foretold by Our Lady were fulfilled. France was plunged into the horrors of the Franco-Prussian war. The collapse of France, the surrender of Napoleon III and the siege of Paris evoked the terrible outburst of the Communard Insurrection. In the course of this terrible upheaval, Mgr. Duboy, then Archbishop of Paris was taken as a hostage with a number of others, all of whom were brutally massacred.

In 1897, Pope Leo XIII, commissioned Cardinal Richard to be his Legate, to crown solemnly the statue of Our Lady which had been set up sometime after Father Aladel's death in 1865 and about which there had been some controversy.

Our Lady had commanded Sister Catherine to keep secret not only her "Secrets" but the whole fact of the Apparitions, save only to her confessor. Even to the Archbishop that good priest had been unable to name the seer of Our Lady. So closely guarded was this knowledge and so humble was Sister Catherine that even her superior, Sister Dufès, had only heard "a rumour which she did not feel inclined to heed".

Sister Catherine was left without a confessor who knew of her conversations with Our Lady. One day Sister Dufès was amazed when Catherine burst into tears, and enquired the cause. She paused a moment and then replied, "Perhaps I can tell you tomorrow. I shall ask permission of the Holy Mother during Meditation."

Next day Sister Catherine asked to see her Superior, and astounded her with the entire story of all that had transpired, a story told with Our Lady's permission because now Sister Catherine's Mission was complete.

These fresh facts were made known: that Our Lady had asked that an image of herself holding the globe be made and placed in the chapel: that Father Aladel had had a drawing made but had not been able to complete the work: this statue was not to replace or interfere with the figure of the medal, already behind the high altar, because it was correct and should not be touched.

When, eight months later, Sister Catherine died, she was happy in the knowledge that Our Lady of the Globe was soon to be in place. It was Pope Leo XIII himself who authorised the statue and had it erected in the chapel of the Apparitions.

The venerable sister's health failed rapidly. In November 1876 she made the annual retreat at the Rue du Bac and foretold her end that year. On December 31st, at four o'clock, sitting beside her bed, she received her sister, Marie Antoinette, with her two children. At about six o'clock, a Sister with her saw the end was near. The Community was notified and recited the prayers for the dying. After a short interval Catherine sighed gently and was gone. Her prophecy again proved true. She did not live to see 1877.

Her Cause was introduced at Rome in 1895 and was renewed in 1907 when the Servant of God received the title "Venerable". Catherine Labouré was beatified by Pope Pius XI on May 28th, 1933, an occasion which the present author will never forget on earth. The crowning glory was achieved, equal to that accorded a few years earlier to Bernadette of Lourdes, when on July 27th, 1947, Saint Catherine was canonised by Pope Pius XII. Her feast day is December 31st, the anniversary of her passing.

Saint Catherine Labouré was exhumed from her resting place in the Rue de Reuilly and brought to the Rue du Bac on March 22nd, 1933. Her body was in a perfect state of preservation. The eyes which had gazed on the visions of Our Lady, the hands that had rested upon her knees, were all intact. Her relics are now exposed in state, arrayed in the habit she loved so well, under the altar of Our Lady of the Globe, to the right hand of the altar, to the foot of which Our Lady pointed.

The same chair, upon which Our Lady sat at the first Apparition of July 18th, 1830, is preserved and regarded as a priceless treasure, in the same chapel of Our Lady's Apparitions, close to the spot where Catherine lies.

# XXIV: LA SALETTE

S O much, rightly, has been written about Lourdes, Our Blessed Lady's appearances to St. Bernadette, and the things that have happened there since, that we in England are apt to forget the similarly wonderful appearance of Our Lady, and the miracles which followed it, in another mountainous corner of France, at La Salette.

This Apparition of Our Lady took place on a mountain slope, six thousand feet above sea level, a few miles from and within the parish of La Salette village; hence its title. It occurred on September 19th, 1846, rather more than a hundred years ago and twelve years before St. Bernadette's momentous experiences. So, while the centenary is fresh in people's minds, it would seem good to refresh our memories with a recapitulation of what took place.

In 1846, September 19th was Ember Saturday and the Eve of the Feast of the Seven Dolours of Our Lady, or Our Lady of Sorrows. Early that morning, two children, Maximin Giraud, aged eleven, and Mélanie Mathieu-Calvat, aged fifteen, were sent to mind some cows which were grazing on a small plateau about four miles from the village.

Mélanie had been used to this kind of work since she was nine, but for Maximin it was a new experience. His father, a wheelwright in the nearby town of Corps, on the Route Napoleon, had lent him for a few days to help a farmer friend whose shepherd had fallen ill.

The boy had arrived at the farm only a day or two before and had met Mélanie for the first time only the day previous. They were strangers so that there was no question of them having planned in advance any fraud or deceit.

It was a scorching day. There was a bright sun and none of the cloud which is so commonly found in high mountains. At noon the Angelus bells rang in the valley below and the children decided it was time for lunch. They drove the herd to a stream for a drink, and themselves retired to a shady little glen. After they had eaten they withdrew yet further to the cool bed of a dried-up spring where they lay down and fell asleep.

Mélanie was first to wake up. To her dismay the cows were out of sight. She aroused Maximin and with him scrambled up to the level of the plateau. There the children heaved sighs of relief. The cows were safe, grazing some distance away.

Before rejoining the herd, the children had to pick up their lunch bags so they turned back to the glen. Suddenly Mélanie gave a cry, turned to Maximin who was lagging behind, and exclaimed: "Be quick! Look! There is a bright light down there!"

There, just where they had been sleeping a few minutes earlier, was a brilliant globe of light, so dazzling that it hurt the children's eyes as they gazed upon it. While yet the young cowherds stared, this globe seemed to divide and in the midst of the brilliance there appeared the form of a Lady, weeping bitterly, seated upon a rock on the floor of the dried-up stream.

The children stood still, terrified. After a moment, however, the Lady stood up and reassured them, beckoning to them. "Come near, children," she called to them, "and don't be frightened. I have come to tell you some great news."

The children then dared to step up close to the Lady,

who started to give them a wonderful message, so wonderful that there need be no apology for repeating it almost entire.

It is amusing to recall that while the Lady was talking Maximin was rather shy and nervous. He twiddled his hat on his stick, flicked some pebbles about and one of them rolled up to the Lady's feet. But his dog, of which he was very fond but which was supposed to be rather fierce, settled down happily beside the Lady, head on paws, and lay there calmly throughout the Apparition.

Before recounting the message which this beautiful Lady entrusted to the children, and through them to the world, it may be as well to give a somewhat detailed description of this wonderful figure as they saw her.

The Lady was tall, they said, loving as a mother but majestic as a queen. She was elevated a few inches above the grass which her feet did not apparently touch. Her face was of indescribable beauty. Maximin could not bring himself to gaze upon it. Mélanie alone saw the celestial blue eyes which were full of tears, tears which ran down her cheeks and fell scintillating into the surrounding brilliance.

The Lady wore a long, white robe scattered with gleaming, golden sequins. A pure white scarf, edged with roses of many colours, was wrapped across her breast. A bright yellow apron hung from her waist. She was shod with white shoes, likewise decked with pearls, flowers and roses that sparkled in the light. Round her neck hung a chain from which was suspended a long cross, to the arms of which were affixed emblems of the Passion. The Christ on the cross shone with a brilliance even greater than that surrounding the Lady.

A corona of light, like a diadem, sprang from a crown of roses on her head. Other rays of light, all of which blended into the aureole around her, darted from the roses at her feet. Asked later about the intensity of this brilliance, the children could only explain that it was brighter than, but different to anything in their experience; brighter than the sun but not to be compared with it.

From her words it is clear that the Lady speaking could have been none other than the Mother of God, sent by Him to deliver a warning to the world, even as He sent messages by the prophets of old. She said:

"If my people will not submit, I shall be obliged to let go of my Son's hand which is so strong and heavy that I can no longer restrain it.

"For what a long time I have suffered for you! If I would not have my Son abandon you, I am forced to pray to Him without ceasing. But, as for you, you pay no heed. However much you pray, no matter what you do, you can never recompense the trouble I have taken for you.

"Six days have I given you for labour. The seventh I have kept for myself. But that no one will give me. It is this that makes my Son's hand so heavy.

"The carters cannot swear without including my Son's Name. These are two things which make my Son's hand so heavy.

"If the harvest is spoiled, it is all on this account. I gave you warning last year with the potato crop, but you paid no heed. On the contrary, when you found the potatoes spoiled you swore and blasphemed my Son's Name. They will go on rotting. This year, by Christmas, there will be no more."

At this, Maximin looked puzzled because he did not speak French well, but only a dialect. He did not know what the Lady meant by "potatoes". So she repeated her last words in his dialect and continued:

"If you have corn it must not be sown. All that is sown, the animals will eat. The rest, and what they leave, will turn to dust when it is threshed.

"There will be a great famine. Before the famine children under seven will be seized with palsy and die in the arms of those who nurse them. The rest will do penance through the famine. The nut crop will go bad and the grapes will rot."

At this moment the Lady entrusted each child with a special secret which, in fact, they revealed to no one except the Pope at his special request.

Then again she spoke aloud: "If the people are converted, the very rocks and stones will turn to heaps of grain. The potatoes will be self-sown for another year.

"In summer, only a few old women go to Mass on Sunday. The others work. In winter, when they have nothing else to do, the boys go to Mass just to mock at religion. The world takes no notice of Lent. People go to butchers' like dogs."

Then the Lady asked a question: "Do you say your prayers properly, children?"

Both answered, "Not very well".

"Then you must be sure and say them carefully every night and morning; never less than an 'Our Father' and a 'Hail Mary', when you can do no better."

The beautiful Lady then reminded Maximin of an occasion when his father had shown him some diseased wheat, and concluded: "Well, children, you must do your best to make all this known to my people."

The Lady now crossed over the bed of the dried-up stream, never walking but always gliding over the surface of the grass, taking the brilliance with her, and followed a path to the higher, level ground. Here she turned and repeated her last words: "Well, children, you *will* pass all this on to my people?" Then she was raised up about five feet from the earth and slowly melted away into clear space, taking the shining light with her.

Thus to the most unlikely of witnesses, two totally illiterate peasant children in one of the most remote parts of Europe, did God through Our Blessed Lady choose to impart a Message as dramatic as it was grave.

The world, "Her people" indeed, had so far forgotten themselves that they blasphemed the Holy Name, broke the Commandments, ignored Sunday, made mockery of religion. Unless there was reconciliation, the hand of her Son could no longer be restrained. Dire punishment would follow unless there was repentance, when abundance would be the reward.

In point of fact, the chastisements cautioned by Our Lady were incurred. In 1845 there had occurred the first phase of the potato famine. In 1846 this was so severe that early in 1847 Queen Victoria had to appeal to Parliament for relief in what is known to history as the Irish Potato Famine. Likewise the wheat shortage was so severe that it is estimated more than a million people died in Europe. In the same year began the terrible grape disease which decimated the vineyards all over France.

The children, Mélanie and Maximin, did their work nobly and with heroism. At home there were few who wanted to believe them, but their masters, the farmers, were astonished that such ignorant children were able to relate accurately a complicated "message", both in French, which they did not understand, and in dialect, which showed the exactness of what they said.

The Mayor heard of it and taxed the children with dire threats of imprisonment if they did not retract, and promises of ample rewards if they did. Bags of money were dangled before their eyes. Maximin received a good beating from his father, a wheelwright given to drink, who was later converted and died repentant.

A few people suspected the truth and climbed up to the plateau to make sure that no one could have been hiding there. There was not even a bush that could have afforded concealment. Instead, it was found that the spring, where the Lady had sat, which was always dry after June, had burst forth and was flowing freely down the hillside. They bathed the eyes of a nearly blind small child and she received her sight instantly.

In the nearby township of Corps, there was a woman, bedridden, with an incurable complaint. A novena was made to Our Lady "of La Salette" for the first time. Water from the spring was given. On the last day the patient was completely and lastingly cured.

The Bishop then appointed two Commissions and for five long years the most searching enquiries were made. The news spread. Cardinal Wiseman from England sent deputations to enquire. Bishop Ullathorne of Birmingham arrived with a group of friends. They went home with convincing stories.

All over France, in as many as eighty places, Bishops appointed canonical commissions which gave judgment that cures granted through the use of Prayers to Our Lady of La Salette and use of the water from the spring were miraculous. Many hundreds of remarkable favours were granted and recorded.

The news reached Pope Pius IX and he asked the children to convey to him the secrets which they had refused to impart to anyone else. They agreed, and special ambassadors carried these "secrets" in letters to Rome. When His Holiness read them, he became very grave, and it was only a matter of weeks before official pronouncement was made as to the veracity of the Apparition of Our Lady of La Salette, and it was declared that the faithful might accept it. This was in 1851.

A magnificent basilica, with pilgrim hospices, was built on the site of the Apparition, six thousand feet above sea level. The figure of Our Lady of Reconciliation of La Salette was approved by the Pope and a Special Legate was sent to crown it solemnly in the Pope's name. The hospices are open all the summer months of the year and can accommodate fifteen hundred pilgrims.

At the same time, a new Congregation of Priests was founded and given recognition by the Holy See—the Priests Missionaries of Our Lady of La Salette. In course of time these missionaries have established houses and colleges in many parts of the world, in addition to France; in particular, Madagascar, Canada, Brazil, Poland and the United States. They have two Missions in England, at Dagenham and Rainham, Essex.

To further their work and to assist in spreading Our Lady's message of penance, a confraternity was founded—almost instantly raised to be an Arch-confraternity—of Our Lady of La Salette. Many impressive indulgences were conferred upon this Archconfraternity by Pope Pius IX, and these have been considerably increased by succecding Popes. Every Pope since then has played some part in increasing the devotion to Our Lady of La Salette.

One of the first churches, if not actually the first, to be given that dedication is in England, at Bermondsey, London. It was dedicated in 1849 within three years of the Apparition.

Likewise England played a leading part in the development of the Confraternity. The first branch in England was established a few weeks after it was created and approved, at Newman's Oratorian Chapel in Alcester Street, Birmingham.

The warnings of Our Lady of La Salette, made a hundred years ago, are as effective and as necessary today. When was there a time when anxiety over famine and food shortages was graver? Or when was an unrepentant world more threatened with the chastisements resulting directly from its infidelity?

It is good to know that it is still possible for English people to join the Archconfraternity. What better way could there be of showing one's concern in these threatening days than by doing so? The headquarters in England of the Archconfraternity are to be found care of the Missionaries of La Salette, 52 Goresbrook Road, Dagenham, Essex. Full details would be sent to all who cared to enquire. The conditions are simple and practical and the spiritual benefits are immense.

Of the secrets and message of La Salette, Pope Pius IX exclaimed: "These are the secrets of La Salette: Unless the World Repent it shall Perish!"

From La Salette today comes a fresh reminder of that grave warning, coupled with those more recently given at Fatima and Beauraing. Who can dare to ignore them?

## XXV: THE MESSAGE OF LOURDES

RELIGIOUS thought in France had been seriously
disturbed and the tempo of the national spiritual
life quickened by the events, first at the Rue du
Bac and Our Lady of Victories in Paris, then at La
Salette. It was not that Apparitions of Our Lady were
new in France. The amazing series at Le Laus in
1664 was but typical of many another. The
Apparitions of Notre-Dame de l'Osier, to a withy-cutter
in Savoy; the rescue of the shepherdess from the River
Gave at Bétharram; the astonishing origin of the shrine
at Garaison; these are instances of numerous other
Apparitions that played an important part in keeping
Our Lady's Kingdom true.

It was in 1858, twenty-eight years after the revelation
of the Miraculous Medal, and twelve after La Salette,
that the third and greatest of the nineteenth century
sequences of Apparitions of Our Lady was vouchsafed
to Bernadette at Lourdes. It cannot be maintained
that Bernadette was influenced by the previous
appearances; it is doubtful if she gave them a thought
during the period of her experiences. Yet the knowledge gained through the canonical enquiries into these
earlier manifestations must have been of great value
in guiding the authorities whose duty it was to
determine the nature of what took place at Lourdes.

The authenticity of the Apparitions in Paris and at
La Salette was pronounced in 1835 and 1851. Our
Blessed Lady may be said thus providentially to have

paved the way for what she vouchsafed at Massabielle.

The story of Our Lady's Apparitions to Bernadette has been related so often that it would be purposeless here to reiterate it. In the whole survey of literature, French or English, which abounds on the subject, there is none clearer, or more accurate, than the admirable pamphlet *Bernadette of Lourdes* by Father Martindale, S.J., published by the Catholic Truth Society of London. So carefully has this been compiled, so well have been avoided those "colourful details" that are, in fact, accretions which hide the wood with trees, commonly found in books such as Lassare's and Estrade's, that this pamphlet becomes an invaluable corrective to mistaken ideas.

Attention here must be devoted to two particular aspects of the story—the actual appearance of Our Lady as Bernadette saw her, compared with her two earlier appearances: and the words of her message, revealed as the Apparitions progressed, stage by stage, in the conversations at the grotto.

St. Bernadette described the Blessed Virgin thus: "She had the looks of a girl of sixteen or seventeen. She was dressed in a white robe fastened at the waist with a blue sash. On her head she wore a white veil falling behind almost to her feet which were covered, partly by her dress, partly by yellow roses. On her right arm there hung a rosary with white beads on a golden chain that shone like the two roses on her feet. She was alert, young and surrounded by light."

All four witnesses are agreed that the "Lady" each saw was beautiful beyond words; all had the same difficulty in finding words strong enough to describe what each had seen. When Bernadette was asked how beautiful Our Lady was, she replied that to gain any idea it would be necessary to go to heaven. "When the vision vanished," she explained, "I was astonished to find myself still on earth." Likewise all four

children are agreed, in effect, as to the aureole of light
which surrounded Our Lady.

At the Rue du Bac, St. Catherine Labouré remarked
that the chapel was lit up: "as if for a midnight Mass".
It was just such a brilliance which first attracted
Mélanie's attention at La Salette, where both she and
Maximin reported that the beautiful Lady was
surrounded by a light so dazzling that it hurt the eye.
St. Bernadette's description of the same phenomenon
was that it was at once brighter yet softer than the sun

An attempt was made later to get Bernadette to
describe the kind of cloth of which Our Lady's dress
was made. She was taken to a shop and shown many
kinds but none was good enough. The shopkeeper
showed her a lovely piece of silk. "How about this?"
he asked. "Nothing like it." "But, Mademoiselle,
in all Lyons you will find no fabric more silky or
white." "And what does that show," replied
Bernadette, naïve and unperturbed, "except that the
Blessed Virgin did not have her dress made by you!"

That dress, probably, was made from spun and
woven light.

Of the roses, Bernadette said that they shone brighter
than any gold.

The single Apparition at La Salette was unexpected.
In the convent chapel, Saint Catherine Labouré was
in no way forewarned of the three visions in 1830.
Likewise the first and second Apparitions at Lourdes,
on February 11th and 14th, were unannounced;
though Saint Bernadette certainly paid her second visit
to the grotto in the hope of renewing her celestial
experience. And, although she learnt much from Our
Lady in those two Apparitions, yet no word was
spoken.

Through Mme. Millet's influence, the child was
allowed to pay her third visit on the 18th, in company
with her friend and one or two others. This was the

*Our Lady Ascending.    The statue at
La Salette*

(Page 193)

*A familiar Lourdes scene—the procession of the Blessed Sacrament outside the Rosary Chapel*

(Page 202)

first occasion when Our Lady spoke to her, the first when there were adult witnesses of her behaviour and reactions.

At La Salette, Our Lady spoke first in French and then in Dauphiny dialect. At Lourdes she spoke entirely in patois. Bernadette had been given pen and ink and paper and had been told to ask the mysterious visitor her name and wishes. Our Lady answered: "It is not necessary to write what I have to say," and then laughed.

On a later occasion, in 1871, at Pontmain, when Mme. Barbadette went to fetch her spectacles to see the Vision, Our Lady seems to have been highly amused. Otherwise her expression ranged from gracious and smiling serenity to the other extreme, of anguish and sorrow.

In the meantime Bernadette had requested her friends to withdraw a little way. Now they suggested that she ask that they might come back. Our Lady replied: "Nothing need prevent their return . . . Will you do me the favour of coming here for fifteen days?" The Mother of God asks a child to do her a favour! Here again, Our Lady demonstrated exactly the same degree of courtesy that was experienced at La Salette and in Paris. Even though the Queen of Angels spoke with a humble village child, her requests were pleas, not orders.

The effect on the child's manners of these contacts with the Queen of all Queens was remarkable. In all their conversations it was notable that Bernadette behaved with a courtesy far above anything she could have learned at home. People asked her who had taught her to behave so politely. "I don't know how I behave," was Bernadette's unassuming answer. "I just do what the Lady does. She greets me and I greet her in the same manner." Whatever action Bernadette performed during this and the subsequent

Apparitions, she did so with a modesty and grace that astonished onlookers.

The other message given to Bernadette during this third Apparition was prophetic: "I do not promise to make you happy in this world, but in the next." Saint Bernadette had much to suffer both physically and mentally on account of these Apparitions, but when she was canonised there must have been many to whom this prophecy recurred as particularly poignant.

It was decided to allow the child to keep her appointments. Next day, taking a candle with her, she hastened to the grotto at an early hour, with a group of five or six friends. The fourth and fifth visions passed by without any particular message to the world. Her friends noticed, however, that now she began making large and solemn signs of the Cross, a practice she retained all her life. They questioned her and were told: "I was making them too fast, I had to go slower to keep time with the Lady". Another friend remarked: "You make your signs of the Cross very well". She replied: "I don't know how I make them. I don't think anything about it. I do what the Lady does." This, then, was the lesson to the world of the fourth and fifth Apparitions.

The sixth visit was on a Sunday, when there was given the clear instruction: "You will pray to God for sinners." While Our Lady gave this command she looked towards the spectators and wept. In response, tears streamed down Bernadette's cheeks. "I cried," she explained, "because the Lady did".

The seventh Apparition was on Tuesday the 23rd, without incident. Next day the Lady came again and the Apparition lasted an hour. Bernadette turned to the crowd and called out: "Penance! Penance! Penance!"

The tenth Vision was perhaps most dramatic and for Bernadette certainly the most critical. She found

Our Lady right inside the cave, who commanded her: "Go drink at the spring and wash in it," pointing to a certain spot on the earthy floor of the grotto. Obediently the child scraped away the sand, drank of the muddy water which welled up, and washed her face. Worse and worse, to the indignation of the onlookers who mocked her as mad, she plucked and ate several blades of grass.

Curious link with the past. In feudal days, it was the custom each year to offer blades of grass from that very spot to Our Lady at Le Puy, Grande Châtelaine of Lourdes. The muddy spring continued to flow and, where before there had been only a damp patch, henceforth, uninterrupted, was to flow daily twenty-seven thousand gallons of crystal, pure water. At the time, people thought that the source had a miraculous origin. This undoubtedly helped to increase their sympathy with Bernadette and to tide over the difficult years until the Lourdes' devotion was formally recognised.

As at La Salette, however, it was no new spring that was revealed. It had always trickled away behind the rubbish which littered the grotto. But Bernadette was inspired to reveal it and never again was its presence ignored. A few days later, Louis Brouillette, the carter who had lost his eye in an accident, regained his sight through use of the water. Thus began the great mission of healing which has been associated ever since with Lourdes.

There is no record of any message on the next three occasions, February 26th, 27th or 28th, though it is said that Bernadette performed her usual acts of penance; prostrating, kissing the ground with such fervour that the onlookers were led to follow her example.

On March 1st the child took a friend's rosary to the grotto. She bowed when the Lady appeared, and began to tell her beads. Many others imitated her. The Lady asked Bernadette where her own rosary was. "Let us see it," she requested; and when it was pulled out of a pocket, the Blessed Virgin told her little friend to "use that".

Thus far, the clergy had taken no official cognisance of events at Massabielle, though Abbé Dézirat, of another parish, had witnessed and been impressed by Bernadette's behaviour on March 1st. Out of courtesy, an aunt had taken her to see the Curé, the celebrated Abbé Peyramale, some days previously, but he had gruffly rebuffed her. Now, on March 2nd, the Lady formally asked her messenger to tell him that she wished there to be a procession to Massabielle on Thursday, the last day of the fortnight.

Poor Bernadette! She was received with such scorn that she left with the second part of her message undelivered and, with characteristic courage, had to return. "The Lady in white whom I see at the grotto bade me tell the priests to build a chapel there, even a small one."

March 3rd found a crowd of several thousand beside the Gave. Bernadette did not see her Visitor until late evening. She explained what had happened in Our Lady's own words, the longest single speech of hers recorded at Lourdes. The Lady had not come that morning because people were present who had come merely to gape at the child's face during the Apparition, and who were unworthy of that because they had spent the night in the grotto, dishonouring it.

The Curé had told Bernadette to ask that a rosebush should blossom then and there as a proof of the Apparitions. When she heard the request, the Lady smiled again.

March 4th marked the last of the promised fifteen days. Immense crowds gathered expecting some climax, but the Apparition followed its usual course.

Bernadette, who had been so true to her promise, knelt
for an hour in ecstasy. Afterwards she reported that
the Lady had smiled at the Curé's requests, had bowed
as graciously as ever at the close of the Vision but
had not said good-bye, from which it might be
concluded that there would be further visits.

For three weeks Bernadette did not go near the
grotto but at last, on March 25th, she awoke very early
and set forth to Massabielle at about four o'clock,
where she found the Lady awaiting her.

Up to then the child had always insisted on referring
to her visitor as the "Lady". If anyone suggested
to her that it was the Mother of God, she demurred:
"I do not know that it is the Blessed Virgin. It is a
beautiful Lady."

As soon as Bernadette reached the grotto, therefore,
on this great feast-day of the Annunciation, she asked:
"Madame, will you be so good as to tell me who you
are?" The Lady let her ask this question three times.

"At my third request," Bernadette told afterwards,
"she assumed a serious air. Then she joined her hands
and raised them breast high . . . she looked heaven-
wards . . . slowly separated her hands and bent over
towards me, and said:

*"Qué soî l'Immaculado Councepcion."*

"I am the Immaculate Conception."

No words can sum up the tremendous significance
of the pronouncement better than those of Father
Martindale in his pamphlet: " . . . None had now any
doubt as to who the Lady was. On the feast
commemorating her own great Annunciation, Mary
had announced to the child and to the world that it
was herself who had appeared among them; and from
the wild rosebush of the grotto there began to breathe
forth into all peoples the fragrance of the mystic Rose
of God."

At the Rue du Bac it was Mary Immaculate who

showed herself and inspired St. Catherine Labouré with the Miraculous Medal. It was there that she revealed her preference for the ejaculation "O Mary, conceived without sin, pray for us who have recourse to thee".

At Our Lady of Victories, Father des Genettes was catapulted into his gigantic task by Our Lady's command: "Consecrate thy parish to the Holy and Immaculate Heart of Mary". With these two signposts to point the way, the great journey in faith began which was to culminate in 1854 when Pope Pius IX, above all "Our Lady's Pope", proclaimed the dogma of the Immaculate Conception. Four years later the Virgin Immaculate crowned her sequence of Apparitions, in Paris and at La Salette as well as beside the Gave, with her own proclamation, and with it set her seal of approbation, as it were, on the Church's Declaration of Faith.

The seventeenth Vision occurred on April 7th and the final one on July 16th, Feast of Our Lady of Mount Carmel. By then, the authorities had barricaded the grotto and Bernadette was obliged to kneel on the further side of the river. Yet it seemed to her that Our Lady was as near as ever.

It was not until Pius IX expressed a personal desire to know the secrets given to them at La Salette that Maximin and Mélanie could be persuaded to divulge them in closely guarded, sealed envelopes to the Sovereign Pontiff alone. Whatever may have been the subject of those confidences, they were sufficiently grave to disturb the Holy Father. Today all discussion of them is strictly prohibited.

It appears that Our Lady confided likewise a number of secrets to Bernadette, but no inducement could persuade her to reveal a jot or tittle of them.

"Would you tell your secrets to the Pope?"

"The Blessed Virgin told me to tell no one. The Pope is someone."

"Yes. But the Pope has the authority of Jesus Christ."

"The Pope has authority on earth. The Blessed Virgin is in Heaven." Thus reasoned the "ignorant" little peasant girl, who some maintained was mad. She steadfastly refused to discuss the matter further.

Such was the Appearance of Our Lady at Lourdes —as the Immaculate Virgin Mother of God—and such was the fullness of her message which, in the course of eighteen visits, she chose to deliver to the world through that very humble servant of God who is now a glorious Saint in Heaven. Thus sprang into being the Lourdes we know today, which, with the possible exceptions of Fatima and Loreto, is the greatest shrine of Our Lady, and the most frequented, in the world.

Our Lady asked for a chapel. Three churches have been built at Massabielle where every year hundreds of thousands of Christians receive the Sacraments of Penance and the Holy Eucharist. These three churches are the Crypt, or Lower Church, opened in 1856 by Mgr. Laurence; the Upper Church of the Immaculate Conception, consecrated in 1876 by a Papal Legate is of Minor Basilica rank; the third, the Rosary, was begun in 1883, completed at a cost of three million francs, old time value, and was opened in 1889. It, too, is of Minor Basilica rank. At the altar within the grotto, Masses are said without interruption from dawn till noon during pilgrimage time; and sometimes in the Rosary Square the Holy Sacrifice is offered before crowds of 50,000 and even 100,000 of the faithful.

Our Lady asked for a procession. On all occasions when there is public Benediction of the Sick, Our Blessed Lord is carried, in the Sacred Host, through seried ranks of the faithful, acclaimed even as He was acclaimed at Jerusalem on the first Palm Sunday. At the close of each day the Rosary is said publicly at the grotto and this is followed by another procession in which every pilgrim carries a candle protected from the wind by a paper shade and during which the famous Lourdes hymn is sung.

Our Lady asked for Penance. The hill behind the older basilica is crowned with a truly dramatic, impressive, Way of the Cross, which it is the duty of every pilgrim to follow. And near the entrance to the church is the Pénitencerie, a narrow chapel containing twenty-four confessionals. On all occasions every possible opportunity is offered so that every pilgrim may have the grace of a good Confession.

But nowhere in her conversations does it seem that Our Lady ever promised miracles or cures. At her instance, water flowed from the grotto floor, and it was not long before people began to realise its wonderful propensities. Quite near the grotto have been built the Piscines, or bathing-places, with nine baths. It is worthy of record that, in spite of the low temperature of the water, no fatality has occurred among the sick on account of their immersion, and no infectious disease has been known to have been spread thereby.

The world has responded thus much to the call of Lourdes. In 1935, for example, on the occasion of the great Jubilee, Masses were said day and night for three days and more than a million pilgrims visited the grotto. In the course of a recent, typical year, 800,000 organised pilgrims arrived by train, not counting any who came by road or independently.

Little of the Lourdes that St. Bernadette knew remains. Her humble home is transformed into a "sight" rather than a shrine. The church she knew has been replaced by something more modern. The grotto bears rather more resemblance. The source is pent in. The muddy floor is beautifully paved. The piles of rubbish have been swept away. No sticks may be found for hungry children to sell. Instead the rocky walls are covered with a forest of crutches and other such votive offerings, and blackened with the soot of a million candles.

The niche in the rock where Our Lady Immaculate stood is there, enshrining Fabisch's statue (of which Saint Bernadette is alleged to have exclaimed: "But not like her! There is as much difference between day and night") that has been copied and recopied in well nigh every city in every continent of the globe.

Of necessity, the mother of so many regrets, there have been changes drastic and "improvements" many. It could not have been otherwise. But in spite of them, Lourdes, the pilgrim's Lourdes, remains eternal and the same. The same grotto, the same stillness, the same music of the Gave rippling close by; and the same consciousness that this was indeed the place Our Lady chose to rank among the greatest of all her sanctuaries.

## XXVI: OOSTACKER

EVEN when present-day travel bans are lifted there are difficulties which may well deter a good many people who might otherwise be only too glad for an opportunity to visit the famous Grotto beside the Gave at Lourdes; difficulties of distance, expense and so forth.

It will come, therefore, as a welcome surprise to many to learn that there is an important Lourdes shrine in Belgium, only a threepenny tram ride from Ghent station; an easy and not very costly journey from London. The story of this sanctuary is sufficiently inspiring to draw many thousands there each year.

The shrine itself, the basilica and its domain, are so attractive and have so much to offer pilgrims that it is curious how few English Catholics seem to think of adding their numbers to the multitude. For Oostacker, which is the name of the nearby village that gives its title to the shrine, is not merely a Lourdes imitation. It is a very real and historic centre of Marial devotion, and a place where on innumerable occasions Our Lady has chosen to manifest her extraordinary powers as Mediatrix.

Fourteen years after the Lourdes Apparitions, the Marquise de Courtbourne, who owned the château at Oostacker, decided to build a large aquarium wherein to house and display her fine collection of rare fishes. The aquarium was designed to look like a big cave with the glass-fronted tanks set along the walls of the interior.

The site chosen for this erection was known in the

family as "the hermitage" because a brother of the Marquise had lived there for some years in solitude in a small châlet. He had been a Trappist, but was obliged to resign from his monastery because of ill-health. Here he had spent his remaining days in prayer and meditation, withdrawn from the world.

As soon as the aquarium was ready, the Marquise invited her friend, the parish priest, to come and inspect it. Knowing his patron's great interest in the then fairly recent events at Lourdes, the good priest suggested that it might be possible to incorporate a figure of Our Lady as she had appeared to Saint Bernadette in a cleft in the rocks of this artificial cave.

This was done and the Marquise invited as many of the parishioners who cared to attend to be present at the blessing of this unostentatious shrine. At once it assumed a place of great popularity in the people's affections and Sunday by Sunday parties of them sought permission to visit the grotto. By the following year, 1873, the stream of visitors had so increased that it was decided to make the grotto always accessible to the public. Raised thus to the dignity of a public shrine, the parish Priest solemnly blessed the statue on June 29th, before a congregation of more than two thousand.

The pilgrimage was inaugurated. It was for Our Lady to do the rest. Within a year, Oostacker was to be famous throughout Europe, a name on the lips of good Catholics in many lands, a shrine visited by organised pilgrimages from Holland and France as well as Belgium.

From the first, the response to prayers at this grotto seemed to be especially direct. Many were the instances of small "cures" and favours reported to the clergy. On September 9th, 1874, a more pronounced cure was granted. A woman who had been ill for twelve years, quite unable to walk and unresponsive to any treatment prescribed by well-known specialists, was brought to Oostacker. After a few moments' prayer, she suddenly rose from her bath-chair and fell on her knees, entirely well.

From that moment miracles—ecclesiastical commissions of enquiry have pronounced them to be such —became frequent. The most sensational, perhaps because the most spectacular and the one most widely reported, was that in the case of Peter de Rudder, which took place in 1875.

Peter de Rudder was a labourer who had been severely crushed when a heavy tree had fallen across his body. Among other injuries, his leg was smashed a few inches below the knee and the bone was literally pulverised. That was in 1867. For a year his life was in danger because of a gangrenous infection. From time to time, large splinters of bone worked themselves out through a gaping wound near his ankle. The marvel is that none of the surgeons had ordered his leg to be amputated.

For eight years de Rudder lay incapacitated from work. His savings were long since spent and he was living in penury on a small pension. Then the news reached his village of the wonderful favours being granted at Oostacker and he resolved at all cost, and regardless of pain, to make the journey there.

By the time de Rudder reached Oostacker he was exhausted, for he had perforce to drag himself on his crutches for long distances. He fell, worn out, onto a grassy bank in front of the simple figure of Our Lady. Overcome with thirst, he asked for some water from a little fountain which had formerly trickled through the fish tanks. Then he prayed with fervour.

After some moments he was seized with a curious sensation urging him to throw down his crutches and advance through a series of pews towards the shrine. This he did, and when he reached the entrance to the aquarium he suddenly realised what had happened. "What has happened?" he cried in a loud voice. "O Mary! Thank you! Thank you!"

As soon as Peter had recovered from the shock of this marvellous intervention, assistants took him to the château where he was professionally examined. His leg was whole and intact. Whereas that morning, when he left home, the shin-bone had been flexible, like a piece of rubber, now it was firm and solid, able to take his full weight without pain. The site of the fracture was marked with a faint blue line, but otherwise the leg might never have been injured. Even the festering sore, through which a bone-splinter had emerged only recently, was healed.

Peter de Rudder was afterwards examined by scores of medical experts, including the surgeons and bone specialists who had tried for so long but in vain to produce a cure. His case has become classic, well known in the annals of medicine.

No physical explanation of the cure has ever been produced. When, in later years, Peter died, he bequeathed his leg bones to the Bishop in the interest of science. They are preserved with attested records for all, and any sceptics, to examine. Accurate casts of them have been affixed to a plaque beside the figure of Our Lady as a public testimony.

As a direct result of this and other miracles, Oostacker was recognised as a major shrine of Our Lady. A church, since raised to basilica rank, was built beside the grotto, which remains outside, carefully preserved in the same condition as it was in Peter de Rudder's day. It was blessed in 1877 by the Jesuit Provincial, and to this day the shrine, basilica and domain are under the guardianship of the Jesuit Fathers.

Oostacker has become the Belgian Lourdes, not that its existence has in any way diminished the devotion that Belgium has towards Lourdes itself. But whereas ordinary folk can travel to the south of France only upon occasion, vast numbers can and do visit Oostacker every year.

The contrast between Lourdes and its Belgian counterpart is great. The former is grand—the queen of all Our Lady's shrines—with its esplanade, its churches and, above all, its unique grotto—the place which Our Lady chose for her eighteen appearances. But Oostacker is simple. The domain is more like the village green of some obscure country hamlet. The twin-spired basilica is rather like the parish church of a country town. The poplar-lined drive, bordered by a dyke, is like many another Flemish country lane.

The pilgrim who does not expect grandeur, however, need fear no disappointment. For all that the mighty cranes of the great new graving-dockyard for deep-sea vessels tower in forest-like masses only a mile or two away on the horizon, here will be found just the same fragrant charm and peace that one meets at the grotto beside the Gave; a delicious peace and spiritual calm that one learns to recognise as being associated in some mysterious way with all such places chosen by Our Lady for her own.

There are Calvaries, and Ways-of-the-Cross, and Ways-of-the-Rosary as added encouragements to the pilgrim, for prayer and devotion. Inside the basilica, surrounded by a thousand plaques and tablets, ex-voto and in thanksgiving, there is a magnificent shrine of Our Lady of Lourdes, crowned by order of the Holy See.

But, somehow, for most people, the artificial mound which constitutes the fabric of the old aquarium, and the simple, unspoiled "Lourdes Grotto" put there by the Marquise, provide all the inducement that is needed. It is hard to tear oneself away to run for the tram which takes one back to Ghent.

## XXVII: PONTMAIN

PONTMAIN is famous as the site of the French national votive offering to Our Blessed Lady given at the conclusion of the Franco-Prussian War, partly as an act of expiation, partly in thanksgiving, for many mercies in spite of almost crushing defeat.

A small agricultural community, at that time of some five hundred souls, it is hidden away in the remote north-west corner of Mayenne, thirty miles from the See-centre of Laval, where the borders of Brittany and Normandy meet.

When the new year of 1871 dawned, there were few who had heard of Pontmain, fewer still who dreamed that within weeks it would be spoken of with awe throughout the Catholic world or that, generations hence, pilgrims would be journeying thither, as to Lourdes and La Salette, from far and wide.

That new year did not dawn happily for France. It marked one of the gravest crises which the country has had to face. The 1870 war had resolved itself into catastrophe. The Germans had entered Paris. Their armies had thrust deep, carrying death and ruin into the heart of the country. An unusually severe winter added misery to misfortune. With heroic fortitude, the defenders retreated step by step, fighting every inch, towards the Atlantic sea-board. The battle of Le Mans had laid Mayenne and Brittany open to the invaders.

The evening of January 17th, 1871, found all the

faithful of those departments united and urgent in their prayers for deliverance. Every local shrine of Our Lady was thronged with anxious suppliants; not least that of Nôtre-Dame d'Avenières at Laval, where the next German attack was expected at any hour. Pontmain shared the same peril.

It is well known that the stubborn French peasant will carry on with his immediate tasks, even when battle rages all round. Such was the experience of many in our forces in Normandy during the last war. So then it was at Pontmain. A local smallholder, César Barbadette, knew that even if the morrow brought Germans, that night his beasts must be fed. Soon after five o'clock, he called his sons Eugène and Joseph, aged twelve and ten, to help him cut up some fodder in the adjacent barn. A quarter of an hour later a friend, Jeanette Détais, pushed open the heavy door and came in with some news about the farmer's step-son at the front.

Urged by some impulse, Eugène went to the open door and looked out. He himself explained later that he had just gone "to look at the weather". It was intensely cold. Ice and snow glistened on the roofs of nearby cottages and the church across the way. The stars were brilliant. But the boy was puzzled. There was a curious blank space in the sky immediately above the house opposite. He regarded it and then, suddenly, between a triangle of specially brilliant stars, he saw the figure of a beautiful woman smiling at him. He was still staring when Jeanette took her leave. He asked her: "Look Jeanette, there above Augustin Guidecoq's. Tell me what you see."

"No, Eugène, I can see nothing."

Hearing the question, the others came to the door. The father seemed equally blind but Joseph, without hesitation, replied: "Yes! A tall, beautiful Lady!"

"How is she dressed?"

*OOSTACKER. The shrine of Our Lady of Lourdes in the Basilica and (below) the simple Grotto where Peter de Rudder was cured*

(Page 214)

*Our Lady of Pontmain, on the le*
(Page 219)
*and (below) the shrine of Our Lad*
*of Pellevoisin*
(Page 228)

"I see a tall, beautiful Lady in a blue dress covered with stars. She has blue shoes with gold buckles." He added that she wore a black veil on which was set a crown that widened out at the top, with a red line round the middle.

M. Barbadette was vexed. He took a second look and said: "You see nothing. If there was anything, we could see it as well as you. Come, finish the cutting at once. Supper must be ready."

The boys obeyed without a murmur but their thoughts were so sincerely on what they had seen that he sent Eugène to have another look.

"She is still there!" he cried.

"Go, then, and fetch your mother. Just tell her I want her." While Eugène was gone, Joseph slipped out and stood gazing at the sky, spellbound.

Mme. Barbadette's first action was to box her son's ears for forgetting to say "please". Then she found Joseph clapping his hands and shouting: "She is beautiful", so she smacked him too, telling him that he would be attracting all the neighbours.

Although she could see no more than her husband, Mme. Barbadette was deeply moved at her boys' admiration. They were not given to lying. Called upon later to give evidence under oath, both parents admitted that they could remember no previous instance of untruthfulness.

"Perhaps it is the Holy Virgin," she suggested. "Since you see, come into the barn and say five Our Fathers and Hail Marys."

This done, the boys declared the Lady was still there, so Mother Victoire, as Mme. Barbadette was called, went for her spectacles. Thus armed she scanned the skies, to the Lady's apparent amusement, for her smile widened. "Assuredly you see nothing at all," declared the bewildered mother. "You are little liars." The boys were shocked. They had not been called that before. Quietly they went back to their job.

After supper Mme. Barbadette reconsidered the matter. She sent Eugène and Joseph back and as they still persisted, she called in one of the nuns from the convent-school, Sister Vitaline, to advise. The Sister failed to see anything, but suggested that other children might, though not adults. She returned with three little girls from the convent; Françoise Richer, Jeanne-Marie Lebossé and Augustine Mouton. The last named could see nothing but as soon as Françoise reached the convent door she exclaimed that there was **something beautiful** "over M. Guidecoq's house".

When they arrived at the barn, both she and Jeanne-Marie were able to give a description of the Lady which tallied with the boys'. Another child aged 6, Auguste Friteau, who died soon after, saw the vision for ten minutes from his grandmother's arms; and a baby, aged two, squealed with delight at something which enchanted him in the same direction.

Another Sister ran and fetched the Curé, Michael Guérin, a celebrated priest renowned for his love of Our Lady, the possibilities of whose cause for beatification are being examined. He twitted the nun who fetched him, saying she scared him. But as soon as he reached the barn he realised that this was no case of hysteria or deception. Without interfering, he stood in the background and listened to the description of an apparent change in the vision being given by the four children.

A red cross had appeared on the Lady's breast; then an oval band of the deepest blue formed all round her, within the starry triangle which was clearly visible to all present, even though they could see no figure. These stars offer important evidence. Although the Apparition must have been in the direction of the constellation of the Great Bear, the three stars did not in any way correspond. Although some sixty people saw them that one night, the next they were gone.

At this juncture, certain onlookers began to argue about the nature of the event. Immediately the Lady became sad. When he heard of this, the Curé intervened for the first time, asking all to kneel and say the Rosary. The children, however, did not seem to hear, but remained standing, entranced. As the decades of the Rosary progressed, the figure began to increase in size and the stars on her dress multiplied. A cluster of forty, in pairs, gathered beneath her feet. By that time the onlookers were perished with cold so M. Barbadette flung open the barn for them. The children remained outside, erect, oblivious to the cold.

The Curé asked the nuns to sing the "Magnificat" and then the "Litany of Loreto". Now a long streamer began to unroll at the Lady's feet and these words, in simple French, were revealed: *"But pray, my children"*.

At that moment a passer-by, come from Laval, and unaware of what was happening, called in to the kneeling people: "You may well pray! The Germans are at Laval." The message in the sky continued to unfold: *"God will soon answer your prayers"*.

The crowd took this as prophetic and cried out: "The war is over. We shall have peace." But twelve year old Eugène rebuked them: "Yes! But go on praying."

If there was any doubt in the minds of the witnesses that the children were enjoying an Apparition of the Blessed Virgin, this was now removed; for the words on the streamer were replaced with a second message: *"My Son allows Himself to be moved in compassion"*.

At this, Our Lady's hands were raised shoulder high, palms outward, and she smiled more radiantly than at any time before. As swiftly this phase changed; she lowered her hands and, becoming ineffably sad, clasped a blood-red crucifix which appeared; surely nothing which four children could have imagined or invented simultaneously. On top of the cross was a second cross-bar, gleaming white, and upon it, in bold red letters, were the holy names, JESUS CHRIST.

Four small "candles" had appeared at four points within the blue oval. While the crowd sang "Parce Domine", these lit up and the crucifix faded, giving place to two luminous crosses which seemed to spring up from Our Lady's shoulders. Little by little the sadness passed and once more she began to smile. Finally, she extended her hands in much the same posture as that of the Miraculous Medal. A white cloud, visible to all, then began to blot out the space between the three stars. Our Lady's figure melted away, feet, body and, lastly, her head. The Apparition was gone.

At sunset that same evening, the German Commander-in-Chief announced in Le Mans: "My troops enter Laval tonight." A few hours later, coincident with the end of the Apparition, a totally unexpected order was handed to General Schmidt, forbidding him to take Laval. Next day the Prussians withdrew about ten miles. This is historic fact, humanly inexplicable. Catholic France accepted it as the outcome of Our Lady's intervention at Pontmain. Eleven days later the armistice was signed.

The subsequent history of the voyants is not without interest. Eugène became a secular priest and died, rector of Châtillon-sur-Colmont, in 1927. Joseph became an Oblate of Mary Immaculate and died a holy death in the house of his Congregation at Pontmain in 1930. Jeanne-Marie became a religious of the Holy Family nuns and died at Bordeaux in 1933. Françoise entered Abbé Barbadette's service and died in 1915.

The good Curé sent word of these events at Pontmain as soon as possible to the Bishop of Laval, but he remained silent. In the meantime, the news spread. Five hundred people attended a Mass of Thanksgiving at Pontmain on January 23rd. Six days later a pilgrimage of as many Bretons arrived: on February 6th a group of priests and layfolk from Coutances.

Then, on March 10th, General Charette, with a chaplain and several Zouave officers, arrived. They submitted the children to a terrifying examination, even threatening them with their swords. At the end the General remarked simply: "I believe".

Before long the Bishop visited the hamlet and set on foot a formal enquiry, as a result of which he declared from the pulpit his own personal belief but added his decision to hold a further inquest. A new tribunal was appointed, of prelates unlikely to be led astray through emotion, or easily deceived. A board of medical specialists, psychiatrists and alienists was chosen. As a result of their independent but unanimous findings, after consultation with the Holy See the Bishop was able to deliver formal judgment that a "veritable Apparition of the Immaculate Virgin had been vouchsafed at Pontmain"—Cultus was authorised, under title of Our Lady of Hope of Pontmain.

Father Guérin died in 1872 and was succeeded almost immediately by a Community of Oblates of Mary Immaculate who began at once on the building of the French National Votive Offering, in the form of a great twin-spired church. This was consecrated in 1900 and raised to basilica rank in 1905.

In 1877, permission to say the Mass of the Immaculate Conception at Pontmain was accorded by Pope Pius IX. In 1919, however, a new request was made, through Cardinal Dubois, for the privilege of an Office and Mass proper to Our Lady of Pontmain.

This was unusual as three voyants were still living. Pope Benedict XV ordered a new and severe enquiry. Although forty-eight years had elapsed, the two priests, witnesses, were able to give evidence and one of the chief doctors of the original panel. On April 16th, 1920, Mgr. Grellier was able to deliver a new judgment and the appeal for a special Mass was renewed. But Pope Benedict died and it was Pius XI who announced that Rome had given recognition in "its most beautiful form".

It is, perhaps, unique that the Holy See has authorised a proper office during the lifetime of two voyants who were thus required to recite in the lessons the story of their experiences and their own answers to questions asked by the tribunal.

As at the scenes of her other Apparitions, Our Lady seems to have set her seal on Pontmain with a number of attested miracles. One of the most noted instances is the case of Maria Vaugeois who suffered from a malformation of the spine. On August 14th, 1899, she assisted at the Mass for the Sick at Pontmain. Next day, after a long period of prayer in the new basilica, she was suddenly and completely cured. The cure was certified by three independent doctors.

Every day hundreds, at times thousands, of pilgrims throng to Pontmain, army veterans prominent among them. In spite of this popularity, the outward appearance of the village, which is only a little larger now, has not greatly changed. In a field immediately behind Augustin Guidecoq's house, the basilica towers up, like a miniature Cologne Cathedral. At the cross-roads stands the church, much as Pére Guérin left it, with many of his gifts still in place.

Nearby is the barn and the adjacent Barbadette home. The barn is fitted up as a chapel, the walls of which are decorated with scenes of the Apparition. Here there is a daily recitation of the great event.

Further up the street is an unpretentious house within which the pilgrim will find a very interesting collection of objects associated with the voyants and the history of the Sanctuary. In addition there is a truly marvellous collection of pictures of many hundreds of Our Lady's shrines, with replicas of many of her images.

There are two or three, quite primitive, hotels and as many souvenir shops. There is no railway—the best approach is from Mont St. Michel, the easiest from Laval, by motor coach. The Oblates of Mary Immaculate have a large monastery, surrounded by a park, with open-air altars and procession ways. Everything at Pontmain has one object and one objective; to render homage and thanksgiving to Our Lady of Hope.

In March, 1944, the Catholics of France repeated their vows to Our Lady of Pontmain, for deliverance from fresh German occupation. The ceremonies of the seventy-fifth anniversary offered a great opportunity for the fulfilment of those vows. Led by the Papal Nuncio and numbers of Bishops, an immense crowd foregathered for a triduum of functions, reminding the world that in the rôle of Deliverer, Our Lady of Hope is as effective in the twentieth century as she was in the days of the Barbary pirates and the crusades. Although, theologically, Pontmain cannot be said to rank with Lourdes, or Loreto, it is none the less a truly great and important seat of Marial devotion.

The statue in the basilica was honoured with the dignity of papal coronation at the instance of Pope Pius XI, in 1934, by the late Cardinal Verdier.

# XXVIII: PELLEVOISIN

COMPARED with Pontmain, the events known as the Apparitions of Our Lady of Pellevoisin, in 1876, which resulted in the formal recognition of the Sacred Heart Scapular, and the establishment by Papal Brief in 1896, of the Archconfraternity of Our Lady All-Merciful, form a great contrast.

Whereas the former place has been enriched with a fine basilica, a national votive offering, and the establishment of a fine domain, supervised by a religious order, Pellevoisin has remained in quiet seclusion, not to say oblivion, with almost none of the external adornments that are usually found at pilgrimage centres. It is, nonetheless, a remarkable shrine and, if only to complete the story of the nineteenth century Apparitions of Our Blessed Lady, something of its history may well be included in this series.

Pellevoisin, like Pontmain, is a small village with few pretensions. Its name, derived from the Latin *belli vicus,* place of war, is a reminder of some battle between Gauls and Romans in the days of Julius Cæsar. A warrior and his men were buried in a tumulus of exceptional magnitude. Today a gracious statue of Our Lady stands beneath a fine chestnut tree on its summit.

The village is in the department of Indre, and so in the Archdiocese of Bourges, and lies between Chateauroux and Tours, connected with the outside world by a single track, narrow-gauge line from

Buzançais, and two trains a day. It is a peaceful, sunny spot.

The surrounding countryside, a gently undulating plain, devoid of mountains, forests, or even rivers, has little to enliven it, but is quietly beautiful in its pastoral simplicity. There are few places in France more withdrawn from the world, or which lend themselves better to the quiet spirit of contemplation.

The village consists of a pretty, wide street of forty or fifty small houses leading to a good early-Gothic church dedicated to St. Martin of Tours. A few yards distant, half hidden by a dense shrubbery, is the comfortable-looking Convent of Dominican nuns, built fifty years ago. Before then, a solitary house stood there, a coach-house with two tenements, separated from the lane by some rough wooden palings; a building onto which has been joined intact the convent, as being the focus of Marial devotion at Pellevoisin, scene of the remarkable cure of a humble maid-servant.

Estelle Faguette was born in 1843, near Châlons-sur-Marne, of poor parents who soon after migrated to Paris in search of work. Estelle came under the influence of the Sisters of Charity, and so of the Miraculous Medal, and joined the Children of Mary in the parish of St. Thomas Aquinas. At eighteen, she entered the novitiate of the Augustinian Nuns of the Paris Hotel-Dieu but suffered a severe tumble and, after nearly three years, was obliged to relinquish her aspirations. Through her friends, the Sisters of Charity, she obtained employment with the Countess Arthur de la Rochefoucauld, who became very fond of her and gave her work compatible with her strength. By degrees, a severe internal tumour developed and then pulmonary consumption, from which Paris doctors declared no possibility of relief.

The Countess owned property at Pellevoisin and arranged for Estelle to spend her last days in one of these two tenements near the church, looked after by some nuns of the Order of Providence of Saumur. Her condition grew steadily worse, aggravated by mental anxiety that she was leaving her parents uncared for.

The patient lingered until February, 1896, when acute peritonitis intervened. On the 13th, Dr. Hubert of Buzançais called and told the Superior, Sister Marie-Theodosie, that Estelle had perhaps five hours to live. The parish priest, Abbé Salmon, gave the Last Sacraments which brought her exquisite peace of mind.

Entirely resigned, she begged that a message be sent to her mistress for tapers to be lighted for her at the shrine of Our Lady of Victories; which request was fulfilled, significantly, on the very next day, the 14th. Contrary to all expectations, Estelle was alive and fully conscious that night. Arrangements had been made for her funeral, and a grave in the local churchyard had been ordered by the nuns.

During the night of the 14th-15th, it seemed to Estelle that a demon appeared, half human, half animal, with a shaggy mane, horrible, grinning and stinking. This vision lasted several minutes and greatly terrified the dying woman. Then it seemed to her that Our Lady appeared near the bed and reassured her: "Fear nothing," she said, "you know well that you are my child".

Estelle was left full of optimistic happiness—a condition, by the way, not uncommonly associated with tuberculosis. The doctor, however, was astonished to find her alive next morning. The Curé, to whom she confided her strange story, was kindly sympathetic, having regard for the sad state of the poor woman; but he personally dismissed the matter as being one of entire illusion.

Three successive nights it seemed to Estelle that she experienced similar Apparitions, with the difference that each time the demon appeared further away, and that Our Lady gave her added assurance, first that she would be "dead or cured by Saturday", then, on the following night, that she would be cured on the Saturday.

Estelle became so positive in her assertions that the priest deemed it prudent not to remain the sole recipient of her strange prediction. He persuaded her to share her confidence with some other discreet persons, in order that they might bear witness to the exactitude of her prophecy. In spite of the fact that three doctors had declared death inevitable and imminent, seven people heard the patient repeat Our Lady's promise that she would be cured on February 19th.

But on the Friday her state was so much worse that the story seemed a mockery. The sore caused by her tumour was much larger and gave excruciating pain. Her right arm was paralysed, her breath feeble to the extreme. The Curé promised to give her Holy Communion next morning if she was still able to receive the Host.

He came at half-past six to hear Estelle's confession and she told him she was better, although her right arm was still helpless. The Curé promised to come back with the Blessed Sacrament after Mass.

At half-past seven he returned, followed by a number of those who were privy to the prophecy. As soon as Estelle had received Holy Communion, he spoke to her: "Poor Estelle. You have been brave and resigned. Now have great faith in Our Lady and, to show that all you have told us is not just a fantasy, will you make the Sign of the Cross with your right hand?" Immediately, without the least effort, she raised her arm and made a large sign. "Again!" cried the priest, with tears in his eyes. A second time, Estelle raised her arm, calling out that she was fully cured; then she rose and got out of bed.

Her friends immediately examined her. Her eyes

were clear, her breath fresh and regular, her movements co-ordinated; the inflammation had gone, the sore was completely healed; there was no trace of any illness or ill health whatsoever. Estelle left her bed as brightly as if she had just enjoyed a night's sleep. "What struck me most," declared the Sister Superior, "was the speed with which her skeleton was covered with flesh, plump and healthy."

Estelle Faguette, thus marvellously cured—the miraculous has never been pronounced upon—lived at Pellevoisin until August 23rd, 1929, when she died at the age of eighty-five. Wonderful though her recovery was, and even had there been in it certain proof of Our Lady's intervention, which there seems no particular reason to deny, it is doubtful if Pellevoisin would have become widely known. But during the alleged Apparitions, five in number, which preceded her cure, Estelle claimed to have been recipient of commands and promises from her heavenly visitor. In the fifth visit, the Lady was said to have stated:

"I am all-merciful and have power over my Son . . . If you wish to serve me, be simple so that your words and deeds agree . . . One can be saved in any state (of life). Where you are, you can do much good and publish my glory." The Lady then saddened. "What distresses me most is the lack of respect for my Son . . ." (here there is marked resemblance to the message of La Salette) ". . . both in Holy Communion and during prayer, when the mind is often distracted. I say this of those who pretend to be pious . . . Publish my glory, but, before you speak, take advice from your Confessor. You will have setbacks— people will treat you as a voyante, as a fool. Pay no heed to that. Be faithful and I will help you."

Abbé Salmon had heard all this prior to Estelle's recovery which, it seemed to him, came as confirmation of her story. He was prudent, and neglected to take no testimony available. Certificates and letters were obtained from the doctors and witnesses of the cure, and a written statement was made by Estelle. But, even so, it might be said that there was little to involve Pellevoisin, apart from some local recognition of a very great favour—miracle even—granted by the Mother of God to one of her more humble clients.

For several months there was little development. Estelle did not go back to her work immediately. Perhaps it was considered wiser for her to remain in the Archdiocese, pending enquiries, and close to the scene of her cure. She felt baffled because there seemed little for her to do to fulfil her promise to work for Our Lady's glory.

At about half-past ten on the Eve of the Visitation of Our Lady, and, incidentally, of the consecration of the basilica at Lourdes, Estelle was saying her prayers in her little room when she realised the presence of the Blessed Virgin, as in February, surrounded by a soft light.

Our Lady, it seemed to her devoted subject, was dressed in a white robe, fastened at the waist with a white cord, with a long white veil hung from her head to her ankles. She appeared in the midst of a transparent, bluish cloud and, at times, rays of light streamed from the palms of her hands, as in the Visions of Saint Catherine Labouré. Furthermore, her figure was surrounded, from head to foot, by a large aureole, or oval, of roses, white, yellow and red, which gave forth an exquisite scent. It seemed to Estelle, too, that she carried on her breast a white scapular with the image of the Sacred Heart of Jesus. She appeared very close, at about the height of the fireplace, and looked at her client with marked tenderness. Estelle declared later: "When one has seen the Blessed Virgin, one wants to die to see her again," a remark similar to Saint Bernadette's.

Thus began the second phase of visions in which the woman who had received such extraordinary favour was inspired to establish a work that has in fact spread far and wide. In all, Estelle enjoyed fifteen such experiences, five in February prior to her recovery, the others on July 1st, 2nd, and 3rd; September 9th, 10th and 15th; November 1st, 5th and 11th; and the Feast of the Immaculate Conception. This last was undoubtedly the most beautiful.

It seemed to Estelle that, during the course of these visions, her celestial visitor spoke freely to her, often for many minutes at a time, largely on the subject of her own spiritual life. It is impossible to relate all that was said, though verbatim records in Estelle Faguette's own writing are preserved. Much was a resumé of the messages given at Pontmain, Lourdes, La Salette and the Holy Chapel, Paris. For example, taking up the thread of the warnings given to Maximin and Mélanie, Estelle reported that Our Lady said with marked sadness: "As for France, what have I not done for her? She still refuses to pay heed. Very well, I can no longer restrain my Son. *France will suffer much.*"

At another time she said: "You have already proclaimed my glory. Go on doing so. My Son has souls devoted to Him. His Heart has so much love for me that He cannot refuse my requests. Through me, He will touch the hardest of hearts. I have come especially for the conversion of sinners."

On September 9th, Estelle was saying her Rosary when the glorious vision was renewed. She was given the most fruitful message of all: "For a long time my Son's treasures have been made known. Let them pray." Here Estelle said she was given to understand that Jesus had shown, through Saint Margaret Mary, the glory and the power of the devotion to His Most Sacred Heart.

Then the Mother of Our Saviour held up the little

piece of white flannel which formed the scapular on her breast, and exposed a red Heart surmounted by a Cross, surrounded by a Crown of Thorns, wounded with a lance. From the wound fell drops of blood and water. The Heart stood out vividly against the white background.

As Our Lady held it forward, she uttered these words: "I love this devotion." Then, looking round the room she added: "It is here that I shall be honoured."

Estelle learned by intuition, she explained, that it would be her duty to promote devotion through a scapular made after this pattern.

The last Apparition was vouchsafed after the High Mass on December 8th. The room had, in the meantime, been changed into an oratory for the use of the local Children of Mary, with the explicit permission of the Archbishop. A shrine, with a figure of Our Lady of Lourdes surrounded by roses, had been made on the mantelpiece. Estelle entered soon after midday, with several of the Sisters. The Apparition began at once. The Curé and the Countess de la Rochefoucauld were fetched and, with a number of others, crowded into the room for the remaining period of the ecstasy.

After telling Estelle to call to mind all that had been told her in the previous Apparitions, the Lady said: "You will see me no more," and gave her own scapular for her servant to kiss. Then she continued: "Go yourself to the Prelate and give him the copy you have made. Tell him to help you with all his power, and that nothing would be more agreeable to me than to see this badge on each one of my children, in reparation for the outrages that my Son suffers in the Sacrament of His Love. See the graces that I pour on those who will wear it with confidence, and who help to make it known."

Again it seemed as if a shower of graces, sparkling like diamonds, poured from the hands of the Mediatrix of All Graces. "These graces are from my Son; I take them from His Heart; He cannot refuse me."

With regard to the blank side of the scapular, Our Lady told Estelle: "I reserve it for myself. Submit what you think best. The Church will decide."

The Prelate, the Most Reverend Charles, Prince de la Tour d'Auvergne, Archbishop of Bourges, had been watching these events at Pellevoisin with much concern. He agreed to receive Estelle at once and kept her two days, cross-examining her, with the result that he wrote to Abbé Salmon urging him to have a number of scapulars made as soon as possible.

He then appointed a Commission of fifty-six ecclesiastics, under the Vicar General, to enquire into matters. Of them all, one alone refrained from giving an opinion. The rest were unanimous, that the Apparitions were indubitable and of supernatural character. Even so, the Archbishop forebore from pronouncing on the subject at once. Several years had elapsed in the cases of the Rue du Bac, La Salette and Lourdes. But he was prepared to act in other directions. He laid the findings of his Commission before the Roman Congregations and gained blessings for his project from Pope Pius IX.

This was to found at Pellevoisin a Confraternity under the protection of the Mother-all-Merciful, to radiate devotion to the Sacred Heart through the newly designed scapular. On the first anniversary of the revelation, he blessed the Chapel at Pellevoisin and said Mass therein, after which he himself enthroned the new statue of Our Lady of Pellevoisin, *toute miséricordieuse*.

Mgr. Chigi, Papal Legate in France at the time, was one of the first to join the Confraternity and to accept a scapular. In the following year, before he

*Our Lady of Fatima*

(Page 240)

*Our Lady of Beauraing officially erected
in 1946*

(Page 252)

*and (below) the "Beautiful Lady" as
she appeared to Mariette Beco at
Banneux*

(Page 260)

had time to take steps which he obviously contemplated, the Archbishop died.

If Pope Pius IX had assisted in promoting the Mission of Pellevoisin, Leo XIII did more. In 1896, at the request of Cardinal Boyer, he raised the Confraternity to Archconfraternity status, without pronouncing in any way on the character of the Apparitions. Three days later the Pontiff bestowed an extraordinary number of indulgences to be gained on the dates of the chief appearances.

In 1900 Estelle herself was accorded the great privilege of a visit to Rome, with the Duchess of Estissac, the Countess's sister-in-law, and a long audience with the Pope; from whom she solicited and obtained approval for the scapular "for the entire world".

Before the end of the year tragedy had occurred. The bitter trials foretold came to pass. Estelle became the object of an abominable calumny which put the cause of Pellevoisin into grave difficulties. The author of this injustice, maladroit rather than wicked, confessed and retracted long after, but not before his pernicious story had reached the Bishop's House and the Vatican. The Pope, who had been prepared, it is said, to give the Apparitions his highest sanction, suspended judgment; suspended, without in any way expressing disapproval or reducing the recognition already accorded to the scapular and Archconfraternity.

Certain revisions were made in 1904 to the rules and privileges of the Archconfraternity. The Congregation of Rites, by decree of April 4th, 1900, had already approved the scapular. This was renewed, under the signature of Cardinal Vanutelli, but the title of the Archconfraternity was fixed as that of the Mother of Mercy, and with the instruction that, in all future instances, images of Our Lady of

Pellevoisin should not depict the Blessed Virgin *wearing* the scapular. Far from condemning, this decree gave great encouragement to parish priests to institute the Archconfraternity in their parishes.

Finally, because enemies were all for interpreting various instructions from the Holy See as condemnations of the Apparitions, Cardinal Merry del Val wrote in 1907, to Cardinal Coullie of Lyons and to the Archbishop of Bourges that: "neither directly nor indirectly" had any decree of the Holy See approved (or disapproved) these Apparitions, and the sole prohibition had been against speaking of them "as Apparitions approved by the Holy See".

"It is in this sense," the Cardinal wrote in his official capacity, "and in no other, that the letters of the Sacred Congregation of the Council must be understood."

And how about Pellevoisin today? Is it still a centre of pilgrimage? Certainly. Large numbers of well-organised pilgrimages go there every year, often led by bishops. In particular each year, on September 9th, there is a great rally, often led by the Archbishop of Bourges and supported by a number of other diocesans.

The house of the Apparitions is now adjoined to a large Dominican Convent. A grille divides the nuns' choir from the altar and shrine in the room where Estelle was restored to health. There, about twenty-six nuns daily sing the Divine Office. A fine park surrounds the convent, where the ceremonies of the more important pilgrimages take place. The parish church, the same fine Gothic church which Estelle and Abbé Salmon knew, is the official and worthy seat of the great Archconfraternity which is said, with its numerous affiliations, to number about two million members.

Although no formal pronouncement has been made

on the subject of the Apparitions, all that was asked in them has been accomplished. Estelle neither desired, nor sought for, personal credit; expected only the bitterness which was her lot, and the calumnies from which she has been completely exonerated.

She was laid to rest in the local churchyard where her tomb is treated with respect by the local inhabitants. On the stone are engraved these two words, addressed to her in the course of the Apparitions: "Sois Simple"—"Be simple".

Pellevoisin has to offer just that which Our Lady seems to have intended—a place of retreat from the noise and tumult of the world and a profound opportunity to make reparation, through Our Lady of Mercy, for the sacrileges and offences committed against the Sacred Heart of her Son.

# XXIX:  THE MESSAGE OF FATIMA

FOR twenty-nine months, the World War of 1914-18 had rumbled on with all its attendant horrors of poison gas, flame-throwers, and aerial bombardment of civilians when, on May 5th, 1917, Pope Benedict XV decreed the Crusade of Prayer for Peace. In particular, he asked for unstinted use of the Rosary, and inserted the invocation "Queen of Peace, pray for us", immediately after that addressed to the Queen of the Most Holy Rosary in the Litany of Our Lady generally called the Litany of Loreto.

The launching of this Crusade was no act of optimism, with the end of the war in sight, but a desperate eleventh hour remedy. On the Western Front the conflict wallowed, stalemated, in a sea of mud and blood. Daily casualty lists of appalling length reported the sacrifice of countless young lives in hideous circumstances. In the East, the Czarist Regime had already begun its headlong fall and no one could foretell the horrors that would follow the left-wing revolution. Lenin and Trotsky arrived in Petrograd on April 16th.

Remote from this bloodshed, but deep in a country which had only recently suffered from bitter civil war, whose king was living in exile, and where the plums of office had been snatched by materialistic anti-clericals, was a group of hamlets which formed the parish of Fatima, in the diocese at that time of the Cardinal Patriarch of Lisbon.

The remote country hamlets of Europe, in the days before wireless brought the most distant cottage within a few seconds of the latest city news, carried on their

240

usual way of life with a stolid indifference. The daily sweat of wringing an existence from a stubborn soil did not allow much time for reflection upon the latest alarms from Paris or Moscow. A number of Catholics struggled bravely on in defence of their Faith, resentful of the often scurrilous attacks of a free-thinking Press on their Pastors and their Creed. Many of the half-hearted had lapsed, or salved their consciences with an occasional attendance at some Feast-day. As usual, country places remained more loyal than towns. Thus it was in the hamlet of Aljustrel, in the parish of Fatima. People carried on as in the past, poor, lacking many modern amenities, but by no means penurious or as ignorant as the absence of book-learning might tempt half-educated townsfolk to believe. They who for generations have had to make their living from the soil teach their children the same way from an early age. In particular, flocks must be watched and kept on the move lest, by over-grazing, they destroy valuable pasture. This is a job quite small children can manage, more profitably than their elders who have harder manual labour to perform.

Therefore, on Sunday morning, May 13th, 1917, three cousins, Lucy dos Sandos, aged ten, Francis and Jacinta Marto, aged nine and seven, set out to tend their sheep in a valley known locally as the Cova da Iria. Watching sheep does not require a child's whole attention and they started to play at building houses when, soon after the midday Angelus, they were startled by a brilliant flash of lightning. Not a cloud could be seen but, fearing a tempest, they started for home. A second blinding flash frightened them even more and they would have run, but were brought to a standstill by an extraordinary sight. A few feet away, resting on the foliage of a little evergreen oak, was a dazzling globe of light, in the centre of which they could see, more glorious than the sun, the figure of a beautiful Lady. She seemed to be less than eighteen years of age and was dressed in a white robe, fastened at the neck with a gold cord, which reached down to her bare feet. A white veil, richly embroidered with gold, covered her head and reached to her ankles. Her hands were placed together, in an attitude of prayer; from her right hand hung a rosary with a silver chain and cross, and luminous pearls for beads.

If the globe of light and the sunshine call to mind the beginning of the Apparition of La Salette, so do the first words spoken by the Lady. "Don't be frightened. I shall not harm you."

After several moments of awe and astonishment, Lucy summoned up her courage and spoke:

"Where do you come from?"

"From Heaven," the Lady replied.

"What have you come here for?"

"To ask you to come back here every month on the same date until October, when I shall tell you who I am and what I want you to do."

Thus began the most startling, the most extraordinary, the most ominous and best attested of all recorded series of acknowledged Apparitions of the Blessed Mother of God.

In variant form the three children went through all the trials and tribulations suffered by those others to whom she has deigned to appear. They were scoffed at, treated as liars and young criminals, persecuted, threatened with death, cast into gaol. But they persisted and, as with Saint Bernadette, managed somehow to fulfil their promise to keep their tryst in the Cova da Iria, on the 13th of June, July, September and October. On August 13th they were locked up in prison but in spite of the children's absence, many people witnessed certain phenomena associated with these Apparitions, and Our Lady appeared to the three six days later at another pasture called Valinhos.

**Already** many books have been published, giving in detail the text of the Conversations conducted by Our Lady with Lucy and Jacinta. Francis always saw the Vision but never heard the Lady speak. Likewise there has been much written on the subject of various secrets given to Lucy, some of which have been published since, in accordance with Our Lady's apparent wishes. One of the most authoritative of these books is one easily obtainable: *More about Fatima,* by Rev. V. Montes de Oca, C.S.Sp., which is based very largely on the work of Father Gonzaga da Fonseca, S.J., Professor at the Biblical Institute at Rome, one of the greatest authorities on the subject of Fatima. Father Fonseca's book, "Le Meraviglie di Fatima", comes (in its fourth edition) from the Vatican Press with the imprimatur of the Vicar General of the Vatican City. Such an imprimatur, of course, does not involve in any way the infallibility of the Church, any more than the revelations of Fatima constitute truths of Faith. It constitutes, however, an unusually sound guarantee that the events of Fatima have been subjected to official enquiry, in obedience to all canonical regulations. It is not necessary, then, to repeat in detail the entire text of what transpired. Sufficient here to record the more important utterances and requests made by Our Lady of Fatima.

On June 13th, the Feast of St. Anthony, the children gave up attending the annual parish feast to be present at the Cova da Iria. Then Lucy was asked to recite the Rosary every day. On this occasion several witnesses, unable to see the Lady, observed that the sun grew dim at the moment of the Apparition and that the branches of the tree where Our Lady appeared bent as if beneath an invisible weight. All heard the loud report, as of a rocket, which marked the end of the Vision, and saw a white cloud which moved away from the tree in an easterly direction. The third

Apparition was attended by a crowd of several thousand people. The previous instruction, to say the Rosary, was amplified; with the additional command: "Sacrifice yourselves for sinners and say often, especially when you make your sacrifices, 'Oh Jesus, it is for love of Thee, for the conversion of sinners, and in reparation for offences committed against the Immaculate Heart of Mary'."

The Lady then taught the children to insert a prayer between each decade of the Rosary: "Oh Jesus, forgive us our sins, save us from the fires of hell, and take to Paradise all souls, especially those that have need of mercy". All present again witnessed the dimming of the sun, and the white cloud which mingled with the branches of the tree, departing at the close of the Apparition, with the same loud report.

Before August 13th, civil authority, strongly anti-clerical, intervened, delighted to have the opportunity of exposing, as they thought, a clear example of ecclesiastical fraud. The sub-prefect of the region, Arthur d'Oliviera Santos, took the three youngsters into custody and, after vain attempts to squeeze out anything that could be interpreted as retraction, had them put into gaol with adult criminals, threatening them with dire penalties. During re-examination, Santos told the gaoler to get ready a cauldron of boiling oil. Then, one by one, the children were taken out, for all they knew to die. When it came to be Lucy's turn, he told her: "Your sister is already dead. The same fate awaits you unless you confess." But the girl let herself be led away, to what she thought was certain death, unshaken. In prison, the children knelt and offered their misery for the honour of the Immaculate Heart of Mary and for the conversion of sinners. They were detained until August 15th, when the magistrate could find no further excuse for detaining them.

Although no Apparition occurred on August 13th, the crowd assembled saw the white cloud settle on the tree after the flash of lightning and then float away, after a short interval, in the direction from which it had come.

On August 19th, Lucy, Francis and Jacinta were rewarded for their constancy by an unpredicted Appearance at another pasture, Valinhos. The Lady asked for processions, with great honour, of Our Lady of the Rosary, and concluded by exhorting them to pray fervently, especially for those whose souls are lost because there is nobody to pray or make sacrifices for them.

All the civil authorities' attack did was to publicise the events at the Cova da Iria. It is estimated that thirty thousand were present on September 13th. Although this figure may be an exaggeration, it is clear that exceptionally large numbers were gathered there.

This time, Mgr. John Quaresma, the Vicar General, attended incognito, in order to report to the somewhat sceptical, but deeply concerned, Cardinal Patriarch. Various external phenomena were clearly visible. A globe of light appeared from the east and settled on the usual tree, followed by the cloud seen previously. Then, from the clear sky, began to fall a rain, like manna, of white petals which dissolved before they came within reach. This phenomenon was repeated on several occasions; notably May 13th, 1918, and March 13th, 1924.

The children received further guidance and instruction. A promise, made in June, that a great miracle would be performed on October 13th, was renewed though, on account of the August interference, its magnitude was to be reduced. The Lady gave approval to the suggestion that part of many offerings left at the oak-bush should be used to build a chapel.

She also promised to heal certain sick but not others, because, she said, Our Lord did not have confidence in them.

The Vicar General also saw the globe of light rise and depart.

October 13th was, by prediction, the greatest day. An amazing crowd of not less than fifty thousand foregathered, expecting the extraordinary miracle. Had they been disappointed, had the "apparitions" been simply hoaxes, it is well-nigh certain that the children would have been lynched. The day dawned cold and wet. The fields were a sea of mud. The Apparition began, as usual, with thunder, lightning and the arrival of the cloud.

First of all the Lady proclaimed her identity: "I am Our Lady of the Rosary. I want a chapel built here in my honour where the Rosary must be recited every day." Later she warned: "Men must change their ways, not to offend Our Lord, who is already greatly offended. They must say the Rosary and do penance for their sins."

"If men repent, the War will soon end."

Then the Blessed Virgin extended her hands, as on the Miraculous Medal, and beams of light poured from them. To the children were shown, after the manner of the Pontmain Apparition, three scenes, first of the Holy Family, with St. Joseph and Our Lady representing Our Lady of the Rosary; then of Our Lord, as a fully-grown man, blessing the world, beside the figure of Our Lady of Sorrows; thirdly, Our Lady of Mount Carmel, with scapular in hand.

But while the three children were gazing on these strange representations, the crowd was being treated to a very different spectacle. The sun, which had hitherto been obscured by clouds, broke through; but with the kind of light associated with eclipses. Then the orb began to shake and tremble, and to spin wildly like a fierce Catherine-wheel, casting beams of light of all colours. It was fantastic to see and watch the faces of fifty thousand people turned upward to gaze upon this horrific event. For four minutes, the sun seemed to spin; then paused, to spin again for as many minutes; and then a third time. This extraordinary sight, recorded in no known observatory, was witnessed impartially by friend and foe alike. Fifty thousand people of various races and creeds, and no creeds, observed it. People living several miles away, unaware of what was happening at the Cova da Iria, gave identical reports.

After the third wild spin, the sun seemed to break away from its place in the sky and then to rush forward, zigzagging in its course, as if about to plunge onto the heads of the terrified spectators. Many, believing their last hour to have come, made hasty acts of contrition and fell on their knees, imploring God's mercy. Bitter sceptics and virulent critics were instantly convinced, to remain faithful until the present day; for many who witnessed this unparalleled spectacle are living. Then, stopping short in its fall, the sun zigzagged back to its normal place and brilliance in the unclouded sky.

This solar phenomenon of October 13th, 1917, was described in many of the Portuguese newspapers of the period. That it was witnessed by many thousands of people, of all conditions and classes and viewpoints, and by people several miles away, as well as by those present in the Cova, precludes any explanation on the grounds of collective illusion or mass hysteria. Neither can the most stringent critic in any way produce or maintain any suggestion of fraud or artificiality. No known mechanism, however scientifically constructed, is capable of reproducing similar affects under comparable conditions.

Portuguese Catholic authority watched events at

Fatima carefully and prudently. Whatever opinions may have been held until October 13th, the solar prodigy changed the situation. The most violent anti-clerical newspaper was obliged to admit as much next morning. Curious reflection. When did any daily newspaper in this country make reference to these events, as thrilling as any volcanic eruption or display of aurora borealis?

On November 3rd, the Patriarchal Curia prescribed a serious enquiry into "Fatima". Two months later, the Pope re-established the ancient Diocese of Leiria, to include Fatima, and one of the new Bishop's first duties was to conduct this investigation. In due course the Canonical Commission began its task and, after numerous sessions, over long years of painstaking work, made its final report in a document of thirty-one chapters, April 14th, 1929.

At last the Bishop was able to act. On October 13th, 1930, before a gathering of a hundred thousand people at Cova da Iria he proclaimed: (1) that the visions with which the children were favoured were worthy of credence; (2) that the cult of Our Lady of Fatima was officially authorised.

The National Pilgrimage of Thanksgiving followed, May 13th, 1931, led by the Cardinal Patriarch of Lisbon and the Portuguese Hierarchy, supported by three hundred thousand pilgrims, a high percentage of the total population of the country.

It was further revealed during the enquiry that Our Lady had made other statements to the children which had not immediately been made public. On May 13th, they had seen Our Lady reveal her Immaculate Heart surrounded by thorns, afflicted by the sins of the world, asking for reparation and penance. On July 13th, they were shown a vision of Hell, after which the Blessed Virgin told them:

"You have just seen Hell, wherein are cast the souls

of poor sinners. To save them, the Lord wishes to establish in the world devotion to my Immaculate Heart. If people do as I tell you, many souls will be saved, and there will be Peace."

"The War will end. (This was in 1917.) But if people do not stop offending the Lord, another worse than this will start during the next Pontificate."

The Spanish Civil War, in which Russian, German and Italian troops took active part, was indeed the first round in the universal conflict which thus began in the Pontificate of Pius XI.

This revelation continued: "When you see the night lit up by a great unknown light, know this to be a sign from God that the punishment of the world is at hand, by war, famine and persecution against the Church and Holy Father.

"To prevent this, I shall ask for the consecration of the world to my Immaculate Heart, and for Communion of Reparation on the first Saturdays of each month.

"If my requests are heeded, Russia will be converted and there will be peace. If not, she will spread her errors through the world, provoking wars and persecution against the Church. Many will be martyred. The Holy Father will have much to suffer. Several nations will be destroyed. But, in the end, my Immaculate Heart will triumph."

Appalling prophecy, yet pregnant with hope. Can it be said that the world, or any part of it, has obeyed or heeded these requests?

Portugal was consecrated to the Immaculate Heart of Mary, at Fatima, on May 13th, 1931.

On October 31st, 1942, Pope Pius XII associated himself with the closing celebrations of the Fatima Jubilee by consecrating the world, and Russia in particular, to the Immaculate Heart of Mary.

On July 16th, 1948, at the conclusion of the great

pilgrimage of Prayer and Penance to Walsingham, Cardinal Griffin, Archbishop of Westminster, made the solemn act of Consecration to the Immaculate Heart of Mary on behalf of England.

Furthermore, in its desire to promote devotion to the Immaculate Heart, the Holy See has extended the Office and Feast to the universal Church, for August 22nd.

In wise anticipation, the Bishop of Leiria, diocesan of Fatima, bought a large area of land surrounding the scene of the Apparitions and allowed Mass to be said there on occasion as early as 1921. This estate today constitutes the sanctuary of Fatima. The first small chapel was destroyed by atheists in the following year. It was soon rebuilt at the site of the evergreen oak which, regrettably, was torn to pieces by souvenir hunters.

Almost immediately, local authorities were faced with the necessity of supplying water for the press of pilgrims. It was decided to dig out a huge cistern to collect rain water. Workmen had hardly begun digging when they struck a hitherto unsuspected spring, so copious that it has never since failed to meet the heavy demands made upon it. On October 13th, 1928, a child, blind and dumb from birth, was cured. A second wonderful cure took place in May, 1929, again with use of water from this newly discovered spring, in the heart of the Cova chosen by Mary. Since then, a considerable number of cures has been attested. The Benediction of the Sick with the Blessed Sacrament, as at Lourdes, and the use of water from what is now called the Miraculous Fountain, fitted with taps, form important acts of all big pilgrimages.

Nearby stands the simple, almost primitive, chapel of the Apparitions wherein is the statue of Our Lady of Fatima recently crowned at the instance of Pope Pius XII. On the hillside overlooking the domain, on the very spot where Lucy, Francis and Jacinta had played at building houses, rises the basilica of the Immaculate Heart of Mary, 270 feet long and 165 feet high, with altars in honour of each of the fifteen mysteries of the Most Holy Rosary.

Other important buildings include the hospital for the many sick and the medical bureau. It is officially stated that about a thousand cures of diseases of all kinds have been recorded; though, wonderful as this may be, and undoubtedly is for the individuals so blessed, comparatively few may be certified as miraculous. The Church in her wisdom is ever jealous of the use of this epithet.

It is stated that one sixth of the total population of Portugal goes to Fatima each year.

This, then, is the essence of the story of the birth of a twentieth century addition to the many great sanctuaries of Our Blessed Lady. Every episode of it has happened within the last thirty-three years, within the lifetime of a great number of people now living. The facts are readily available, nothing relative is hidden, though certain secrets entrusted to Lucy remain secret. Fatima is open to all, Catholic and non-Catholic, Christian and atheist alike. The story is unimpeachable. If one desires witnesses, there are many. The principal voyante, Lucy, is a Carmelite nun; her companions died, as predicted, quite soon after the Apparitions. Those who require miracles to strengthen their faith, or to substantiate the message given by the three children, must ask themselves what more can be offered. The blind see, the deaf hear, the very sun has paid tribute.

Mary has shown the way by which the world may be converted and led to peace. Fatima, then, is more than "just another shrine". It is a blazing torch, a beacon, to guide humanity towards the triumph of Her Immaculate Heart.

# XXX:  BEAURAING

MANY of those who, rightly, are paying close attention to the subject of Our Lady's Apparitions at Fatima, in 1917, tend to the belief that they are the latest of all recognised appearances of the Blessed Mother of God, and so to disregard, albeit unwittingly, another highly important sequence that was vouchsafed fifteen years later to five children at Beauraing.

Beauraing is a typical, largish village in the Walloon area of Belgium, twelve miles from Dinant. Its inhabitants are simple, industrious country-folk who, especially prior to 1932, were touched with something of that curious Walloon indifference in matters religious which puts them into such marked contrast with their Flemish neighbours. By no means a tourist centre at the time, it attracted many visitors to its great feudal castle and to the nearby celebrated Caves of Han.

It was in this setting that occurred, between November 29th, 1932, and January 3rd, 1933, no less than thirty-three episodes that ecclesiastical authority has decreed may be accepted as true Apparitions of Our Blessed Lady and which permit Beauraing to be ranked with Lourdes, Fatima and La Salette as a chosen sanctuary of the Immaculate Virgin.

As the Bishop of Tarbes and Lourdes publicly declared last summer in the pulpit at Lourdes: "The cultus of Our Lady of Beauraing completes magnificently that of Lourdes . . . Lourdes and

Beauraing are the complements of one another. Thanks must be given to Our Lady for having visited both Lourdes and Beauraing.''

After more than ten years of scrupulous investigation by theologians, doctors and scientists, all acutely conscious of their task, the Bishop of Namur, in whose diocese these events occurred, issued, in 1943, the decree authorising the *cultus* of Our Lady of Beauraing and the propagation of the Message there revealed to the children and by virtue of a special decree of approval from the Holy Office, dated December 7th, 1942.

The subject is too vast to be enlarged upon in a few paragraphs. Already many books have been written. This summary may be taken as a simple guide to the more outstanding episodes.

On the evening November 29th, 1932, two children, Férnande Voisin, aged 15, and her brother Albert, 11, went to meet their sister, Gilberte, 13, who was due to come out of the convent school at half-past six. They were joined by Andrée Degeimbre, 15, and her sister, also Gilberte, 9½, who had planned to take part in some practical jokes on the way home, ringing doorbells of certain irascible neighbours.

Gilberte Voisin, whose father was an official at the local railway station, attended the school run by the Sisters of Christian Doctrine in a large house that backed onto the main line, at a corner where the street passed under a stone viaduct. A fair-sized garden, with tall railings, bordered this street and a Lourdes grotto had been built which partly hid the unsightly embankment.

Just as Gilberte was coming out of school, Albert exclaimed that he could see a bright light moving by the viaduct. The others turned expecting to see the reflection of a motor's headlamps. Simultaneously all five children were conscious that they were gazing upon "the figure of a lady, dressed in a long robe of pure white"; and, as instantly, that the lady they saw was none other than the Blessed Virgin, walking to and fro on the embankment.

No one at home gave the slightest credence to this story, and the older children were almost convinced that they had been deceived. But there was no more bell-ringing! Next evening they went, as usual, to meet Gilberte Voisin, half hoping, half fearing what might happen. There was an almost exact repetition of the previous night's events. The children ran into Madame Degeimbre's house crying out in triumphant tones: "We've seen her! It *is* the Blessed Virgin, and she is much more beautiful than her statues!"

Mme. Degeimbre was furious, forbade her two children to go again to the convent and told M. Voisin that he must go himself in future to fetch his daughter.

But reason prevailed. The whole village was laughing, so Mme. Degeimbre armed with a big stick went with the four children to meet Gilberte on December 1st. Scarcely had they reached the garden when the children saw Our Lady face to face on the path in front of the grotto. She had a crown of golden rays shining on her head. Mme. Degeimbre could see nothing, ordered the four to run and fetch Gilberte Voisin, and started to thrash the bushes. Immediately the children returned, the Vision reappeared, as glorious as ever.

Gilberte Degeimbre, the youngest, was overcome with emotion at what she saw, so exquisite was the beauty of the Vision. She had to be taken home and was left there with Gilberte Voisin. Soon after eight, the other three children returned, together with several adults. Now the Apparition was renewed, on the lowest branch of a small may tree, just inside the garden fence beside the road. This was the site of the remaining appearances.

Mme. Degeimbre was so struck by the effect on, and the behaviour of, the children that she herself was unable to doubt further. M. Voisin searched with a torch but could find no trace of fraud. They fetched the parish priest who was, throughout, a model of prudence. He smiled, agreed to say a Mass in honour of Our Lady on December 8th, and advised them to discuss matters with no one.

Next morning the Reverend Mother of the convent intervened. She scolded Gilberte Voisin most severely, forbidding her ever again to mention such a "ridiculous story". She forbade the others to enter the garden any more and told Fernande that, being the eldest, she was old enough to know better. She ordered the gate to be locked at dusk and a fierce dog to be set loose inside.

The next evening, December 2nd, all five children returned with their parents and certain well-known Catholic men of the parish. Again the Apparition appeared at the may-tree, and the children saw much more than on the previous nights. Questioned immediately afterwards, and separately, they agreed that Our Lady was dressed in a white robe that reflected a blue kind of light. It was Albert who asked the first question proposed: "Are you the Immaculate Virgin?" The Lady smiled and nodded her head. "What do you want?" The simple reply was given —the first words uttered by Our Lady at Beauraing, and heard by all five children—"Always be good".

Thus the Apparitions continued. The children were told in particular to come "on the day of the Immaculate Conception". That evening there was a crowd of 15,000 spectators, including the Commissioner of Police and several secret police. The grotto was illuminated, but, at ten minutes past six, as soon as the children arrived, escorted by their parents and a number of specially chosen doctors and psychologists, they saw Our Lady, radiant and glorious, in the usual place.

Because Gilberte Degeimbre was so much the the youngest, the scientists considered that she would be the least inclined to any possible fraud. At the very start, Dr. Maistriaux saw she was weeping and asked why. "Because she is so very beautiful," was the reply. A few seconds later she failed to answer and it was found that she was in complete ecstasy. Each child was examined in turn by different doctors and found to be in a similar state.

Dr. Leurguin, of Houyet, put a lighted match under Gilberte Voisin's left hand, long enough to cause a smart burn. There was no recoil. Other doctors pinched, slapped and pricked the five children without response. They even stabbed a pen-knife into Albert's face. When electric torches were shone into their eyes, they remained insensitive.

In the meantime, the huge crowd was saying the Rosary. As soon as the last decade was finished the children cried out with tears: "She is gone".

Later Fernande explained: "I could see nothing, neither fence, nor tree, nor crowd: only the Holy Virgin who smiled at us".

But what surprised the panel of doctors most was the fact that they could find not the slightest trace of burning on Gilberte Voisin's hand, not even a blister or sign of scorching! All she could say to her father after her examination was: "Just think of it! They tried to tell me they had pricked me and burned me!"

The visions continued, thirty-three in all. On December 17th, Our Lady asked for a chapel to be built so that people might go there on pilgrimage. Four days later she declared: "I am the Immaculate Virgin"; and a few days later: "Soon, I shall appear for the last time".

It was on December 29th that, as the Blessed Virgin

opened her arms in her usual gesture of farewell, she first revealed on her breast a Heart of Gold, surrounded by an aureole of intense light.   In this manner, because that golden heart was directly symbolic of her Immaculate Heart, an important link was established between this sequence of visits and the prodigious series at Fatima, sixteen years previously.

Next evening, she commanded: "Pray!  Pray very much", and again revealed the brilliance of her Heart, which was displayed a third time on the last day of the year.

On January 1st, 1933, Gilberte Voisin was told to: "Pray always".   Two days later, as had been foretold, there was the final apparition.  To each child a separate command was given.   To Andrée it was: "I am the Mother of God, the Queen of Heaven . . . Pray always . . . Good-bye".   Gilberte Voisin was then told: "I will convert sinners.   Good-bye."  To Albert, just "Good-bye".   To Gilberte Degeimbre the same. Finally Fernande was asked two questions.  "Do you love my Son?  Do you love me?"

When Fernande had replied "Yes" to both, Our Lady concluded: "Then sacrifice yourself for me. Good-bye."

Afterwards the three youngest children admitted that Our Lady had entrusted each with a secret which might be told to no one, not even to each other.

The subsequent story of Beauraing is too lengthy to discuss in a short space.   Unbalanced people falsely claimed to have enjoyed further Apparitions.   One professor claimed to have solved the mystery of the original lights by a test which convinced few others; and to have disproved the episode of the trance by means of a photograph taken at a later date under rather questionable circumstances.   Bitter attacks were launched, some of which came from England.   The ecclesiastical    authorities    commanded    the    most exhaustive enquiries. Before they were complete, the Bishop died. It was his successor, fresh and quite independent of all that had gone before, who resolved the matter.

Never once during months of severe cross-examinations, physical and psychological tests, often confronted with cleverly devised traps, did the children make a mistake. By degrees the character of certain amazing cures which soon took place, the beauty and clarity of the Messages reported, and the enormous number of spiritual conversions which were brought about, dispelled doubt and scepticism.

The first year brought no less than two million pilgrims. On one single Sunday, twenty-five thousand people received Holy Communion in the parish church. At last, the Bishop of Namur, in his Pastoral of February 2nd, 1943, approved the *Cultus*, in the darkest moment of Belgian history. In August, 1946, on the Feast of the Immaculate Heart of Mary, who revealed herself as Our Lady of the Golden Heart, the Bishop blessed the official statue to represent Our Lady of Beauraing, and inaugurated the new Marial Domain.

In the course of ten years or so the Feudal Castle which crowns the village, and its entire enclosure, has become the property of the sanctuary. A superb chapel has now been erected close beside the site of the Apparitions. (The actual spot is quite undisturbed and is still very much what the children knew.) The garden between the Convent and the railings serves for public functions. A fine open air altar stands on the site of the old grotto. The may-tree is railed in, with bronze railings which are designed to serve as a gigantic votive candle stand. The recognised figure of Our Lady of Beauraing is enshrined in the open air, immediately beneath the boughs of the tree where the children saw her. The Castle is become a retreat house and in its delightful grounds there is rising a magnificent basilica which will be without rival in Belgium.

And the children? What of them? They have remained charming, unspoiled, normal and healthy-minded people. Fernande Voisin trained as a nurse and is now married. Motherhood is her vocation. She has (1948) four children, Rose-Marie, Michel-Marie, Emmanuel-Marie and Noël.

Gilberte Voisin, after professional training, became a qualified teacher but she too married, in 1945, and has at least one small son, about two years old, also Michel-Marie.

Albert Voisin did his military service and served in England, Ireland and Germany. He recently gained his diplomas in education and has gone to teach in the Congo mission field.

Andrée Degeimbre married a Flemish horticulturist, and has two daughters.

Gilberte, her young sister, was married in 1947. M. and Mme. Voisin still live in Beauraing. M. Voisin, brave patriot, was arrested by the Germans for his share in the Resistance and narrowly escaped execution.

Mme. Degeimbre was forced to give up her little business owing to the importunity of so many questioners, and now lives with Andrée at her farm. All are devoted, practising Catholics and not one of the "children", now grown up, with the benefit of years of experience, has the slightest idea but that each one of them did really and truly see, and converse with, the Mother of God at Beauraing.

# XXXI: BANNEUX

GREAT was the stir in Belgium caused by the reported appearances of Our Lady at Beauraing. Atheistic critics might have been expected to scoff, but there were many devout Catholics who earnestly wished for guidance in the matter. Before ever that series of Apparitions, since accredited by ecclesiastical authority, had been completed, prayers and novenas were being offered throughout the country for a right judgment.

Unknown to anyone in the district, but in union with the nuns of several convents, the parish priest of Banneux, a hamlet in the diocese of Liège, ten miles east of that city, was making just such a novena to end on January 16th, 1933. The previous evening, a Sunday, had seen the Bishop, Mgr. Kerkhofs, kneeling in his cathedral before the Blessed Sacrament exposed, to set the seal on his decision to consecrate his diocese that year to the Immaculate Heart of Mary, in accordance with the requests made at Fatima.

At that same moment, Mariette Beco, born March 25th, 1921, one of the youngest, and certainly poorest, inhabitants of Banneux, was pressing her nose against the window of her home, waiting impatiently for her brother Julien to come in. It was seven o'clock and she was hungry for supper. Her father, a hard working labourer and a badly-lapsed Catholic, had gone to bed early. Her mother was busy in the back room. It was a dark, moonless night and cold. A petrol-lamp was burning on the table.

Suddenly Mariette gave a cry, "Mother! There is a woman in the garden!" Mme. Beco hurried to the window but could see only a vague form under the trees by the roadside in front of the house. A strange fear seized her. She exclaimed, "Perhaps it is a witch!"

Afterwards, Mariette described her experience thus: "First I put my head on one side, then on the other. I thought it was caused by the lamp, so I moved the light. But the beautiful lady was still there. I was frightened and called my mother. She said, 'Perhaps it is a witch!' But I noticed a blue girdle like that on Our Lady in church and said: 'Oh no! It is the Holy Virgin'.

"Mother answered, 'As if that is likely!' but I insisted that it was Our Lady, as she was smiling at me."

From that moment, Mariette no longer feared. She took her beads—a rosary she had picked up one day in the road, but never used—and said six decades, keeping her eyes fixed on the Lady, who moved her lips at the same time. Then the Lady beckoned to Mariette, who tried to run out to her. But Mme. Beco would not allow her to do so. She drew the blind and bolted the door.

Next day Mariette was made to tell her father, who laughed and called her a fool. Julien was intrigued and suggested that the "figure" was a reflection from some icicles. They tried in vain to reproduce it. That day, too, Mariette had told one other person, her bosom friend, Josephine Leonard, aged 10, and she went to the presbytery and told the Abbé. He, supposing wrongly that Mariette had heard about Beauraing, and fearing an "epidemic" of visions told her not to spread stories and to forget about it. The story, however, reached the Abbé just as he concluded his novena.

Until then Mariette had been the most backward of all the children at catechism, so much that, lacking parental sympathy, she had given up and lapsed. Next morning, however, found her at Mass and then at catechism, knowing her lesson perfectly, probably for the first time. The Abbé was astonished. Remembering what Josephine had told him, he questioned Mariette and packed her off with a sharp warning "not to go imagining things". But he was so deeply impressed that he made a careful record of what the child had told him.

That evening, January 18th, 1933, at seven o'clock Mariette ran into the garden before she could be stopped. Her father followed, to find her kneeling by the gate, praying quietly. It was cold and dark. Just as he reached the child, she flung out her arms and cried out in rapture, for at that moment she beheld the Lady a few feet away, separated from her only by a "bright cloud of light".

M. Beco was thunderstruck. Although sadly lapsed from the Faith, and unable to see anything, he could nevertheless sense the presence of an "immense power of sanctity", as he explained. He stood for a few moments and then hastened to fetch the Abbé.

The following morning, completely converted, he made his confession and was restored to the Sacraments, an event which the Abbé had considered most improbable.

Unfortunately the priest was out when M. Beco called, but a friend, a practising Catholic, went back with him just in time to see Mariette stand up and walk onto the highway. "Where are you going?" they called to her. "*She* is beckoning me," was the answer.

Slowly the child made her way along the road, following the Lady, who seemed to glide rather than walk, keeping her eyes fixed on Mariette. Three times she stopped at points about a hundred yards apart and each time Mariette knelt, then got up and followed on until they reached a spot where a small brook flowed out of a bank into a ditch by the roadside. Here the child, obeying the Lady's command, knelt and plunged her hands into the water.

She explained later that the Lady had told her: *"This spring is set apart for me"*; and then, on departing, had added *"Goodnight"*.

On this occasion Mariette was able to give a clearer description of the Lady to her questioners. Asked whether the Lady resembled the figure of Our Lady of Lourdes in the church, she "could not say". Her robe was long and white and hung to her feet, but left the right foot bare. Later she saw a beautiful rose on the foot. She wore a blue girdle and rays of light shone from her head. She was rather more than five feet tall, bending slightly to the right with her hands raised to her breast and pointing upwards. There was a rosary on her right arm, but Mariette could not recall seeing a cross on it.

A third apparition was experienced at the same hour on the 19th, the following evening. On this occasion, Mariette obeyed the instructions given her by a wise Benedictine whom the Abbé had called in for advice. Almost as soon as the Lady appeared, in the same place, she asked, "Who are you, Madame?" Then those standing near heard her repeat the reply given to her, "Ah! The Holy Virgin of the Poor!" Over and over again, in later cross-examinations, Mariette insisted that the Lady said to her, *"I am the Virgin of the Poor,"* and that she herself, by instinct, had added "Holy".

Then, as on the previous night, with the same halts and kneelings, she returned to the spring. "Madame," she asked as told, "You did say yesterday 'This spring is set apart for me'?" There was a moment of silence while the gracious Lady smiled. Then she nodded and added, *"For all the nations . . . For the sick . . . I come to relieve the sick"*. To which Mariette replied, simply, "Thank you". The Lady then added, *"I shall pray for you. Au revoir,"* and faded into the darkness of the night.

In all, there were eight appearances, five others being on January 20th, February 11th, 15th and 20th and, finally, March 2nd. During the fourth apparition, Mariette asked if the Lady wanted anything and was told, *"I would like a little chapel"*. The Lady then put her hands on the child and blessed her, who staggered and fell into a swoon. A doctor present carried her indoors where she soon revived.

It was not until February 11th that the fifth Apparition occurred, when the message was given, *"I come to relieve suffering. Au revoir."* It was a matter of complete astonishment to Mariette that this was the seventy-fifth anniversary of the Apparition to St. Bernadette at Lourdes.

On Saturday, the 15th, the child asked for a sign. The reply was, *"Have faith in me . . . I shall trust you . . . Pray earnestly"*. It was then that Mariette was entrusted with a great secret . . . "Something I mustn't tell anyone, not even father or mother". When the Lady vanished on that occasion, Mariette wept for a long time. No inducement has ever persuaded her to divulge her secret. She still says "My secret is locked inside me".

On Monday, the 20th, Mariette went to pray as usual at the spot of the Apparitions and had just finished when she knelt down again. A third time the Lady appeared to lead her to the spring. This time she was not smiling but exhorted her urgently, *"My dear child, pray hard. Au revoir."*

These "au revoirs" were the only indication that the cycle of apparitions was to continue. "Au revoir" means "until the next meeting".

It was on March 2nd that the final appearance occurred, the last Apparition of Our Lady *so far* to receive official recognition by ecclesiastical authority. It was pouring with rain, but Mariette went as usual to say her rosary. When she reached the third Glorious Mystery she was checked by a violent gust of wind and saw—for the last time—the Mother of God in her glory. She stood before her chosen messenger, just as she had stood before St. Bernadette, St. Catherine Labouré, the Children of La Salette, at Beauraing and at Fatima, and looked at Mariette for a long time without smiling. Then she said: *"I am the Mother of the Saviour, Mother of God. Pray hard."* And again she gazed on the child during a long period of silence. Mariette answered with a rather abrupt "Yes". Finally, Our Lady spoke the parting word, *"Adieu"* —"Good-bye"—and, a second time, imposed her blessing.

Mariette fell into a second swoon. She did not witness Our Lady's departure, but she knew from that one word that the series of visits was ended. Yet for many years it has been her practice to repair whenever possible to the scene of the apparitions, to recite the Rosary at seven o'clock. So inconspicuous has she (now married, and mother of a fine family) made herself that it is doubtful if any one other than neighbours could distinguish her.

Such is the straightforward and simple story of the Apparitions at Banneux, which were granted in response, as it were, to the novenas for the verification of Beauraing. For several years Mariette and her recitations were subject to every conceivable test. The fate of those who claim to have experienced apparitions of Our Lady is rather terrifying. Untruth could hardly survive. She was examined by panels of doctors and psychiatrists, men of world-wide repute. This is a typical verdict given by one, before the Commission of Enquiry instituted by the Belgian Primate. "I cannot find any suspicion of hysteria in Mariette. I have come to the conclusion that neither Beauraing nor Banneux have any place in the medical sphere."

Testimony does not depend solely upon doctors. The favours obtained afford additional reason for accepting Apparitions, not that the Church considers such graces as proofs but rather as presumptions in favour. So remarkable have these favours been at Banneux that they have excited scientific interest comparable to the cases at Lourdes.

In addition, cases of conversion from schism, heresy and paganism are as frequent and as fully attested. It is not surprising that Banneux has become a great centre of impressive pilgrimage. In spite of its remoteness, its poverty, the opposition of violent anti-clericals, the repugnance of the Nazis during their occupation of Belgium, obstacles have been swept away.

A chapel was soon built on the site of the Apparitions; the spring has been enclosed; piscines have been built for the bathing of the sick; hospices erected for their care; chapels of perpetual adoration have sprung up; a vast site has been purchased for a basilica, the cornerstone of which was laid by the Papal Nuncio to Belgium, in the presence of the Bishop and many prelates in 1948. In 1934, one year after the Apparitions, the Bishop approved the establishment of the world-wide "International Union of Prayers".

In 1942, as a result of the unanimous verdict of the Ecclesiastical Commission, supported by rescripts of approval from the Holy See, he authorised by Pastoral Letter the cult of Our Lady of Banneux, Our Lady of the Poor.

In 1947, in a second Pastoral Letter, the Bishop was able to repeat, ''Today, after five consecutive years of observation and prayer, we are happy to renew and confirm this approbation and declaration''.   Thus the cult of Our Lady of Banneux, the most recent of all the Apparitions approved, takes its place beside La Salette and Lourdes.   Truly has this century been blessed with three such amazing series of apparitions as those at Fatima, Beauraing, and of Our Lady of the Poor, at Banneux.

# BIBLIOGRAPHY

## TO VOLUME ONE

THIS bibliography does not pretend to be exhaustive. The author has, in fact, made use of several hundred volumes and articles in his search for material for the study of the shrines discussed herein. In addition to a brief general list, the reader will find, under separate headings, the titles of a number of works, either of outstanding importance or more readily available to the ordinary busy reader, bearing on the subject of individual shrines. It is much to be regretted that so few of these are in English, though English references, usually of secondary importance, are given where possible.

---

## I.—GENERAL

1.—*Akathistos Hymn:*
Blackfriars, Oxford, 1947.

2.—*La Belgique à Marie;* H. Maho:
Brussels, 1927.

3.—*Celebrated Sanctuaries of the Madonna;* J. Spencer Northcote, D.D.:
London, Longman Green, 1868.

4.—*Culte de la Sainte Vierge en Afrique;* R. P. Delattre:
Paris, Desclée, 1907.

5.—*I Giardini di Maria;* Carolina Bertini:
Pisa, Salesian Press, 1940.

6.—*Hodegetria Eikon;* Compiled by G. P.:
"Eastern Churches Quarterly," April, 1944.

7.—*Histoire Illustrée des Pèlerinages Français;* J. B. Drochon:
Paris, Plon, 1890.

8.—*Le Livre du Pèlerin;* Abbé Jamar:
  Liége, Demarteau, 1884.

9.—*Les Madones Anciennes Conservées en Belgique;* Comte J. de
  Borchgrave d'Altena:
  Brussels, Cercle d'Art, 1945.

10.—*Mariologie de St. Bernard;* Dom Dominique Nogues, Abbé
  Général, O.C.:
  Paris, Casterman, 1947.

11.—*Mary's Praise on every Tongue;* P. J. Chandlery, S.J.:
  Roehampton, Manresa Press, 1924.

12.—*Mater Christi;* Carlo Cecchelli:
  Vols. I and II, Rome, Fr. Ferrari, 1946, 1948.

13.—*Mount Sinaï Revisited;* Eric Burrows, S.J.:
  "The Month," January, 1944.

14.—*L'Art au Mont Sinaï;* Chanoine M. David:
  Paris, Lethielleux, 1937.

15.—*Notre-Dame de France;* Michel Christian:
  Paris, Tegui, 1938.

16.—*Notre-Dame de Milin (Burcin, Isère);* anon.;
  Lyons, Lescuyer, 1943.

17.—*Notre-Dame de Diocèse de Verdun;* Mgr. Charles Aimond:
  Paris, Gigord—St. Paul, 1943.

18.—*Onzième Centenaire de l'Abbaye de Beaulieu;* "Le Trésor";
  Maurice Gady:
  Société Historique de la Corrèze, 1948.

19.—*Our Lady's Dowry;* T. E. Bridgett, C.SS.R.;
  London, Burns Oates, 1894.

20.—*Pèlerinage de Paris;* A. Gabourd:
  Paris, Perisse Frères, 1863.

21.—*Pietas Mariana Britannica;* E. Waterton, F.S.A.:
  London, 1879.

22.—*Russian Icons;* David Talbot Rice:
  London, "King Penguin" Series, 1947.

23.—*La Sainte Vierge;* Mgr. M. Besson:
  Geneva, l'Echo Illustré, 1942.

24.—*Les Sanctuaires de Marie en Belgique;* Gonzalve Rodriguez, O.F.M.:
Renaix, Leherte Fils, 1924.

25.—*Santuari Mariani d'Italia;* D. Alfonso Salvani, O.S.B.:
Rome, St. Paul Press, 1933.

26.—*Sculpture Belge de la Fin du Moyen-Age;* P. Pradel:
Brussels, Edition Cercle d'Art, 1947.

27.—*La Vierge Notre Médiatrice;* Maurice Vloberg;
Grenoble, Arthaud, 1938.

28.—*Vierges du Dauphiné;* Abbé Cavart:
Lyons, Lescuyer, 1940.

29.—*Vierges du Jura;* anon.:
Lyons, Lescuyer, 1940.

———

30.—ST. MARY MAJOR, ROME:
*La Madonna di S. Luca in S. Maria Maggiore;* Pico Cellini:
Rome, Istituto Grafico Tiburino, 1943.

31.—LORETO:
(a) *Santa Casa di Loreto;* Antonio Pagani, Sac. Dot.:
Rome, Desclée, 1907.
(b) *Loreto and the Holy House;* G. E. Philips:
London, R. T. Washbourne, 1917.
(c) *Il Santuario di Loreto;* P. Angelo di Camarino:
Pesaro, 1923.

32.—WALSINGHAM:
(a) *Walsingham;* H. M. Gillett:
London, Burns Oates, 1946.
(b) *Pilgrim's Walsingham;* ibid:
London, Samuel Walker, 1948.
(c) *What to see in Walsingham;* Fr. Gilbert, O.F.M.Cap.:
Walsingham, 1948.

33.—CHARTRES:
(a) *Chartres, Its Cathedral and Monuments;* A. Clerval:
Chartres, Renier, 1926.
(b) *Monographie de la Cathédrale de Chartres;* Etienne Houvet:
Chartres, 1939.
(c) *Le Viole de Notre-Dame;* Yves Delaporte:
Chartres, 1927.

34.—EINSIEDELN:
    (a) *Histoire du Monastère d'Einsiedeln;* P. Odilon Ringholz:
        Benziger, 1904.
    (b) *Notre-Dame des Ermites;* Dom Sigismond de Courten,
        O.S.B.:
        Benziger, 1938.
    (c) *Our Lady of Hermits;* Translation by Marian Lindsey:
        Ibid, 1938.

35.—MONTSERRAT:
    (a) *Guide Historique;* Official:
        Barcelona, 1909.
    (b) *Montserrat Mountain;* Official:
        Ibid. 1928.

36.—HAL:
    (a) *Notre-Dame de Hal;* Juste-Lipse:
        Brussels, Greuse, 1849.
    (b) *Basilique Notre-Dame de Hal;* Remy Janssens:
        Hal, 1947.
    (c) *Notre-Dame de Hal;* by the Pastoor-Deken of Hal:
        1908.

37.—LE PUY:
    (a) *Le Puy en Velay;* André Chanal:
        Le Puy, Jeanne d'Arc, 1942.
    (b) *Notre-Dame du Puy;* J. M. Philibert:
        Ibid, 1942.
    (c) *Le Cloître du Puy;* André Chanal:
        Ibid.
    (d) *Notre-Dame du Puy;* G. and P. Paul:
        Ibid.

38.—ROCAMADOUR:
    (a) *Notre-Dame de Roc-Amadour;* E. Albe:
        1926.
    (b) *Notes et Documents sur Roc-Amadour;* E. Albe:
        "Revue Religieuse de Cahors," 1916.
    (c) *Roc-Amadour—Etude Historique;* E. Rupin:
        1904.
    (d) *Documents Nouveaux sur Rocamadour;* Ludovic de
        Valon:
        Marseilles, 1928.
    (e) *Defense de la Tradition de St. Amadour;* J. T. Layral:
        Paris, Vic et Amat, 1912.

39.—AVIOTH:
    (a) *Histoire de Son Pèlerinage;* Abbé R. Adam:
        Sedan, Balan, 1934.
    (b) *Sanctuaires de la Vierge dans Luxembourg;* Brochure
        Mariale, No. 9:
        Comité Marial, Namur, 1943.

40.—LUXEMBURG:
   (a) *Histoire de Notre-Dame de Luxembourg;* L. Kuntgen,
       S.J.:
       Luxembourg, P. Brück, 1866.
   (b) *La Cathédrale de Luxembourg;* Michel Faltz:
       Luxembourg, S. Paul, 1946.

41.—FOURVIERE:
   (a) *Notre-Dame de Fourvière;* Mgr. L. Deyrieux:
       Grenoble, "Revue les Alpes," 1943.
   (b) *La Basilique de Fourvière;* Sainte-Marie Perrin:
       Lyons, Lescuyer, 1942.
   (c) *Fourvière;* Chanoine J. M. Gaillard, (Rector):
       Lyons, Lescuyer, ibid.

42.—MONTAIGU:
   (a) *Scherpenheuvel;* E. P. Leopold, O.C.D.:
       Courtrai, 1947.
   (b) *Histoire de Notre-Dame de Montaigu;* Parts I and II:
       J. Fr. Pallemaerts:
       Antwerp, 1947.

43.—LUJAN:
       *Our Lady of Lujan;* by a Passionist Father:
       Buenos Aires, C.T.S., 1918.

44.—OUR LADY OF GOOD COUNSEL:
       *The Virgin Mother of Good Counsel;* Mgr. G. F. Dillon,
       D.D.:
       London, Burns Oates, 1894.

45.—OUR LADY OF PERPETUAL SUCCOUR:
   (a) *Ausführliche Geschichte des Muttergottesbildes von der
       immerwährenden Hilfe;* Clemens Henze, C.SS.R.:
       Rome, Sant' Alfonso, 1939.
   (b) *Story of Perpetual Help;* Clarence A. Seidel, C.SS.R.:
       Rome, Sant' Alfonso, 1936.

46.—LE LAUS:
   (a) *La Vénérable Benoîte Rencurel;* Felix Vernet:
       Paris, Lecoffre, 1931.
   (b) *Vie abrégée de la Vén. Benoîte Rencurel;* Pierre
       Médan:
       Paris, ibid, 1936.
   (c) *Histoire des Merveilles de N. D. du Laus, tirée des
       archives du Sanctuaire;* F. Pron:
       Gap, 1875.
   (d) *La Vénérable Soeur Benoîte;* A. Juge:
       Lyons, 1899.

47.—OUR LADY OF VICTORIES:

   (a) *Notre Esperance;* Louis Blond:
       Paris, Editions Franciscaines, 1941.
   (b) *Notre-Dame des Victoires;* Louis Blond:
       Paris, ibid, 1941.
   (c) *Centenaire de Notre-Dame des Victoires;* L. Blond:
       Paris, ibid, 1936.


48.—THE MIRACULOUS MEDAL:

   (a) *La Vénérable Catherine Labouré;* Edmond Crapez, C.M.:
       Paris, Lecoffre, 1917.
   (b) *La Bienheureuse Catherine Labouré;* Lucien Misermont,
       C.M.:
       Paris, Lecoffre, 1933.
   (c) *The Book of the Miraculous Medal;* by a Vincentian
       Father:
       London, Sands, 1940.


49.—LA SALETTE:

   (a) *Holy Mountain of La Salette;* Archbishop Ullathorne:
       Altamont, N.Y., 1942.
   (b) *Our Lady of La Salette;* Wolfgang Fortier, M.S.:
       London, Burns Oates, 1931.
   (c) *Histoire de l'Apparition de la Mère de Dieu à La
       Salette;* Louis Carlier, M.S.:
       Paris, Desclée, 1914.
   (d) *La Salette; Précis Historique;* E. Picard, M.S.:
       Villeurbanne, Chambefort, 1941.
   (e) *La Grâce de la Salette;* J. Jaouen, M.S.:
       Paris, Editions du Cerf, 1946.
   (f) *Notre-Dame Réconciliatrice;* J. Sougey, M.S.:
       Grenoble, 1946.
   (g) *Actualité de La Salette;* Yv. Estienne:
       Grenoble, 1945.


50.—LOURDES:

   (a) *Annales de Notre-Dame de Lourdes:*
       Lourdes, Imprimerie de la Grotte.
   (b) *Lourdes;* Aileen Mary Clegg:
       London, Sheed & Ward, 1929.
   (c) *Bernadette of Lourdes;* C. C. Martindale, S.J.:
       London, C.T.S., 1946.
   (d) *Histoire de Notre-Dame de Lourdes;* L. J. M. Cros, S.J.:
       Paris, Gabriel Beauchesne, 1901.
   (e) *Histoire de Notre-Dame de Lourdes d'après les Docu-
       ments et les Témoins:*
       Ibid, vol. I, 1925: vol. II, 1927: vol. III, 1927.

51.—PONTMAIN:

   (a) *Notre-Dame de Pontmain;* Mgr. Michel Even:
       Grenoble, Revue les Alpes, 1946.
   (b) *Le Mystère de Pontmain;* Mgr. Paul Richaud, Bishop of
       Laval:
       Paris, Bonne Press, 1946.
   (c) *Michel Guérin;* un serviteur de Marie:
       Laval, Goupil, 1935.
   (d) *L'Evénement de Pontmain; Récit de l'Apparition* by
       Abbé A. M. Richard:
       Pontmain, new edition, 1946.
   (e) *L'Apparition de Notre-Dame de Pontmain;* Récit d'un
       Voyant, Joseph Barbadette, O.M.I.:
       Brussels, 1938.
   (f) *Nouveau Mois de Marie de Notre-Dame de Pontmain;* H.
       Auguste, Vice-Rector:
       Rennes, Nouvelliste, 1933.


52.—PELLEVOISIN:

       *Notice sur Notre-Dame de Pellevoisin;* Mgr. P. Bauron:
       Lyons, St. Eucher, 1938.


53.—FATIMA:

   (a) *Our Lady of Fatima;* Archbishop Finbar Ryan, O.P.:
       Dublin, Browne & Nolan, 1945.
   (b) *More About Fatima;* V. Montes De Oca, C.S.Sp., trans-
       lated by J. da Cruz, C.S.Sp.:
       Dublin, Gill & Son, 1945.
       Based upon—
   (c) *Le Meraviglie di Fatima;* Gonzaga da Fonseca, S.J.:
       Vatican Press (Fourth Edition), 1941.
   (d) *Fatima;* Mgr. L. Picard:
       Ham (Belgium), 1944.


54.—BEAURAING:

   (a) *A Beauraing cinq Enfants;* Paul Piron, S.J.:
       Liége, Soledi, 1943.
   (b) *Beauraing: Mémoires et Documents;* G. Maes, C.SS.R.:
       Liége, Redemptorists, 1936.
   (c) *Précis des Apparitions à Beauraing;* Dom Hugues
       Delogne, O.S.B.:
       St. Maurice (Switzerland), 1947.
   (d) *Beauraing;* Prof. A. Schellinckx, M.S.C.:
       Namur, Godenne, 1934.
   (e) *La Coeur Immaculée de Marie;* G. Maes, C.SS.R.:
       Beauraing, 1933.
   (f) *La Vierge au Coeur d'Or;* L. Michel, C.SS.R.:
       Beauraing, 1946.

BEAURAING—*continued*.

(g) *La Belle Histoire de Beauraing;* Chanoine H. Massart,
  Administrator:
  Brussels, Universitaires, 1948.
(h) *Beauraing, Documents Episcopaux;* The Bishop of
  Namur (Mgr. Charue):
  Secretariat, Beauraing, 1946.
(i) *Lettre Pastoral;* Mgr. Charue, Bishop of Namur:
  July 25th, 1947.
(j) *Discourse of Bishop Théas of Lourdes:*
  Lourdes Bulletin, April 4th, 1944.
(k) *"La Voix de Beauraing":*
  Secretariat, Beauraing, Monthly.


55.—BANNEUX:

(a) *La Vierge des Pauvres;* Dom Idesbald Van Houtryve,
  O.S.B.:
  Louvain, Mont Cesar Abbey, 1947.
(b) *Notre-Dame de Banneux;* Amand Géradin:
  Brussels, Marechal, 1947.
(c) *Pastoral Letters of Mgr. Kerkhofs, Bishop of Liége;* of
  March 19th, 1942 and March 19th, 1947:
  (Liége, H. Dessain).


56.—*The Blessed Virgin in the 19th Century;* Bernard St. John:
  London, Burns Oates, 1903.


57. *Les Visites de la Saint Vierge à la France au XIXe Siècle;*
  Marie André:
  Paris, Alsatia, 1946.


58.—*Notre-Dame Parmi Nous;* Hyac. Marechal, O.P.:
  Grenoble, Editions "Revue des Alpes", 1944.

AN INDEX will follow at the end of the Second Volume.